# Praise for Dr. Sylvia Rimm

□

"Dr. Rimm is a welcome voice of calm and reason—someone who offers practical advice, with almost immediate results. She's a guardian angel for families who need a little or a lot of guidance."
—KATIE COURIC, NBC *Today* show

"Dr. Rimm's book provides . . . a rich array of suggestions . . . the kind of down-to-earth advice parents desperately seek when struggling to motivate their underachievers."
—THE WASHINGTON POST

"Only two, the Boston pediatrician Dr. T. Berry Brazelton and the British psychologist Dr. Penelope Leach, have achieved near Spocklike popularity with parents. . . . In her own mild-mannered way, Dr. Rimm is scrambling to pull ahead of the pack."
—NEW YORK TIMES

"These books are smart and caring and full of insight. I've read parts again and again."
—JACQUELYN MITCHARD, mother of five, journalist, and author of *The Deep End of the Ocean*

"Sound, practical advice and a great deal of wisdom about the most challenging task that many of us ever face—parenting!"
—SALLY M. REIS, PH.D., associate professor in the department of educational psychology at the University of Connecticut

"Rimm brings both public appeal and strong credentials to this sensible guide to raising children, addressing both common annoyances and deeper issues. . . . This practical and wise book is a good selection for public libraries and . . . is sure to be popular."
—LIBRARY JOURNAL

"Mix of common sense, ethics, and commitment to kids earns Sylvia Rimm respect."
—CLEVELAND PLAIN DEALER

"A wise and sensitive observer of children."
—JEROME KAGAN, PH.D., professor of psychology at Harvard University

ALSO BY DR. SYLVIA RIMM

*Why Bright Kids Get Poor Grades
And What You Can Do About It*

*Raising Preschoolers*

# How to Parent So Children Will Learn

Previously published as
*Dr. Sylvia Rimm's Smart Parenting*

DR. SYLVIA RIMM

ILLUSTRATIONS BY HARRY TRUMBORE

THREE RIVERS PRESS
New York

Grateful acknowledgment is made to the following:
The National Association of School Psychologists for permission to
reprint the Position Statement on Students with Attention Deficits.
Copyright © 1991 by the National Association of School Psychologists.
Reprinted by permission of the publisher.

Houghton Mifflin Company to reprint
Kohlberg's Stages in the Development of Moral Values.
Theodore Sizer, *Religion and Public Education.*
Copyright © 1987 by Houghton Mifflin Company. Reprinted with permission.

Published by Three Rivers Press, a division of Crown Publishers, Inc.,
201 East 50th Street, New York, New York 10022. Member of the Crown Publishing Group.

Originally published in hardcover by Crown Publishers, Inc. in 1996.

Random House, Inc. New York, Toronto, London, Sydney, Auckland
www.randomhouse.com

Three Rivers Press is a registered trademark of Random House, Inc.

Printed in the United States of America
Design by Susan Hood

Library of Congress Cataloging-in-Publication Data
Rimm, Sylvia B.
[Smart parenting]
How to parent so children will learn ;
illustrations by Harry Trumbore.—1st pbk. ed.
Originally published: 1st ed. New York : Crown Publishers, ©1996.
"Previously published as Dr. Sylvia Rimm's Smart Parenting."
Includes bibliographical references and index.
1. Parenting.   2. Child rearing.   3. Achievement motivation in children.
4. Self-reliance in children.   5. Academic achievement.
I. Rimm, Sylvia B., 1935-   How to parent so children will learn.
II. Title.
HQ755.8.R535   1997        97-8570
649'.1—dc21

ISBN 0-609-80121-X

10  9  8  7  6  5  4  3

This book is dedicated to my parents,
REVA AND HARRY BARKAN

To my mom, who modeled for me that "women can do every-thing."

To my dad, who affectionately advised me that when it rained, I could walk between the drops.

I thank my parents for courageously immigrating to the United States, thus providing me with this country's opportunities for learning and achievement.

# CONTENTS

# ACKNOWLEDGMENTS

I would like to thank the children who have come through Family Achievement Clinic and their parents for sharing their lives with me and providing the feedback to confirm that my parenting recommendations are effective. I'd also like to indicate my appreciation to both Wisconsin and Cleveland Public Radio for giving me the extensive audience of parents whose questions I answer regularly, thus permitting me to focus on the main practical concerns of most moms and dads. I want to acknowledge as well those parents in my radio, TV, and personal audiences who permit me to feel assured that my parenting advice is practical, realistic, and up-to-date.

NBC's *Today* show producer, Patricia Luchsinger, receives a special thank-you for introducing me to millions of parent viewers who correspond with me regularly. Thanks so much to Steve Friedman, the former executive producer of *Today*, and now to the current executive producer, Jeff Zucker. Thanks to Katie Couric and Bryant Gumbel, whose delightful interviews help me to answer parents' needs. Thank you also to Michael Bass, Linda Finnell, Janet Schiller, and the many other *Today* show staff who help make my monthly national appearances so effective.

My sincere appreciation is extended to my editor, Peter Ginna, and to my agent, Pierre Lehu, for their helpful reviews of my book.

Thanks especially to my publications staff, Joanne Riedl, Marilyn Knackert, Jeremy Knackert, Marian Carlson, and Barbara Ruder, for their help in the preparation and proofreading of my book. Thanks also to the staff of the public library in Watertown, Wisconsin, for their help in compiling the lists of recommended books for children. My appreciation goes forever to my husband, our children, their spouses, and even our grandchildren for their continuous encouragement and support. Finally, my appreciation is extended to the families who reviewed my manuscript and made suggestions and comments that were so helpful.

# PREFACE

I have written this book to give you, as "smart" parents, the foundation for fostering a home environment that encourages children's love and respect for learning. As cornerstones provide the basic elements of the foundation to a building, my book provides the basic four cornerstones for raising your kids to love learning and value achievement. I hope these cornerstones will help you to build confidence in your parenting and to prevent and solve problems.

My experience comes from working with families in both clinical and media settings. My role as child psychologist on NBC's *Today* show has permitted me to give parenting advice to millions of viewers in a series called "Raising Kids in the '90s."

My public radio program, *Family Talk with Sylvia Rimm,* which is broadcast nationally, has afforded me opportunities to converse with parents all over the country. My newspaper column, syndicated by Creators Syndicate, also provides me the opportunity to answer my letters in writing each year. Altogether I receive literally thousands of letters and phone calls from parents and family members seeking advice.

My clinic, Family Achievement Clinic,* which specializes in

---

* Family Achievement Clinic is part of Westlake Healthcare Associates and is an affiliate of MetroHealth Medical Center. It is located at 2001 Crocker Road, Cleveland, Ohio 44145.

working with bright children who aren't performing to their abilities in school, permits me to have direct therapy experience with children and their families. The Model, which I developed at Family Achievement Clinic in Wisconsin and continue to use in Cleveland, Ohio, focuses on the child, the home, and the school for reversing underachievement and helping children achieve and feel good about themselves.

There are a few consistent and significant recommendations I give regularly to parents who come to my clinic that have dramatic impact on children's school learning and achievement experiences. Out of the literally thousands of questions I answer regularly for parents, teachers, radio, newspaper, and television audiences, there emerge some basic commonsense themes that make critical differences. I have boiled down those themes to the four chapters in this book to guide you in parenting your children wisely toward learning from birth to young adulthood. At the end of each chapter, I have selected a few representative questions I have answered in my columns or on radio and television. These are all real questions from parents, and they serve as case examples of the principles described in the chapter.

*How to Parent So Children Will Learn* was originally published in 1990. This updated and expanded version of that book includes many new issues to reflect the continually changing and challenging needs of parents in our society. New and expanded topics include the new importance of fathering, two-parent working families, parenting suggestions for immigrants, foster care and adoption, selection of child-care providers and the role of those providers, the impact of TV heroes, attention deficit disorders, test anxiety and test-taking strategies, and the importance of organization for achievement. I have also included many other changes that can be made at home and school that I have already described in my earlier books.[1, 2, 3]

Readers who have read my book *Why Bright Kids Get Poor Grades* may find that a few of the sections in this book are similar to some in that book. That is because many readers of this book will not have read the first book because their children are not underachieving. Some important principles must be addressed to *all* parents, not just those with underachieving children. Those principles are so critical to smart parenting and effective learning that even if you've read them in my first book, they bear repeating. Of course, readers will find many new suggestions in this book that can't be found in my first book.

Parents often ask me about my own parenting experience. They even assume that all my "good commonsense advice" must come from parenting my own four children. It is true that from time to time a memory of my children's upbringing reminds me of a good solution to a parent's problem. However, parenting four children is not enough experience to provide the variety of expertise I require in my many roles as a psychologist. Perhaps what I learned most from my own parenting experience is, first, the importance of staying united as parents. Second, and equally important, I learned humility, which permits me to communicate with you and continue to be sensitive to what a difficult and sometimes frustrating responsibility parenting is.

# INTRODUCTION

Parents often wonder why some children enjoy school, love learning, and achieve so well in the classroom, while other children, who are equally capable, are so negative about school, avoid learning, and underachieve. Even smart parents may find themselves baffled because the bright, happy child they used to know may have "shut down" to learning. The shutdown sometimes begins as early as first grade, although many children turn away from education in middle school or high school or even in college.

Intelligent children don't automatically fulfill their early promise. People often blame schools for children's problems. Indeed, schools and teachers are very important and do make a major difference in encouraging children's learning. Positive school experiences increase the likelihood of positive life experiences. Education continues to provide the most effective path toward upward mobility, success, and life fulfillment.

You, as parents, have the most dramatic, positive impact on your children's education, not only during their childhood, but for their entire future. Teaching your children to learn and achieve will enhance their confidence and their potential for life satisfaction. Accepting them as underachievers or assuming achievement will not provide them with happiness and will only take away their confidence. Yet, fostering achievement at home is more difficult than it has been in past generations. Thus, parents can't rely so easily on their own childhoods to guide them toward parenting their children. Families have changed so dramatically that the rules that come from past family research are not as readily applicable to present generations. The variations of familial arrangements that provide home environments for children include stepfamilies, single-parent families, grandparent families, families with homosexual parents, families that use child-care providers, adoptive and foster families, and undoubtedly others that I have not thought of. The complexities have also multiplied for traditional two-parent families. Television, the Internet and video games, violence, divorce, two careers, overburdened educational systems and overburdened parents, drugs, peer pressures, and increased competition are only a few of the environmental stressors that have risen dramatically in one generation. Ethnic, cultural, and religious differences make for increased heterogeneity within and among families.

All in all, moms and dads seem to find themselves bewildered about parenting. They know for sure that they can't love their children too much, but most other parenting guidelines and books leave them floundering in confusion and contradiction. Nonetheless, there are highly predictable home and school environments that guide capable children along paths on which they will learn and feel good about themselves. The four chapters that follow will provide you with the foundation that will almost inevitably lead your children toward learning and achievement.

Smart parent planning begins from before birth and extends to young adulthood. Parents can't control their children's environments entirely, but they can set some main directions that virtually assure achievement. "Smart" families need a game plan, some rules, and some reasonably clear strategies and goals. That's what my book is about—assuring a love of learning and accomplishment while recognizing that overall happiness for your children is the true goal of parenting.

Happy parenting! May your experiences provide you the joys that it has for my husband and me.

# HOW TO GET THE MOST OUT OF THIS BOOK

"Smart" parents are usually busy, and finding time to read a whole book is no longer easy. Although you will want to read this book more than once and refer to its subject index when in need, I've tried to make even your first reading parent-friendly.

Each chapter begins with an advance summary that focuses on the learning objectives of the chapter. My illustrators have captured some familiar family settings. I hope you'll chuckle at those that strike home and read the text surrounding the pictures that most apply to your family. I've used boldface type to lead you directly to **Parent Pointers,** which you can apply even before completing the book. Boxes surround activities and conversations that can immediately help you with your children. You don't have to read everything to make simple changes. You may wish to use a colored highlighting pen to mark text that is significant to you. If your child's other parent(s) wishes to read your copy of the book, suggest they use other colors for highlighting. Although the resulting text will become very colorful, the color coding can then be used to concentrate on specific helpful communications between you and the child's other parent(s).

If you enjoy a question-answer format, you may wish to turn to the end of each chapter to review some parent questions, along with my responses, before you read the chapter. Then, for a comprehensive and more detailed discussion of those topics, you can return to the beginning of the chapter.

You'll notice some positive results in your children almost immediately, although some changes will take patience. Remember, your children were born with genetic differences in their intelligence, temperaments, and personalities. Your goals are for them to love learning and value achievement to whatever ability they have. My book can help you to do that gradually from before birth to adulthood. I hope, as "smart" parents, you'll find that with a few basic strategies, you'll build confidence in your parenting skills that will permit you to guide your children to achievement and learning.

# How to Parent So Children Will Learn

# In Chapter 1
## You'll Learn How To

- empower your children with the V of Love.

- use praise appropriately to convey values to your children and avoid causing pressures.

- use referential speaking effectively.

- encourage appropriate independence in your children without overempowering.

- interpret what your children are saying to you.

- select appropriate rewards and punishments.

- encourage a positive home atmosphere.

- set limits for children who are too powerful.

- decrease arguments and power struggles with your children.

## CHAPTER 1

# EMPOWERING YOUR CHILDREN WITH THE V OF LOVE

A S PARENTS you've undoubtedly read many books assuring you that you can never love your children too much. Other books have urged you to empower your children. Although I concur with those who say you can never love your children too much, I would caution you to empower them carefully and only gradually with the "V of Love."

Visualize the letter V as a model for guiding the extent of praise, power, and freedom given to your children. When your children are very young, they begin at the bottom of the V with moderate praise, limited freedom and power, and a few choices. As they grow in maturity and are able to handle more responsibility, the limiting walls of the V spread out giving them gradually increasing freedom and power while still providing parental limits. During adolescence, as your children move to the top of the V, they become capable of considerably more independent decision-making and judgment. They can earn and accept higher praise more comfortably. They feel trusted and continue to respect guidance from their parents and teachers. They're thus more competent and have more confidence for moving out of the V into adult independence and personal decision-making.

In some families the V is reversed to look like this: Λ. Children who start at the base of this figure are given too much freedom, too much praise, too many choices, and indefinite wide limits. They become accustomed to having power and making decisions before they have the wisdom to handle their freedom responsibly. However, as these children move toward adolescence, their parents may observe that they don't appear mature enough for so much power and freedom. They observe them making poor choices and worry about the dangers that arise among teenagers. Their teens may choose not to do homework or study and instead become involved with a negative peer group. Cigarettes, alcohol, drugs, promiscuous sex, and AIDS are serious threats from which their parents try to protect them. Thus, parents begin to make demands on their children, which they haven't done before. They set limits and take freedoms away. Adolescents who had too much control as children now feel overcontrolled by parents. They believe they know more than their parents and teachers. Their angry statements reflect their feelings of restriction. "My parents are controlling me. They want too much of me. They expect me to be perfect. All they care about is school. They used to treat me like an adult and now they treat me like a child," these adolescents complain. They rebel, feel increasingly angry, or are depressed. Not only do they fight their parents and teachers, they fight learning as well.

These worried parents overpunish and narrow limits further, resulting in even more anger and rebellion. The oppositional adolescents turn formerly happy homes into armed camps in which underachievement is only one part of the problem. Neither the parents nor the teens understand or communicate with each other. Relative to the power and control these teens once had, they feel powerless.

Once freedom is given, it isn't easily taken away. The resulting adversarial mode may force adolescents to rebel too stubbornly, parents to respond too negatively, and both to lose the positive home atmosphere that can be so valuable in educating children. Children brought up with the inverted V of Love expend their energies protecting the power they believe they should have and the extraordinary abilities for which they were overpraised. This pattern of protection only causes them to build defense mechanisms.

The V-shaped love encourages children to develop their talents, freedom, and power. Developmental empowerment is much smoother and more comfortable for adolescents and parents alike

THE V OF LOVE

and provides the appropriate atmosphere in which children can be inspired to learn.

## PRAISE

Children thrive in an environment of being valued and loved. Praise for children's accomplishments encourages them to continue to accomplish and share their achievements with those whom they please. Attention to their smiles, gurgles, "patty-cakes," and "bye-byes" enhances their communication and their learning. **Reading to children, discussing, sharing interests, and answering their questions expands their vocabulary, their knowledge, and their intelligence.** They soon find that their new vocabulary, knowledge, and reasoning skills empower them to capture adult conversation. They thus learn that intelligence and learning are valued in their home. This is an apparent good beginning to a lifetime of learning. Praise, attention, and positive reinforcement are good for children. **Praise is probably the most effective communicator of adult values and provides parents with a critical tool for guiding**

PARENT
POINTER

PARENT
POINTER

**children.** The expressed pleasure of adults is the most powerful early motivator.

## TOO MUCH PRAISE, TOO MUCH OF A GOOD THING

Some parents who recognize the value of praise make the assumption that if some praise is good, more praise must be better. Other parents assume that if they praise their children in extravagant terms, it will build their children's self-concepts even more. However, both are "too much of a good thing." In their attempts to build children's confidence, some parents can actually praise too much. Too much praise may cause your children to become praise-dependent or "attention addicted." Too extravagant praise may result in your children feeling extremely pressured because they believe they must live up to extraordinary and impossible standards that are conveyed by your praise. **In order to guide your children without pressuring them, praise with the values within which you'd like them to live,** and recognize that they should not be encumbered with impossible expectations. For example, you can praise your children as "good workers" or as "bright," "creative," "kind," or "attractive." It's better to avoid terms like "brilliant," "extraordinary," "perfect," "stunning," "spectacular," "genius," "best," "most beautiful," or "favorite." The former are qualities they can control by their own efforts; the latter may be internalized as impossible goals and are highly competitive messages. Unless your children turn out to be spectacular, brilliant, perfect, and beautiful, they may feel frustrated about their inadequacies forever. They may also blame you for putting pressure on them, although you'll wonder where that pressure came from. Incidentally, if in your enthusiasm and love for your children the extreme words slip out occasionally, there's no harm done. It's the habitual use that's likely to cause problems.

A mother shared with me her surprise at her son's frustration with her high expectations for him. She kept reassuring him by telling him that he was already perfect. She thought that doing so would help his self-esteem; however, it made him feel more and more pressured. Her words of praise were viewed by her son as her expectations; therefore, he assumed she expected him to be perfect.

PARENT
POINTER

Reasonable praise feels like reasonable expectations; extraordinary praise feels like extraordinary expectations.

In most two-parent families, fathers are more involved with their children than they were in former generations. Thus, their praise words will be viewed as Daddy's expectations. If Dad's most frequent praise words relate to a daughter's beauty or a son's athletic skill, girls will believe Dad values appearance above all for them, and boys will assume sports are the first priority in Dad's expectations. I only emphasize this point because my observations of fathers and their children often encourage the "princess" and "jock" images. If children are expected to be intelligent thinkers and learners, overemphasis on appearance and sports will deter their excitement about learning.

Don't praise your children for every accomplishment, word, drawing, or clever insight. Permit them to enjoy the inner rewards of learning and creating. **Be sure to insist that they work and play alone for a little time each day so they can feel the fun of learning and they don't become dependent on praise.** Children

PARENT
POINTER

THE ROOTS OF PERFECTIONISM

who become attention addicted at home are likely to feel, by comparison, attention deprived at school. They may also feel neglected when siblings, with whom they must share the limelight, enter the family. Their sense of specialness, which was dependent on continuous praise, may disappear when they find they must share attention.

Children who have been attention addicted may shut down to school learning when they feel attention deprived in the classroom. They may appear to have the symptoms of either inattentive or hyperactive types of attention disorders. They typically don't understand their own feelings, although occasionally children with whom I've worked have called out in class to teachers in despair, "I'm special, don't you know?" or "I'm very, very smart." Several children have shared with me their concerns. In the words of one little girl, "The teacher just doesn't give me enough attention."

PARENT
POINTER
**Moderate praise empowers children enough to feel confident and to love learning;** however, too much praise enslaves them to pressure and dependence. Children who have been told they are the best believe they are expected to be the best. Children who have been admired as perfect believe that they must be perfect. "Perfect" and "the best" don't exist in the real world. Don't imprison your children with impossible goals in the hope of building their self-confidence.

When two parents are working, and their children are being cared for by child-care providers, there are some special issues to discuss with them related to praise. Because praise conveys adult values to your children, it will be important to communicate your values to those important adults with whom your children spend many hours. If a nanny comes to your home daily or you're taking a preschooler to a caregiver who only cares for a few children, their
PARENT
POINTER
praise or lack thereof will influence your children. **It's best to give the caregiver in writing some words you like to use and some you'd rather not use to encourage your children.** Of course, if your preschool children are in a day-care center, you'll have little say about what words the day-care provider uses, but you do have a choice of providers. If you observe in a day-care center for a
PARENT
POINTER
few hours, you can easily notice the atmosphere. **A negative environment in which children are being frequently criticized**

**is certainly not a good place for your children.** A negative environment only encourages your children's negative behaviors. You should also be sensitive to overpraise or comparative praise. Actually overpraise is less likely to occur in such a center because attention is shared by multiple children right from the start. Comparative praise can be quite common and can be damaging if your child is always either negatively or most positively compared to others.

## THE REFERENTIAL SPEAKING EFFECT

Discussion among adults about children may have an even more powerful effect on children's behavior than direct praise or negative statements. I've coined the term *referential speaking* to describe this conversation that takes place frequently between parents, among parents and other relatives, between parents and teachers, and, yes, even among teachers, within children's hearing. The description of children's activities, behaviors, and misbehaviors, as if the children are not listening, may empower them or cause serious problems and feelings of limitations for them. As with praise, referential speaking can encourage children to have a realistic self-concept, may cause them to feel pressured, or may result in discouragement.

Lest you think that only unintelligent people speak "referentially," let me assure you that *all* parents, relatives, and teachers sometimes speak referentially, and it's not a function of lack of intelligence. Referential speaking is talk by persons who feel most comfortable with spontaneity and are in a hurry. They may be busy and not have the time or opportunity to speak confidentially and thus describe their children to other adults without thinking about the impact on those children.

**Referential speaking is not all negative. Referential speaking about children can set intentional expectations that are positive and can provide a sense of positive control for them.** For example, if you say to your spouse, "I notice that Elizabeth's really persevering in her efforts; she's showing initiative and doing more than what's expected," Elizabeth will be encouraged in her perseverance and effort if she is hearing your conversation (even from

PARENT
POINTER

another room). She can control these abilities, which represent positive qualities.

What kinds of referential speaking are harmful? **Referential speaking that makes children feel inadequate or incapable is *always* harmful.** Referential speaking that empowers children to manipulate adults is also harmful. Here are some examples of harmful referential speaking:

# Case 1

Amy comes to kindergarten screening with her mother. Her mother introduces Amy to the teacher, who welcomes Amy to the classroom. Amy doesn't say anything. Her mother feels embarrassed. She explains in Amy's presence, "I'm sorry that Amy isn't saying hello, Mrs. Smith, but she is very shy. She's always been very shy."

Amy has probably heard five thousand (or more) times before she ever entered school how shy she is. Mother feels the need to explain Amy's behavior because of her own discomfort with Amy's poor manners. She explains to a teacher, to another parent, to a friend, or to a relative why Amy doesn't say hello. What Amy has learned is that she's shy. She thinks that her shyness makes it impossible for her to say hello. Amy assumes that she is biologically, internally, and forever shy. Why would Amy expect to say hello?

How could we change this mother's referential speaking? She could say to Dad or vice versa, "Did you notice how nicely Amy's manners are improving?" When Amy is introduced to the teacher, Mother could ignore Amy's not saying hello and, instead, permit Amy to get right to work. Soon, Amy would learn that she can say "Hello" just like other children.

When parents come to see me about their shy children, I ask them to erase the word *shy* from their vocabulary. The parents find that within a few days or a few weeks their children learn reasonable manners upon greeting other people. We can't necessarily change children's total personalities, nor do we want to, but we can easily teach them reasonable normal social behaviors. Even quiet, sensitive children can learn appropriate manners, and they will learn them if they are not continually labeled "shy" by the important adults in the children's environment. One of the fami-

REFERENTIAL SPEAKING

lies I worked with returned several years later to ask how to handle their previously shy daughter who had since become too aggressive.

# Case 2

Bruce's parents are at a conference with his fourth-grade teacher. The teacher comments, "Bruce seems to be disorganized." Bruce's mother and father agree. They add, "He's disorganized at home. His desk is a mess. His room is a mess. You know, he is our ADHD (attention deficit–hyperactivity disorder) child."

Bruce listens from the back of his classroom. As he hears the familiar tirade about his disorganization and his impulsive behaviors, he feels disorganized and impulsive. He assumes that ADHD means he can't do anything about his problem.

Even if this boy actually has an attention deficit disorder, he can improve his behaviors. Referring to him in this way causes him to feel powerless to control his behaviors. Most parents don't wish schools to label their children negatively, yet they unintentionally label their own children.

## Case 3

What about Brian? He's impossible! Yes, Brian is impossible. He hears it every time his dad is out of town. His mother tells his dad on the telephone how impossible Brian has been. When his dad's at home and walks in the door from work, the first message from his mom is that Brian's been impossible again. What Brian knows is that he's not only impossible, but his mom is powerless to discipline him or guide him. It would be wonderful if that encouraged Brian to be sympathetic to his mother, but as you know, he'll continue to step all over his mother.

How could that be changed? Skip the impossibility of his behavior. Concentrate on the techniques that channel and limit that behavior and referentially speak to Dad or Grandma about his positive and improved behaviors: "Dad, Brian's been a terrific help while you were traveling!" "Grandma, Brian seems to be maturing. He seems to be outgrowing his immature misbehaviors."

Referential speaking has a great deal of impact on children. It truly sets expectations. If you use it positively, provided it is not too extreme, it has positive impact. If you use it negatively, it may have a terrible impact on your children, their attitude about learning, and their self-confidence. **When you see the positive, tell someone. When you see the negative, limit it or ignore it, but don't talk about it if your children are anywhere within a thousand feet.** They have extraordinary homing-in senses when they hear their names. Don't you remember how you tuned in when you heard your parents talk about you? The more you say, the more you'll see.

Here's another example from my personal experience: While I was writing about referential speaking for a previous book, I thought I'd better experiment with Sara, our youngest child. I was always in school or working when she was growing up, so I tried most everything out on Sara. In this case, Sara didn't know about the experiment (although she does now), nor did my husband. He was sitting across from me at the kitchen table in conversation after our day at work. Sara was upstairs in her bedroom doing her homework. I knew that Sara could hear everything upstairs that we talked about in the kitchen. So as part of the conversation with my husband, I simply injected a little bit of preplanned referential

PARENT
POINTER

speaking. I said, "Sara's been working so hard lately. She's getting so much homework done." We continued our conversation. It wasn't ten minutes before Sara came downstairs, saying in haste, "I just came down for a quick drink of water. I'm going right back up to do my homework. I'm really getting a lot done." The experiment worked, and I knew that our positive referential speaking inspired Sara's continued hard work that evening.

Try referential speaking about your children (not your spouse). You can make a difference in a day by speaking referentially to another adult about your children. **Just give a positive message about their efforts or behaviors. Make sure that you're honest and realistic.** You'll discover how powerful adult communication can be for inspiring positive expectations in your children. However, please be conscious of your referential speaking, either positive or negative, because as our grandparents used to say, "Little pitchers have big ears." Your children are listening. Even when you close the doors, they can hear through walls. When you think they are asleep, they seem to absorb your words. Taking walks not only affords exercise but also privacy for those difficult discussions about your children that you don't wish them to hear.

PARENT
POINTER

# EMPOWER YOUR CHILD WITH THE POWER TO BE A CHILD

When children are small, they require small amounts of power. As they get older and grow in maturity and responsibility, they should have expanded power. **Don't treat children as little adults. Give them child, not adult, choices.** Don't consult them in everything or assume that they can share your adult experiences and feelings. Let them look forward to adult privileges and power, and permit them to gradually earn adult status.

PARENT
POINTER

Certain kinds of children are most likely to be "adultized" by their parents: gifted children; only or oldest children; and children of single or divorced parents. Adultizing confers some benefits but also causes some serious risks for children's healthy development.

Children's verbal giftedness increases the likelihood of adultizement because very bright children often display advanced vocabulary, reasoning skills, and sensitivities that cause parents to assume that those children are more mature. They may actually be more mature than their age-mates, but aren't likely to be as mature as they sound. They require the opportunity to play out a reasonable childhood. They are children first, gifted children second.

Only children and oldest children are frequently treated like one of the adults in the family. It's reasonably easy for parents to accommodate one child, and they frequently do so, sometimes at the expense of the other parent. Thus, these children become accustomed to equal adult status, and sometimes, more than equal power. They may sound exactly like little adults as they boss other children or insist on being treated as an equal to their parents.

Single parents and those undergoing divorce frequently choose one child, usually their oldest, as confidant and partner. They may actually view this child as the main purpose of their lives and direct all their efforts toward the emotional sustenance of that child. They may consult with the child about major life issues and even share their bed. They often assure the child that they will always love her more than anyone else in the entire world. They replace the closeness and intimacy that they would normally have with a spouse with their relationship with this favored child. The adultizing of the child may result from the parent's feelings of rejection and vulnerability. Sometimes these parents feel that they must compensate for the child's perceived insecurity because she has only one parent.

Adultized children gain the social, intellectual, and apparent emotional sophistication that emerges from a close and enriched experience with their parent. They may have more mature insights into behaviors than their peers. They may, however, suffer from the feelings of insecurity and powerlessness that emerge with too much adult power. They may feel insecure because they simply don't know how to limit themselves. In classroom and peer relationships, where they aren't given adult status, they may feel "put down" or disrespected in comparison to the way in which they're regarded at home. They actually feel "disempowered" relative to the feelings of being overempowered at home.[1]

The most difficult risk of adultizement is "dethronement." When another sibling is born or the parent remarries, the child may feel irrationally and extraordinarily jealous, although he knows he should be happy about the new member of the family.[2] Dethroned children typically exhibit negativity, anger, or sadness. Their personalities

SINGLE PARENT, CHILD PARTNER

may change so dramatically that parents, teachers, and even doctors may assume they're undergoing clinical depression. Some comments from parents about dethroned children follow:

> "He was a delightful child until I brought our second son home from the hospital; he was like a wild animal thereafter. I couldn't seem to control him at all."
>
> "She was a marvelous little girl until her brother started reading as well as she did. She became obnoxious, unpleasant, negative, and attention seeking. She only seemed comfortable when only the two of us were together."

If you adultize children too early, you will find that they want to run your family, their teachers, and other students. As in politics, too much power corrupts. Such children may become continual arguers who argue about everything. They believe that if they provide sufficient reason, they are *always* right. They say, "Why would I argue unless I was right?"

Those arguing children can no longer see merit in any opinion but their own. As they trap you into the battles you promised your-

DETHRONING AN EMPEROR

self you would handle rationally, you find yourself losing your temper again. "How did this happen?" you ask yourself. Sometimes you feel as if you'd like to kick them. "How can that ten-year-old believe he can run the entire family? Does this child have no humility at all?"

Teachers and parents, offended by such powerful children, try to "put them in their places." Adults respond to these dictatorial, offensive children with a big NO permanently engraved on their foreheads. The children make requests. Adults say no. Adults stop listening. "No, no, no. Go away," they say. "Unfair," the children argue, undaunted. They believe that no one understands them, and almost no one does.

# DIRECTIONS OF POWER: DEPENDENCE AND DOMINANCE

Children may exhibit too much power in either dependent or dominant directions or both. Dominant power is easily identified in aggressive children who want to monopolize attention or in those who argue as described earlier. They are almost immediately viewed as too powerful.

Dependent children who manipulate their adult world in ways that say "take care of me, feel sorry for me, make things easier, help me, protect me, or shelter me" are not usually recognized as powerful. Although their power may result from feelings of powerlessness, and their words and body language suggest that they feel powerless, their requests for help attract and maintain much more adult attention, protection, and assistance than they require. Early adult caretakers did too much for these dependent children, helping and protecting them so much that they unconsciously "push adult buttons" for assistance they believe they need. They don't take initiative. Instead they ask for more and more help at home and in school. Because they are kind and caring and the children's symptoms of power (tears and requests for pity) are very persuasive, parents and teachers continue to protect them, unintentionally stealing from them their opportunities to cope with challenge. As a result, these children don't develop sufficient self-confidence to build the independent power that fosters achievement and accomplishment. Instead, their tenuous control is directed to the hidden manipulation of adults. They hardly ever manipulate intentionally, but they do manipulate effectively and extensively.

The children in the inner circle in figure 1.1 are achievers. They've internalized a sense of the relationship between efforts and outcomes. That is, they persevere because they recognize that their efforts make a difference. They know how to cope with competition. They love to win, but when they lose or experience a failure, they don't give up; instead, they try again. They understand that winning and losing are temporary. They don't view themselves as failures but only see some experiences as unsuccessful and learn from them. No children (or adults) remain in the inner circle at all times; however, the inner circle represents the predominant behavior of achieving children. Outside the circle are prototypical children who represent characteristics of underachievement syndrome. These children have learned avoidance and defensive behaviors to protect their fragile self-concepts because they fear taking the risk of making the efforts that might lead to less-than-perfect performance.

Figure 1.1

# The Inner Circle of Achievers

SOURCE: *Why Bright Kids Get Poor Grades and What You Can Do About It* by S. B. Rimm (New York: Crown Publishing Group, 1995).

The children on the left side of the figure are those who have learned to manipulate adults in their environment in dependent ways. Their words and body language say, "Take care of me, protect me, this is too hard, feel sorry for me, I need help." Adults in these children's lives listen to their children too literally and unintentionally provide more protection and help than the children need. As a result these children get so much help from others that they lose self-confidence. They do less, and parents and teachers expect less. They quietly slip between the cracks, neither they nor their parents or teachers recognizing the capabilities that were exhibited when they were younger.

On the right side of the figure are the dominant children. These children only select activities in which they feel confident they'll be winners. They tend to believe that they know best about almost everything. They manipulate by trapping parents and teachers into arguments. The adults attempt to be fair and rational, while the dominant children attempt to win because they're convinced they're right. If the children lose, they consider the adults to be unfair, mean, or the enemy. Once the adults are established as unfair enemies, they use that enmity as an excuse for not doing their work or taking on their responsibilities. Furthermore, they manage to get someone on their side in an alliance against that adult. Gradually, the children increase their list of adult enemies. They lose confidence in themselves because their confidence is based precariously on their successful manipulation of parents and teachers. When adults tire of being manipulated and respond negatively, the dominant children complain that adults don't understand or like them, and a negative atmosphere becomes pervasive.

The difference between the upper and lower quadrants in figure 1.1 is the degree of and visibility of these children's problems. Children in the upper quadrants have minor problems. They may adjust or outgrow the problems. Parents who understand the potential for their worsening can often prevent them from escalating. If upper-quadrant children continue in their patterns, however, they will likely move into lower quadrants. Most of the dependent children will, by adolescence, change to dominant or mixed dependent-dominant patterns. There are also some children who combine both dependent and dominant characteristics from the start.

Neither of the two extremes, dependent or dominant power, appears to cause major problems at home during the preschool years. Parents often become accustomed to dependency or dominance. They may label their dependent children as somewhat immature and continue to do more for them than they require. They may even acknowledge that their too domineering children seem a little bit "spoiled." They have reasonable confidence, however, that their children's problems will be resolved when they get older, when teachers and the school structure will help their too powerful children adjust.

Dependent and dominant children practice these control patterns for several years before they enter school. It feels to them that these behaviors work well, and they know of no others. They carry them into the classroom and expect to relate to teachers and peers in the same way they have to their family. Teachers may be effective in improving some of the children's ways of relating; however, the more extreme the dependency or dominance, the more difficult it is to modify. Furthermore, teachers may respond instinctively to these children in ways that only exacerbate the problem. The dependency pattern often disguises itself as shyness, insecurity, immaturity, inattentiveness, or even a learning disability. Teachers may also protect these children too much. The dominant pattern does not always show itself in the early elementary grades because the child feels fulfilled by the excitement and power of school achievement. Dominance may also be exhibited as giftedness or creativity, or, not so positively, as ADHD or a discipline problem. If it shows itself as a discipline problem, teachers may unintentionally label these children negatively. The children may be sitting next to the teacher's desk or against the wall with a reputation as being the "bad" kid of the class. Parents often refer to a dominant child as strong willed or stubborn.

Even if some teachers manage these children well in school, the dependent or dominant patterns may continue to be reinforced at home or in other classrooms. If so, the problems will probably surface in later years. Dependent and dominant children are likely to become underachievers because their self-confidence is built on manipulating others instead of on their own accomplishments.

PARENT POINTER

**In granting children appropriate power, we must give them sufficient freedom and power to provide them with the courage for intellectual risk-taking. However, we should also teach sufficient humility so that they recognize that their views of the world are not the only correct ones.** Although we need to empower them enough to study, learn, question, persevere, challenge, and discuss, we cannot grant them so much power that they infringe on parents' and teachers' authority for guiding them. That authority is indeed more fragile for this generation's children than it has ever been.

On May 25, 1989, I sat with thousands of parents and family members at the commencement ceremony of the Johns Hopkins University (our son, David, was among the graduates). Dr. Steven Muller, president of the university, provided a farewell to the audience that seemed to bear an uncanny resemblance to the message about power and freedom that I regularly give to parents. I've excerpted the lines that seem appropriate for your children. As you read it, please substitute "our family" for "this university" or "Johns Hopkins University."

> As we congratulate you on your academic attainments and wish you well, it also seems more timely than ever to remind you . . . that you have received here a great blessing, and that therefore you bear as well a great responsibility. Whatever your field of study, you have been blessed by academic freedom in all fullness. *Veritas Vos Liberabit*—The Truth Shall Make You Free—is the motto of this university. . . .
>
> . . . Let me point out as well that you here today are privileged already to be citizens of the information society; that your education at Johns Hopkins qualifies you for leadership; that the freedom of your education is the world's envy; and that the information technology of tomorrow will make today's mere beginnings look like child's play. . . .
>
> But let me also remind you that knowledge alone is not wisdom; that information is a means, not an end; that the object of free inquiry is truth, not profit; *that freedom without responsibility is animal anarchy.*
>
> . . . Today we celebrate with you your intelligence and your academic achievements. . . . And at Johns Hopkins we invest you with a special trust and mission: to continue your search for truth; to cherish freedom as the only way to truth; to live by the truth that human beings who seek to be free of a master must then *be fully masters of themselves.*

Dr. Muller's message to those graduates should guide you in providing freedom that matches children's capabilities for responsibility so that your family will not resemble "animal anarchy" and so that your children grow to be "masters of themselves."

**The Dependent Pattern: Facilitating Independent Power.** As parents, **be careful not to do for your children what they can do for themselves, or they won't be able to build self-confidence.** If you wonder why these powerful dependent children don't have self-confidence, think of the ways in which you've built your own self-confidence. You didn't build confidence by accomplishing easy tasks. Easy tasks are appropriate for relaxation or vacation; however, they don't build confidence. It's when you attempt a challenge and accomplish something you never before believed you could that you climb one small step up the ladder of self-confidence. In the same way, your children must earn their confidence one small step at a time. No matter how many times you tell them how bright or wonderful they are, you can't anoint them with self-confidence. Unfortunately, they must struggle to earn self-confidence, and just as unfortunately, we as parents must watch that awful struggle. If in the name of kindness we steal their struggle, we only find that we've also stolen that elusive self-confidence.

The mother of a fourth-grade, physically handicapped child named Alex shared with me an example of a dependent manipulation. She had heard me talk about how dependent children are prevented from building self-confidence. She described her son's situation to me, telling me that he had very little confidence. Each morning she dressed Alex to be ready for school because he was slow and she had to get to work on time. I asked her if Alex was capable of dressing himself, and she said he was. I pointed out to her that if he was capable and wasn't dressing himself, then he couldn't have self-confidence.

Alex's mother resolved to change the pattern by insisting that he dress himself independently. She chose a Saturday for fear of attempting the new struggle on a workday. She told Alex that from now on she expected him to dress himself. He protested. She insisted. She said he couldn't leave his room until he had dressed himself. He eyed her imploringly and cried. She left, saying she would come back only after he was dressed. Alex's sobs, cries, screams, and his desperation were hard for her to listen to, so she retreated to the laundry room where she hoped the dryer noise would muffle his cries. As she folded laundry, she kept repeating, "I hate Sylvia Rimm, I hate Sylvia Rimm, I hate Sylvia Rimm." Finally, after two hours, Alex had successfully dressed himself. On Sunday, Alex dressed in half an hour. There wasn't any crying or screaming, just the independent dressing. By Monday, Alex was dressed in ten minutes. Thus began Alex's requests for new challenges. His confidence grew. His relationship with his mother became more positive, and furthermore, even his stepfather acknowledged that he was beginning to like his stepson.

Daniel had a traumatic and difficult birth, which caused his parents to wonder if he would ever be normal. He had multiple surgeries as an infant, so his parents expected him to be slow in his development initially. They worked hard assisting Daniel and even enrolled him in the local public-school program for mentally challenged and handicapped children. When they came to my clinic, they apologized for Daniel's slowness and explained that their other children were indeed intellectually gifted. They described Daniel, an eighth-grader, as needing continual help with both his homework and his classwork. They also acknowledged that Daniel's social skills were inadequate and that he couldn't take care of himself on the

SOMETIMES IT'S REALLY HARD

playground or at home with his siblings. They punctuated most descriptive sentences about Daniel with the words "he's just slow."

I had already reviewed Daniel's WISC-IQ scores and could not believe these parents were describing the child we had tested. Before showing my surprise, I asked if we had tested any of their other children. When they explained again that their other children had no problems, I told them that their "slow" son, whom they and teachers believed needed continual assistance both intellectually and socially, had an IQ of 137.

How could that be? This eighth-grade boy who was so lacking in confidence and so dependent on family and teachers had fooled all the adults in his environment. No one realized how capable he was, least of all himself. These parents, who had worried that their son would not graduate from high school or hold a job, suddenly realized that their son was capable of attending college and reaching for a professional career. I shall never forget the shocked expressions on their faces.

It took only a few months for this young man to become much more independent and several additional months for him to catch up on skills that no one had assumed he could master. By high school Daniel became an honor student. His days of learned helplessness were over, and his confidence grew remarkably. Daniel's parents had encouraged the independence of all three of their other children; it was their oldest son's early development problems that had trapped them, his teachers, and even his peers into assuming he was too "slow" to manage normal classroom achievement and social adjustment.

**Dominant Children.** Children should have choices from early on. You, as parents, are responsible for *providing* and *limiting* those choices. Notice, I emphasize limiting as well as providing. Some parents err in believing that children should have almost all the choices. I often see intelligent parents of toddlers and preschoolers ask these children if they'd like to nap, when and what they'd like to eat, if they'd like to go out to play, and even if they'd like a babysitter to stay with them. When parents ask these children if they want to participate in daily routines that should be expected of children, they confer power to their children that they haven't the vaguest idea of how to use. Although sometimes they are actually so tired or hungry that they accept the opportunity to eat and sleep at appropriate times, at other times the children, although exhausted and cranky, say they prefer not to. At age three they have choices that they are not able to handle. They fuss and argue about simple routines that parents should be guiding them through. Children usually comply when guided positively, and even if they are truly not hungry or tired, a few minutes at a meal or a half hour in the crib will do no harm. It will at least give them the opportunity to eat or fall asleep without a battle. The rule of thumb is: **Don't ask children if they'd like to do something you expect them to do anyway. Simply tell them positively and firmly of the plan.**

PARENT POINTER

Of course, the number and variety of choices increase with the children's increased maturity and responsibility. School-age children should have more choices than preschool children, but even then, planning appropriate mealtimes and bedtimes prevents the home from becoming a battleground. For example, children might select their own breakfast cereal, but skipping breakfast should not be an option. Snacks can be optional but shouldn't displace meals. Children can learn early to choose what to wear to school from an appropriate selection of clothing presented by a parent. However, children don't choose whether or not to go to school.

You're in charge of your children. Be confident in your ability to lead them. Children feel secure following their parents' leadership provided they have become accustomed to accepting guidance. Although they're likely to push limits sporadically to determine the extent of their freedom, they'll respect your noes when they're given firmly and fairly. Children who haven't learned to accept limits in childhood cannot be expected to accept them in adolescence. Parents who have offered their children too many preferences soon find themselves engaged in battle with strong-willed children who expect to do everything their own way.

## WHY DO WE OVEREMPOWER?
## HOW DO CHILDREN THINK?

After you've read about dependent and dominant manipulations and you realize that your children have too much dependent or dominant power, you may find yourself wondering why you responded to these manipulations in the first place. The answer is both simple and complex.

Most good, loving parents project their own feelings onto their children. They try to understand their children's feelings by thinking about how they would feel under similar circumstances, then reason with their children as they would wish to be reasoned with. You listen to what they are saying and try to respond to their requests in the same way in which you would wish that your friends would listen and respond to you.

Now, here's the glitch! Such responses are based on the assumption that children have developed cognitively and morally to an adult level. But they *haven't*. They are still only children. They are not yet capable of adult thinking.

Many of you have taken high school or college courses in psychology. You may have learned about Piaget's stages of cognitive development and Kohlberg's stages of moral development.[3, 4] See figures 1.2 and 1.3. You may have memorized those stages and repeated them back on exams or read about the theories in popular magazines. These theories have been researched, and psychologists, for the most part, have accepted them.

Most parents, however, don't generalize these stages of development to the practical business of bringing up their kids. Instead, many parents, teachers, and counselors treat children like little adults and assume that they're wise and mature enough to express all their needs. We use their literal communications as the basis for guiding them, believing that they always know what they're talking about and what's best for them. Even when they have nothing to say, we coax children to express their feelings. They try to comply and often say what they think we'd like them to. We act on what they say because we believe that they must know what's best for them, although they are mainly telling us what they believe will make us happy or will meet their needs in the next half hour or, at most, the next week.

Please reflect for a few moments upon your own childhood. When did you begin your introspective exploration of your personal values and motivations? When did you begin to interpret what made you feel sad or glad? When did you start to understand why you procrastinated or why you didn't? When did you understand the underlying basis for your elations and depressions?

Figure 1.2

# Piaget's Stages of Intellectual Development

| STAGE | APPROXIMATE AGES* | CHARACTERIZATION |
|---|---|---|
| 1. Sensorimotor | Birth–2 years | Infant differentiates himself from objects; gradually becomes aware of the relationship between his actions and their effects on the environment so that he can act intentionally and make interesting events last longer (if he shakes a rattle, it will make a noise); learns that objects continue to exist even though no longer visible (object performance). |
| 2. Preoperational | 2–7 years | Uses language and can represent objects by images and words; is still *egocentric*, the world revolves around him and he has difficulty taking the viewpoint of others; classifies objects by single salient features: if A is like B in one respect, must be like B in other respects; toward the end of this stage begins to use numbers and develop conservation concepts. |
| 3. Concrete operational | 7–12 years | Becomes capable of logical thought; achieves conservation concepts in this order: number (age 6), mass (age 7), weight (age 9); can classify objects, order them in series along a dimension (such as size), and understand relational terms (A is longer than B). |

continued on next page

---

Figure 1.2 (continued)

## Piaget's Stages of Intellectual Development

| STAGE | APPROXIMATE AGES* | CHARACTERIZATION |
|---|---|---|
| 4. Formal operational | 12 years and up | Can think in abstract terms, follow logical propositions, and reason by hypothesis; isolates the elements of a problem and systematically explores all possible solutions; becomes concerned with the hypothetical, the future, and ideological problems. |

\* The ages given are averages. They may vary considerably depending upon intelligence, cultural background, and socioeconomic factors, but the order of progression is the same for all children. Piaget has described more detailed phases within each stage; only a very general characterization of each stage is given here.

SOURCE: *The Origins of Intelligence in Children* by J. Piaget (New York: International Universities Press, 1952).

---

Young people rarely begin in-depth thinking about their feelings, thoughts, and motivations before late adolescence. For me it began in my sophomore or junior year in high school and continued in college. And it went on. And it goes on. As adults we continue to learn about ourselves. We look back at our childhood motivations with very different insights.

Little kids just respond and repeat back beliefs and opinions. Their cognitive development affects their moral development. Kohlberg tells us that in early childhood children define right by what is rewarded or punished. Later, right becomes what pleases or displeases the important "others" in their lives. Children learn to combine and reorganize adult ideas and restate them. When we hear the ideas we (or someone else) have taught them, we often wrongly respond to them as if the ideas were theirs in the first place. Little kids really need to be little kids until their brain struc-

Figure 1.3

# Kohlberg's Stages in the Development of Moral Values

| LEVELS AND STAGES | ILLUSTRATIVE BEHAVIOR |
|---|---|
| **Level I. Premoral** | |
| 1. Punishment and obedience orientation | Obeys rules in order to avoid punishment |
| 2. Naive instrumental hedonism | Conforms to obtain rewards, to have favors returned |
| **Level II. Morality of conventional role-conformity** | |
| 3. "Good-boy" morality of maintaining relations, approval of others | Conforms to avoid disapproval, dislike by others |
| 4. Authority maintaining morality | Conforms to avoid censure by legitimate authorities, with resultant guilt |
| **Level III. Morality of self-accepted moral principles** | |
| 5. Morality of contract, of individual rights, and of democratically accepted law | Conforms to maintain the respect of of the impartial spectator judging in terms of community welfare |
| 6. Morality of individual principles of conscience | Conforms to avoid self-condemnation |

SOURCE: L. Kohlberg, "Moral and Religious Education and the Public Schools: A Developmental View," in *Religion and Public Education*, ed. T. Sizer (Boston: Houghton Mifflin, 1967).

ture and their experiences permit them to grow gradually into adults. Examine the information you have about your children and their environments before you respond to their expressions of feelings. **Try to remember how you responded as a child instead of interpreting your children's responses in adult ways.** There are many possibilities for what your children really mean (see figure 1.4). Listen to the words of your children and interpret them with your adult wisdom.

PARENT
POINTER

# TAKE-CHARGE TECHNIQUES FOR PARENTS

There are a few such techniques you can use that will help you to lead your children to feeling guided and secure. As your children grow, you'll be able to add to their choices and their power. **Increase their power gradually.** Remember that once power is given, it's not easily taken away. Because my techniques may feel disempowering for some too powerful children, be prepared for some anger, tantrums, or temporary depression. The power we're taking from them is manipulative power—in the long run, they'll be better off without it. The power they'll earn and learn is positive personal power. It will strengthen them and help them to build confidence. The two kinds of power, manipulative and positive, don't fit well together. We must remove the first to achieve the second. It will work. Be patient and calm.

PARENT
POINTER

**Rewards and Punishments.** Kohlberg explains that early stages of morality are shaped by adult rewards and punishments. Although adults have used them from time immemorial to guide children's learning, new theories and new research show when to use—and when not to use—the commonsense approaches of the past. The purpose of rewards and punishments is to aid children's learning—learning to learn, learning to live.

A target provides a model for the continuum and variety of rewards and punishments. The bull's-eye of that target represents *intrinsic rewards.* Intrinsic rewards are the satisfaction of producing quality work or the simple joys of the activity; that is, the children develop interests and are engaged. The enthusiasm and excitement of learning provide intrinsic rewards. Your goal is to encourage

Figure 1.4

# How Do Children Think?

| CHILDREN SAY | PARENTS' USUAL RESPONSE | ALTERNATIVE INTERPRETATIONS |
|---|---|---|
| I need help. | This must be too hard. I should help. | It may actually be too difficult, and my child may need help or . . .<br>My child may be afraid to try.<br>My child is accustomed to being helped too much.<br>My child avoids anything unfamiliar.<br>My child may prefer to play with friends. |
| My teacher doesn't like me. | The teacher has probably said something to hurt my child's feelings. | Perhaps the teacher has, or . . .<br>My child may not be the center of attention in this class.<br>The teacher may be challenging my child.<br>The teacher may have corrected my child.<br>The teacher may not praise as much as my child is accustomed to. |
| The kids are picking on me. | The playground supervisor should be protecting my child. | Maybe the supervisor should or . . .<br>One child said something unpleasant.<br>My child wasn't chosen for the team first.<br>Children are retaliating for my child's aggressive behavior.<br>Kids are picking on lots of other kids, too. |
| I feel sad. | Something terrible must have happened that my child can't talk about. | Possibly true or . . .<br>My child did poorly on a test.<br>My child feels bored.<br>My child didn't get a toy that was wanted.<br>My child got in trouble in school.<br>A friend couldn't come to play. |
| I want to cure cancer and help the world. | My child is so sensitive, caring, and smart. Maybe he/she will cure cancer. | My child may be caring and smart or . . .<br>My child knows that people smile and hug when he/she talks about curing the world.<br>Grandma just died of cancer and he/she misses her. |

continued on next page

Figure 1.4 (continued)

## How Do Children Think?

| Children Say | Parents' Usual Response | Alternative Interpretations |
|---|---|---|
| | | People tell my child that he/she is smart enough to cure cancer and that makes my child feel smart. |
| School is boring. | I wish schools were arranged to challenge bright children. | There may not be enough challenge or . . . There may be too much challenge. There may be a lot of written work. The teacher may not be a stand-up comedian. The child may prefer recess to lunch. |

Source: *Learning Leads Q-Cards, Parent Pointers* by S. B. Rimm (Watertown, Wis.: Apple Publishing Company, 1990).

many bull's-eye rewards for your children's learning experiences. To see the effects of intrinsic rewards, observe a one-year-old dropping blocks into a container, dumping them, then repeating the activity, or notice a high school artist absorbed for hours in a watercolor painting.

As in target practice, the bull's-eye is hardest to hit. Furthermore, it isn't possible for all behaviors to be intrinsically rewarding. Some skills that kids may learn are just not fun; for example, learning math facts or handwriting skills or even making one's bed or doing dishes may not fit into the intrinsically rewarding categories. There are actually many boring tasks that will never be fun either at home or at school but are nevertheless important for learning.

The wider circles that surround the bull's-eye are easier to use and more appropriate for some tasks. They're more frequently used by parents. Outside of the bull's-eye circle is a somewhat larger circle that provides the second-best tools for rewarding and punishing children. This reward category represents attention given by parents, teachers, and close family members. Attention is effective in teaching children to be learners, workers, and thinkers. When im-

AIM FOR THE BULL'S-EYE

portant adults are pleased with children's performances, their praise and interest serve as rewards; their disappointment or lack of interest feel like a punishment. **Your pleasure and your disappointment are highly effective for motivating your children.** Whether or not you use them intentionally to guide your children, you should be aware that your children will be sensitive to your feelings and will, for the most part, try to please you if they believe they can.

PARENT POINTER

The third circle, representing the natural consequences of an activity, provides the next most effective category of rewards and punishments. (You may prefer to interchange circles two and three. They are equally important.) Good grades are a consequence of children's hard work. Poor grades are a consequence of lack of effort. Children who dress themselves independently come to school feeling better than the children who are nagged before school. The first are experiencing positive consequences; the latter, negative consequences. Children who start fights suffer the consequences of starting those fights. Other children will fight back or say mean things to them. Principals or teachers may give them detentions or other consequences. Consequences automatically reward or punish children in their learning.

Sometimes the consequence of an activity doesn't fit the experience. It may, therefore, provide inappropriate learning. Your child may not have studied and yet received an A on the test anyway. Thus, he may believe that school is easy and study is unimportant. Your child may have prepared for a test, but did poorly on the test nevertheless. Sometimes you may not be able to control those inappropriate circumstances; other times you may be able to reorganize the order of learning experiences to create consequences that will automatically reinforce your children; for example, with the morning and homework routines described in chapter 3.

PARENT POINTER

**The personal attention of important adults and natural consequences are preferable to the two broad outer reward and punishment rings of the target.** The fourth ring uses activities as a reward for children's learning performance and withdrawal of activities as a punishment. Parents tend to use—or even overuse—the withdrawal or punishment component of activities more frequently than the reward component. Parents frequently take away activities for long periods of time. The term typically used for withdrawal of social activities is *grounding*. Some parents ground for a day or two, others for a week or two, and still others "for eternity." When children are grounded for what seems like eternity, they feel angry enough to try almost anything. They want to get even by punishing parents. **Although removal of activities is much more effective than spanking or screaming, parents should be careful to remove these activities briefly;** for example, telling a child he can't play his video games for one day gets your point across. Taking video games away for a full week also makes your point clear, but it provides no motivation for your child's improved behavior the next day. Furthermore, if parents keep adding a day for bad behavior, kids give up in despair and think there's no longer a reason to try to do better, or dig their heels in and accelerate the battle.

PARENT POINTER

The final and largest ring of the circle is related to the use of material rewards and punishments, which may include stickers, baseball cards, stars, points, money, gifts, etc. These are referred to as token reinforcements and are probably used most frequently of all. Token reinforcements are effective for short-term purposes. However, they also tend to be overused. Children may learn to negotiate tokens or become dependent on their use. **Token rewards are most effective when they're used temporarily as a bridge to the inner circles of the target and when other less tangible rewards don't work.**

**Overuse of material rewards may result in the unintentional teaching of children to manipulate adults for tokens.** For example, one young man who was getting money for completing his schoolwork stopped doing his work. He asked for an increase in money to continue completing his work. Sometimes children who have been paid for doing home chores will ask for a higher payment for doing the same chores, or they may refuse to do any chores unless they're paid. These are negative side effects of overusing token reinforcements.

When parents use token punishments, they sometimes expect children to pay them for misbehavior; for example, if the children forget to feed their pets, it costs them fifty cents out of their allowance. Again, the occasional shock value of having to pay from their own money as a penalty can sometimes be more effective in getting your children's attention than constant nagging, but overuse will empty your children's meager coffers. When your children have nothing left to give you, and they owe you their next three allowances, they give up in despair, and you're back to relentless nagging. **Use token punishments sparingly.**

My clinic experiences show the effectiveness of token rewards. We use them frequently at the clinic to initiate a study or chore schedule. We emphasize to the children, however, that we're only using them temporarily. We want to help children move toward higher-level reward systems such as improved grades (consequences), improved feelings between family members (positive attention), and most of all, improved self-confidence (intrinsic). In that way, the children understand the plan and the goal of the token rewards. They recognize them as a temporary way to help them change bad habits.

Many parents use the two outer circles of the target most often. As you gain expertise in parenting, you'll find yourself using the three inner circles more frequently.

In summary, rewards and punishments are effective tools for teaching children. Always try to reward as close to the bull's-eye as possible. The entire target is certainly acceptable as long as you rec-

I EXPECT TO BE PAID

ognize that the outer circles are bridges to bull's-eye intrinsic learning. Most important, **don't overreward or overpunish**. If you do, your children will probably rarely reach bull's-eye learning as they learn to depend on and expect negotiations for all their activities.

**Overpunishment and Opposition.** I don't know of a single achieving child who was inspired toward learning through punishment. Yet, parents use punishment so frequently and ineffectively that you might wonder why you find yourself expecting to motivate your children in this way. Parents continue to use punishments because, at first, they seem to work. Children stop their bad behavior temporarily, so their parents feel the punishment is effective. However, if parents overuse punishments, they cause two side effects. First, to prevent the problem behaviors, you'll find that you'll have to use more and bigger punishments; for example, longer and more frequent groundings. You'll soon run out of controls that will punish sufficiently to stop all the bad behaviors. The second side effect is that children who are punished too much resent their parents and want to get even, as indicated in this quotation by one college freshman: "My parents punished me, I punished them back. My parents punished me, I punished them back. You would have thought that I'd have realized that since their punishments didn't work, why would mine?"

Nevertheless, that cycle of punishing and counterpunishing is common. It heightens the opposition and increases negativism within the family. Soon everyone seems to be punishing everyone else, and there's an atmosphere of pervasive anger and getting even. Not only does continuous punishment engender an atmosphere of anger, but **overpunishment may lead to depression for dependent children who lack self-confidence.** These children literally give up. They do not believe themselves capable of doing anything about their problems.

PARENT POINTER

If you're in the habit of overpunishing, you may also be in the habit of shortening or removing these punishments after you realize you've overreacted. That essentially teaches your children that you are all sound and fury, but empty power. They learn to fear you and manipulate you. You provide them with the model for anger and the chance to practice their manipulations. You do all of this because you love your children so much and want so much for them to do well but feel so frustrated with them because they refuse to follow your good advice. You, too, feel powerless. Figure 1.5 gives you some guidelines in your use of punishments.

**Positive Messages.** **Positive statements about expectations increase the likelihood that your children will try to carry them through.** For example, if your children haven't been efficient in doing homework, you may decide that after homework is done, the family will play some games, watch television, read some stories, or have some popcorn (see homework routines in chapter 3). These are positive activity rewards for your children's completing their homework. Children who don't complete their homework cannot participate. To state your expectations positively you would say, "I hope you can finish your homework and do a good job so we can have time to play checkers or Scrabble at seven. I'll be looking forward to it." That statement fosters the child's alliance. Saying it in a negative way, such as, "If you don't get your homework done, you can't play Scrabble with us," provides the same information, but is likely to make children angry. It may prevent them from wanting to finish their work and make them feel as if they're losing an argument. Many parents emphasize the negative and threaten their chil-

PARENT POINTER

Figure 1.5

# Guidelines for Punishment

- Punish calmly.
- Punish briefly. Ten minutes, one day, or one evening are usually sufficient.
- When you take away something like a bicycle, telephone, etc., don't expect children to tell you you're right. They usually say "I don't care" or "That's not fair." They do care or they wouldn't say anything.
- Spanking more than once rarely works. Furthermore, the spanking only models aggression.
- If you're very angry, use time-out for young children. For older children, tell them you're disappointed and you will give some thought to the appropriate punishment. (A little healthy fear while they're waiting will be effective, and time to think about it will keep you rational.)
- Once your punishment is given, don't take it away.
- Be consistent and firm.
- Don't keep adding punishments. That only increases your children's resentment.

SOURCE: *Learning Leads Q-Cards, Parent Pointers* by S. B. Rimm (Watertown, Wis.: Apple Publishing Company, 1990).

dren regularly. Continuous threats prevent children from feeling trusted and good about themselves.

Don't be too hard on yourself if every once in a while you find you're being negative. The frustrations and pressures of parenting may cause all parents to occasionally act more negatively than they'd like to. **Be positive as often as you can.** Positive environments increase the likelihood of positive children. However, negative slips are human, and your children are resilient enough to handle some parental anger.

PARENT
POINTER

**Reasoning and Talk.** All of us would like to be rational parents and have reasonable children, too. You should teach expected behaviors and explain to children the reasons why they're expected to accomplish a task or carry through a responsibility. Reasoning with children helps them to internalize moral values; however, **keep your discussions brief.** Active little children hardly ever hear your

PARENT
POINTER

whole explanation anyway. They turn you off after your first two or three sentences. Beyond that, your voice becomes a mere nagging background, or they'll complain that you're lecturing. If you make your statements brief, you'll be more likely to communicate effectively, and you'll also avoid the continual debating that turns arguers into power strugglers.

**Overemotional Responses.** Many parents are screamers. Mothers and fathers who come to my clinic sometimes claim they tie for best (or worst) screamers. However, mothers tend to believe that fathers scream louder than they do. Mothers often blame screaming fathers for destroying children's self-concepts, although they believe their own screaming does no damage. (It must be the volume of male voices that convinces mothers.) Fathers who hear mothers scream often complain that mothers are too controlling and sometimes criticize their spouses within their children's hearing.

When you scream at your children, it means that you feel powerless to do anything about their behaviors. If you find you constantly scream at your children, be sure to learn to use the time-out and anti-arguing techniques that follow. If you use them correctly, these techniques should reduce your screaming to a minimum. Remember: When you lose your temper, you're out of control. Your children sense that and recognize that you can't manage them. The result is that the balance of power is shifted; they're in control of you. It makes your children feel insecure when they can step on wimpy parents. **Stay calm and in charge (at least most of the time). If you don't feel in charge, pretend you are.**

PARENT POINTER

**Setting Limits by Time-Out.** Some children seem too powerful from infancy. Although they are fed, cared for, and loved, they're not contented, and they push limits. Some parents tell me that by age two their children are controlling them, and they find themselves yelling, screaming, and acting in irrational ways that they never envisioned for parenthood:

"I ask him to sit in the corner and he won't."
"I put her in her room and she comes out."
"I tell him he must eat his vegetables. He eats them and throws them up right at the table."

"I can't control her unless I cry in desperation. Then she
stops and puts her arm around me and comforts me."

These parents can hardly believe they have given birth to such
misbehaving "monsters." The children have somehow discovered
that they're in charge of their caretakers; they have a premature and
severe case of overempowerment. However, there is a great chance
of reversing it when discovered early. **You can take charge and you
must.**

Properly used, "time-out" is an almost magical solution to re-
gaining control of your overempowered children. I have found it
100 percent effective with preschoolers, and with many other children up to age nine or ten. Beyond that, it works with some but not
with others. It's not intended for adolescents.

I know as some of you read this you probably don't believe time-
out works. Parents who come to my clinic don't believe me either.
Not all approaches to time-out do work. However, parents who follow our "cookbook recipe" for time-out come to the next visit smil-
ing, convinced, and ready for the next guidelines. Their children
dramatically alter their behavior because the parents have changed
from followers to leaders. Before, their children were in command

TIME-OUT

and didn't know how to cope with their excessive power. After parents use time-out correctly, the children accept clear limits, and they feel much more secure. The parents are bigger and in charge, and the children are now content to follow their parents' lead.

The time-out described in figure 1.6 is intended only for children who have too much power. More moderate time-outs, such as

Figure 1.6

# Recipe for Successful Time-Outs

- One adult should tell the child briefly that the consequence for naughty behaviors will be to stay in his room for, depending on the age of the child, five to ten minutes of quiet (as determined by a timer) with the door closed. The naughty behaviors should be specified. Don't select all, just the worst (for example, hitting, temper tantrums).
- If the child is likely to open the door when it's closed, lock the door from the outside (some parents loop the end of a rope around the doorknob of the child's room and loop the other end around the knob of an adjacent room). For very powerful children, some kind of lock is initially required. **Never** lock the door when an adult is not present.
- If your child is likely to throw or break things during a tantrum, remove any fragile or precious objects from the room.
- Every time the child misbehaves in the stated way, the child should be escorted to the room without the parent losing his/her temper and with only a sentence of explanation.
- If the child slams the door, loses his temper, bangs on walls, throws toys, screams, shouts, or talks, there should be absolutely no response from anyone. Expect the first few times to be terrible. Set the timer *only* when the child is quiet.
- After ten minutes, open the door to permit the child to leave. There should be no further explanation, apology, warning, or discussion of love. Act as if nothing unusual has happened. *Don't hug!* Repeat as necessary.
- After one week, only a warning of the closed door should be necessary to prevent the undesirable behavior. Give only one warning. *Always* follow through.

SOURCE: *Why Bright Kids Get Poor Grades and What You Can Do About It* by S. B. Rimm (New York: Crown Publishing Group, 1995).

sitting in a chair or going to a room with open doors or a gate, are quite effective for many children. Also, after the powerful child behaves more appropriately, you should be able to give the child one warning and the opportunity to stop the inappropriate behavior. Locked doors are completely unnecessary once children learn they must stay in their rooms, and that happens more rapidly than you would expect even for formerly very powerful children.

Some of you may feel that figure 1.6 describes cruel and unusual punishment that you wouldn't want to inflict on your children. You may be inclined to modify it by explaining to your children after-

Figure 1.7

# Common Mistakes in Using Time-Out

- When children time themselves out, they often slam the door. Parents respond by telling them not to slam the door. The children thus realize they have power over their parents, and they continue to slam the door.
- Sometimes, when the children call out and ask how much time they have left, the parents will make the mistake of talking to or actually arguing with them. The conversation cancels the effect of withdrawn attention.
- Some parents are hesitant about locking the door and will hold it closed or not even close it at all. If the parent holds the door, the child knows that the parent is holding it, and thus the power struggle continues. if it is not closed at all, the child walks in and out proving that the parent is not in control.
- Sometimes after children have thrown things around their room, parents insist that they go back to pick up what they have thrown around. Another power struggle ensues, in which case children take charge of the parent by argument again.
- Sometimes parents use time-out only after they've yelled and screamed and lost their temper. That's too late. It has to be executed reasonably calmly, as if parents are in charge.
- Some parents take all children's toys away or continue to increase the time of punishment, escalating the battle.
- Some parents use time-out too frequently.

SOURCE: *Why Bright Kids Get Poor Grades and What You Can Do About It* by S. B. Rimm (New York: Crown Publishing Group, 1995).

ward how much you love them. If you do, however, you'll cancel the effect of the time-out by giving them a double message. This time-out is effective only because it completely withdraws attention. If it's punctuated by your words of love, your children will continue to control you. It certainly is appropriate to remind them of your love, but not at times when they've misbehaved, and certainly not immediately following their time-out. It simply becomes a confusing double message. Your children will know you love them if you express it at other times.

Time-out is only effective when it shifts power from the children's manipulation to the parents' leadership and doesn't draw undue attention to the children's negative behaviors. Withdrawing power and attention sets a definite limit. It makes it clear to children that they must stop misbehaving. Time-out is effective for all young children.

Some people, even professional counselors, disagree with the concept of using a crib or bedroom for time-out. They suggest that it might create fears of cribs or bedrooms. They fear that time-out in a closed room could upset children too much. Of course, it does seem logical for children to associate bedrooms with punishment if timed-out there; however, it simply does not happen. I have shared my method of time-out with thousands of parents and have never heard of a single child who became anxious about his or her room as a result, nor have I seen any negative side effects of time-out.

I don't really consider time-out to be a punishment but rather a means of limiting inappropriate behaviors. Although time-out in a closed room may be a controversial approach, I continue to recommend it because it works. Calmness, brevity, and consistency combine to make it an extremely effective method. Children may punch a pillow or play with their toys during time-out. By timing them out, you're helping your out-of-control children learn to control and calm themselves independently. Of course, if your children have serious emotional or physical problems, it would be wise to consult a private psychologist to cope with their special needs.

**Setting Limits for Arguers.** If you feel trapped by children who argue constantly, read this section. You've probably tried to reason and discuss; however, before you knew it, you found yourself shouting or losing your temper, and you're not sure how or why that happened. Sometimes, it's not even clear to you what you were arguing about.

Children who argue incessantly often think of themselves as debaters. They frequently hear that they will make good lawyers. **If you have arguers, don't brag to Grandma or a neighbor about your children's creative arguing skills. It will make them more determined than ever to argue until they win** (remember referential speaking). They pride themselves on their reasoning skills and will extend their debating to teachers and friends.

Although you may sometimes enjoy their critical-thinking ability, you also find yourself feeling pushed, frustrated, manipulated, and very negative. When your "debaters" approach, a reflexive *no* appears on your forehead. You may say no before you've even heard their request. However, arguers don't accept noes. They follow you around the room trying to convince you until finally, either out of guilt, frustration, desperation, or just to deliver yourself from pain, you respond with a negative and resigned "All right, yes" at least half of the time.

Even if you have the stamina to stay with your no response, by the time you've completed your argument, you've lost your temper. With at least a 50 percent chance they'll get what they want and a

THE LAWYER

100 percent likelihood that you'll be out of control, your arguers are encouraged to persevere. You've unintentionally increased their arguing skill by teaching them that if they persevere, you may change your decision. You've also enhanced your negative-parent image. If you are sufficiently out of control to threaten or hand out punishments, they can use your irrational response as an excuse for doing what they wanted to do even though they don't have your permission. Furthermore, with a little luck, they'll be able to engage an other adult (parent, grandparent, aunt, uncle, or friend's parent) or at least a friend to side with them against you. None of these situations were what you intended. You feel trapped.

Oddly enough, when you ask a favor of your debating children, they also respond with an automatic "No, why do I have to?" You find yourself following them around the room, providing them with a rationale for your request until finally they respond with a negative "All right, if I have to" or avoid doing it entirely. You wonder why they're so negative when you've been so good to them. They've copied your pattern! Again, you feel trapped.

Children naturally become more skilled in arguing and more determined to win with continued experience. Although it's important to encourage critical thinking and discussion, a regular arguing mode is more of a power struggle than a discussion. Furthermore, these children are accumulating experiences in which they always or often win power struggles. This habit of arguing will make it difficult for them to live or work with others in the future.

The goal of my anti-arguing routine (see figure 1.8) is to teach you to encourage thinking and reasoning but to discourage power struggles with your children. The suggestions give children the opportunity to respect the experience and intelligence of their parents and teachers, while retaining their own rights to think, question, and discuss. This isn't an easy balance to maintain, but children who have heard my discussion of the anti-arguing routine on my public radio program tend to like this approach. They say it at least gives them a fair chance to be heard.

**Don't say "I told you so" when your arguers finally give up the battle.** The more determined you are to let them know that you're right, the harder it becomes for them to admit their own mistakes. **It's better to give no attention to the fact that they've come around to your way of thinking.** Time permits them to

PARENT
POINTER

PARENT
POINTER

Figure 1.8

# Anti-Arguing Instructions

1. When arguers come at you (they always choose an inconvenient time because they instinctively know you're vulnerable), remind yourself not to say yes or no immediately. Instead, after they've made their request, ask them for their reasons. If you've asked for their reasons, they can never accuse you of not listening. Also, you'll feel better by not cutting off their expressions of feelings, and they feel better because they've had plenty of time to talk (talking makes them feel smart).

2. After you've heard their reasons, say, "Let me think about it. I'll get back to you in a few minutes" (for a small request; later for a larger one). There are three marvelous benefits to the second step of this arguing process. First, it permits you to continue to be rational (that's what you wanted to be when you accidentally trained your arguers). Secondly, it teaches children to be patient. Third, because arguers are often bright, manipulative children, since you haven't yet responded with either a yes or no, they know that their good behavior increases the likelihood of your saying yes. Therefore, while you're taking time to be rational and while they're learning patience, these lovely dominant children will be on their best behavior. How nice!

3. Think about their request and their reasons. Don't be negatively biased by their pushiness. If your answer is yes, smile and be positive and enthusiastic. Arguers rarely see adults smile.

4. If your answer is no, and you do have the right and obligation to say no sometimes, then say no firmly. Include a few reasons as part of your refusal. Absolutely never change your decision and don't engage in further discussion. Don't let them make you feel guilty. It is healthy for children to learn to accept noes.

5. If they begin to argue again, review with them calmly that you've heard their request, you've listened to their reasons, you've taken time about them, you've given them your answer and your reason, and the discussion is now over. Don't get back into discussion of the initial request.

6. If they continue arguing, and they're below age ten and not too big, escort them to their room for a time-out. If they're too big for you to time them out, go calmly and assertively to your own room and close and lock your door. If they beat on your door, ignore them. Relax with a good book. Finally, they'll learn that parents have earned the privilege of saying no. They'll also have learned that they may continue to have the opportunity to remain children. They may not appreciate the latter at the time. However, your home will become a more pleasant and positive place in which to live, and your children will find that you are positive, fair, rational, but not a wimp, and they'll respect you.

Source: *How to Stop Underachievement Newsletter* 4, no. 4 (1994), by S. B. Rimm (Watertown, Wis.: Educational Assessment Service).

gracefully acknowledge their mistakes. No one loves to be found out as wrong, and insisting that arguers admit their error usually ends in further no-win battles.

Occasionally **admitting your own flawed reasoning in an argument with someone else and modeling your approaches to addressing error will help your children learn how to admit mistakes (that is, if you've ever made any mistakes). Humor helps!**

PARENT POINTER

When you lose your temper in another argument, you know you've handled the routine poorly. Go back and read figure 1.8 again. If you habitually lose your temper, children interpret that as weakness. They will customize their arguments to last until you lose your temper. As they continue to push, you'll find yourself losing your temper more often. Review figure 1.8 again and again. *It works!* Remember, even kids like it.

**If you're the other parent,** the one who doesn't argue with your children, **don't mediate.** That would only serve as a put-down to your spouse. It gives children equal power with your partner before they've earned it. Your mediation attempts will definitely increase their arguing behavior with your spouse. After your children have developed expertise in arguing with your spouse, they'll generalize

PARENT POINTER

TIME-OUT FOR TEENS

PARENT
POINTER

that arguing technique and direct it back to you. **Support your spouse. If you have differences, discuss those when your children are not present. Under no circumstances should you tell your spouse to control him- or herself in front of the children.** That will be viewed as conveying adult status to your arguers or child status to your spouse, and then your children will become openly disrespectful to your spouse (and eventually to you). It's husband-wife sabotage. Parental unity and support for each other is the key to parental leadership (see chapter 2).

**Avoiding Power Struggles.** Two principles regarding power struggles are important in the relationship between parents and children. Both have been described in my book *Why Bright Kids Get Poor Grades and What You Can Do About It.* The first is stated in Rimm's

PARENT
POINTER

Law #10: **Avoid confrontations with children unless you can control the outcomes.** The second principle emphasizes the importance of **staying in an alliance with your children and refusing to become "the enemy."** These two principles should be your guides in dealing with strong-willed children. You now have several new techniques of limiting children's power, which will help them to respect you.

Many children have already been given so much power that they may involve you in power struggles despite your improved techniques. You can learn to change those battles into alliances. This process may call upon the Pollyanna* in you as well as require your most creative talents, but the results are worth it. Here are five examples of how power struggles can be reversed to provide a more positive atmosphere in your home:

# Case 1

Brian's mother nagged him regularly each morning before school. She nagged him to wake up, nagged him to eat breakfast, and nagged him to get dressed. Brian depended on his mother's nagging. Every morning pre-

---

* Pollyanna is a fictional character in a children's book by the same name, authored by Eleanor H. Porter, who always manages to find the bright side to everything.

sented a new power struggle. I recommended the morning routine, which is described in chapter 3, to his mother.

After I reviewed the routine with her, she went home and began using it immediately.

She called me a few days later to complain in exasperation that the routine just wasn't working. Because other parents have had so much success with it, I was surprised. When I asked her to describe her experiences, she reviewed the typical steps. Her final statement was, "And then he almost misses the bus."

I reviewed her description with her one step at a time. Does your son get up independently? Does he get dressed and ready for school on his own? Does he have a pleasant breakfast in a timely fashion? Does he get to the bus on time? Do you find yourself still nagging? She answered yes to all but the last question. Then she said, "But he gets to the bus at the last minute and almost misses it."

I pointed out to her as sensitively as I could that she may have missed the point. Her son had accomplished exactly what it was that she wanted him to accomplish—an independent, non-nagging morning preparation. Now it was important for her to see him as successful and to let him know that she was pleased with his responsible behavior. If she continued to see his success as a failure and a power struggle, his behavior would regress to its initial state. **Parents who continue to emphasize the power struggle even after it's over increase the battles. Keep the goal in mind and don't get caught up in the imperfections of the process.**

PARENT
POINTER

Another example of a covert, less obvious power struggle is the case of a child who feared thunderstorms. Parents hardly ever think that fears can become power struggles; however, they often do, particularly for shy or inhibited children. The following example generalizes the other fears that may become unconscious power struggles:

# Case 2

Andy was afraid of tornadoes. In an attempt to help him deal with his fears, his mom spent a great deal of time explaining the difference between thunderstorms and tornadoes. The more she explained, the more his fear increased. He became hysterically frightened at anything that resembled a tornado. Soon, even a brief thundershower paralyzed him with fear.

I suggested to Andy's mother that she establish an alliance with her son by saying, "I understand your fear of thunderstorms, and I know you'll learn to handle it. I'll help you prepare a storm shelter in the basement. You can even have a radio and a blanket down there so you'll be comfortable. When you feel afraid, you may go down to your shelter and stay there where you'll feel safe. The rest of us will stay upstairs unless there's a tornado, in which case we'll also come down and join you."

With that sense of control over his safety and the disappearance of a power struggle (Mom trying to prove he had nothing to fear), Andy's overanxiety about storms disappeared. He calmly joined the family during thunderstorms and retreated to the basement only when there really was a tornado warning.

Kent provides another example of diminishing a power struggle:

# Case 3

Kent's dad was making a strong effort to build a good father-son relationship with his young adult son who was home from college. As he approached him to chat, he noticed that Kent was eating in the living room, which was off-limits for food according to house rules. Kent's dad, annoyed at his disregard for house rules, began by asking him, "Why are you eating in the living room?" Kent found himself in a no-win situation. He could only give an answer that would displease his dad. He knew that there was no excuse that would be acceptable. Instead, he walked away without any response. His dad wondered how he could have changed that situation to avoid another power struggle.

I suggested to his dad this alternative conversation: "Hi, Son, I wanted to talk with you. Why don't we go into the family room since you're eating? We can talk in there." That would have set the stage for a father-son alliance rather than a power struggle, while also making it clear that the young man was expected to follow family rules. It could have defused the power struggle that took place regularly between father and son. With practice, the relationship between father and son became much more positive.

Here's another example for more practice:

## Case 4

Dawn and her teacher Mr. Rahn were locked in battle. Mr. Rahn had openly criticized and embarrassed Dawn in front of the class. He announced that her work was far below her ability. Dawn related the story to her mother. Mom could empathically feel the embarrassment her daughter was experiencing and wanted to defend her daughter. Mother's defense would have escalated the power struggle between the teacher and Dawn and resulted in Dawn's having an excuse for continuing her poor work. Dawn might have concluded to her mother, "I can't work for Mr. Rahn. He just doesn't like me." (Does that sound familiar?)

Here was my suggestion of what Dawn's mom should say to Dawn: "I know you feel embarrassed. However, even though I feel bad for you, I think the teacher is right in expecting you to do your work with much better quality. Let's talk to Mr. Rahn together and find out how you can improve your work. Then I'll look it over. I want Mr. Rahn to know what a nice kid and an excellent student you can be."

In a separate communication, the mother might talk to Mr. Rahn and indicate that she is supportive of his requirements and her daughter is aware of this. She could also share with the teacher the story of her daughter's embarrassment and assure him that she didn't provide her daughter with an easy way out of his expectations. Now the teacher would know that the mother is not encouraging a teacher-student power struggle but is instead dissipating it and supporting a positive relationship.

Mr. Rahn and Dawn became closer thereafter and even grew to like each other. If the mother had subtly supported Dawn and become too sympathetic to her embarrassment, she would have exacerbated the power struggle between teacher and student.

A further example:

## Case 5

Marissa indicated to her mom on the way out the door to the school bus that she was taking the family electric mixer with her because they were baking cookies for a school benefit. Marissa's mother, seeing her expensive mixer leave the house, became visibly upset. Her fiery protest to Marissa was, "You didn't ask me; that's my best mixer; you can't take it, and bring it right back here now!" Marissa responded angrily, "I need it to-day, and it's for a good cause. I volunteered it, and I have to bring it." Mother's final comment was, "You can't take it; I'm keeping it, and you're grounded for taking things without asking. I'll see you after school and talk to you about it then." That power struggle continued after school when Marissa came home angry and disappointed that she couldn't carry through her responsibility to her student committee. The antagonism accelerated during the rest of the week.

Marissa's mom wanted to know if the grounding was an overpunishment, and how she could get her daughter to stop the continuous arguing. She also wanted advice on how to get Marissa to respect other people's possessions.

I suggested to her this alternative strategy: On seeing Marissa about to take the mixer out the door, she could have asked Marissa why she was taking the mixer to school. After Marissa's response and in light of the lack of time, she could have said, "You can't take that mixer today, but let's talk about it tonight to see how I can help you because I know you're baking cookies for a good cause." That would have immediately relieved Marissa of the pressure of feeling that her mother was opposing her. It would also set an appropriate limit because she had made it clear that Marissa could not take the expensive mixer to school.

After school, when Marissa indicated that the project had to be postponed, her mother could say the following:

- "I wish you had asked me about the mixer and given me enough time to think about it, rather than just announcing that you were taking it as you walked out the door."
- "I would have been happy to let you take the portable mixer, but this one is too expensive for you to take to school."
- "It's for a good cause and I wanted to be supportive, so why don't you take the portable mixer tomorrow? Next time be sure to ask me beforehand so that we can avoid the confusion and the embarrassment for you."

Absolutely no punishment is necessary. This particular adolescent, a very positive young lady, simply assumed that her mother would support her just cause. She was not considerate enough to ask her mother's permission and was not realistic enough to recognize that an expensive appliance shouldn't be taken to school.

Those were both mistakes that she has now learned to correct for the future. If her mother continues in an alliance with her instead of punishing or arguing with her, Marissa will be much more likely to ask for that permission in the future. If Marissa is punished instead, she will be determined to get even and that would mean continuing the power struggle.

These five examples of power struggles provide the following suggestions for parents as they deal with children in power struggles:

- **Express enough confidence in your children to see the right things they're doing rather than only the wrong things.** If you can redescribe their inappropriate action in a positive way, you'll be setting up an alliance instead of more opposition.

PARENT POINTER

- In establishing an alliance, be sure not to make another person (parent or teacher) into the "bad guy." **Reframe your child's relationship with the other person in a way that makes that person your child's ally.** This becomes more possible with practice.

PARENT POINTER

- **Set limits by your behavior and expectation rather than by punishment.** Marissa didn't take the expensive mixer. Kent didn't get to eat in the living room. Dawn didn't get away with poor-quality schoolwork. Andy didn't continue to get a lot of attention about his fear of thunderstorms. Brian found that he had the power to get himself to school on time independently and without his mother's nagging.

PARENT POINTER

As you get more comfortable teaching children to respect limits, you'll find it can be done in an alliance with your children instead of in opposition to them. You'll also find yourself feeling less threatened and better able to guide your children positively. You'll engage in fewer power struggles with your children, and they'll initiate fewer power struggles with you.*

---

* Many other practical suggestions for responding to dependent and dominant children at home and in school are given in my book *Why Bright Kids Get Poor Grades.*

# WHAT ABOUT GENETICS?

As you reflect on your own children who may be too dependent or too dominant, many of you may agree that indeed too much may have been done for them or they were unintentionally overempowered. On the other hand, some of you may be certain that your children exhibited at least some of these characteristics from birth. They seemed fearful and inhibited from the start, or they seemed to have had high energy or were controlling and pushing limits the moment they came home from the hospital.

My clinical observations support your perceptions, and considerable research indicates that children's temperaments are observably different at birth. Of course, differences in temperament also affect whether loving adults do too much for children or overempower them. I have also found from my clinical experience that not all dependent or dominant children begin their lives with extreme temperamental inhibition or extreme will. Whether dependence or dominance is caused mainly by genetics or environment, you cannot change your children's genetic temperament. You can, however, make a great difference in providing an environment that leads children to use their power appropriately.

# QUESTIONS AND ANSWERS

*Dear Dr. Sylvia,*
*What is the best response to a seven-year-old girl who has started saying,*
*"You don't give me enough attention"?*

*Attentive Parent*

Dear Attentive Parent,
Your daughter is undoubtedly expressing real feelings, but the meaning of those feelings needs to be interpreted by you, then reframed and explained to her.

"You don't give me enough attention" could be caused by any or all of the following:

• She may wish for constant attention (attention dependent).
• She could have received too much attention earlier.

- She may have a new sibling and not wish for you to attend to him or her.
- She may actually have found that by saying those words you'll feel sorry for her and give her more attention.
- You may be too busy lately to give her enough attention.
- All of the above.
- None of the above.

This isn't a multiple-choice test, but these alternatives will at least give you a sense of the many possible interpretations of your daughter's words.

As part of growing up, children need less attention than they did earlier. They usually thrive on gradually increasing independence. However, if they had too much attention given to them in the past, or if changes, such as new siblings, divorce, new school, new jobs, etc., suddenly diminish the attention they have been receiving, they feel attention deprived.

I expect you are already giving her enough attention. In that case, explain to her that growing up means doing more on her own, and you're really pleased with her independence. A few opportunities to moderately praise her maturity and responsibility will encourage good feelings about herself and prevent her from depending so much on your attention.

If you really aren't finding enough time for talk and affection, make it a priority on your daily agenda. Her life will fly by quickly, and you will regret lost opportunities with your growing daughter.


## Dear Dr. Sylvia,

*My daughter is an only child. She has an excellent vocabulary, is gifted, but she is a ten-year-old adult. The problem is she doesn't interact or play with her peers. Instead, she reads at recess rather than play. How do you get ten-year-old "adults" to enjoy their childhood?*

*Parents of Adult Child*


Dear Parents,

Only children have some advantages as well as almost as many disadvantages. They tend to be socially independent because they are accustomed to keeping themselves entertained. They often have adult-sounding vocabularies and adult interests because they spend much of their family time with adults only.

Here are a few suggestions to increase your daughter's social experiences with her peers. Invite a similar-age cousin (if there are any) to spend a week with you during the summer vacation, and hopefully, your daughter can visit for a week at his or her home. Have her invite a friend or friends to stay overnight occasionally on the weekend. An even number of children works out better and will avoid the problem of your daughter being the child left out.

Don't take your daughter with you to adult-only activities. Instead, leave her with a baby-sitter or, better yet, at a friend's home. She may be too accustomed to socializing with adults when she is easily included as one of the adults or just given too much attention.

Be sure that she joins some (not too many) social activities such as Girl Scouts, church or synagogue social groups, or school clubs. Definitely include a week or two of summer camp in your plans for her.

Encourage her to develop special interests and to join groups of children during the school year or during the summer who share her interests. When she finds friends with whom she can share interests and activities, friendships will be natural and not forced or pressured. If your daughter participates in at least some of these activities, she will have ample opportunity to learn the comfortable social skills she may be missing at home.

Single children have many advantages, so you don't need to feel guilty about depriving your daughter of siblings. Only children tend to be much more independent, and as she grows up, your daughter's social independence will become a great advantage, so don't force her into uncomfortable conformity now or she will become anxious and worry about loneliness instead of valuing the comfort of her independence.

### Dear Dr. Sylvia,

*I have a five-year-old granddaughter who gets too much attention. She is very attractive. Her parents are both over forty. Her father is a doctor, her mother has a Ph.D., and they consider themselves the experts. Recently, I received a picture of my granddaughter all made up with*

*makeup; she looks like a made-up doll. Do you have a diplomatic sug-*
*gestion to give to parents about sending the wrong messages?*

*Sensible Grandmother*

Dear Sensible Grandmother,
If your granddaughter's makeup was the fun kind that children use
when dressing up, I assume you wouldn't be concerned. However,
it sounds as if you are realistically worried about your children's
emphasis on appearances and your granddaughter's growing up
too soon. These are well-grounded concerns.

Parents who overemphasize appearance, dressing up, and wear-
ing makeup are conveying to their children their value system.
Their children will, of course, try to live up to that value system and
will constantly feel pressure to be admired for their beauty, their
clothing, and their grown-up appearance. They may not learn that
intelligence, perseverance, and kindness are better measures of living well. Furthermore, if adolescence doesn't provide these children
with a sufficient number of admirers, they may feel ugly, unnoticed,
inadequate, and even depressed.

Your own children, who have obviously achieved much intellectually, would not be happy if their daughter valued herself only for
her surface beauty. They are, undoubtedly, so smitten by this mirac-
ulous child that they assume that their overpraise only builds their
daughter's self-esteem. If you can possibly convey to them that, indeed, they will eventually be blamed by their daughter for the pressure she feels during her adolescence, they can use more moderate
and realistic praise to build confidence without pressures. The rule
of thumb I usually share with parents is that appropriate praise
words should be chosen from parents' realistic values that children
will be able to live up to; for example, *bright, good thinking, hardworking, kind, sensitive, responsible,* or *pretty.* Overpraise words such
as *gorgeous, brilliant, smartest,* and *genius,* when used regularly to
compliment children, are impossible for any child to live up to and
will cause adolescents continual pressure and frustration.

## Dear Dr. Sylvia,

*How can we help our tremendously shy three-and-a-half-year-old*
*daughter?*

*Uncertain Parents*

Dear Uncertain Parents,

Shy behaviors can be partly inherited and partly learned. Even biologically shy children can learn appropriate social involvement and usually do if parents don't overprotect or shelter them too much. However, don't insist on so much involvement that your daughter feels constantly pushed. Too much pressure could cause her to retreat further. If you avoid sheltering too much and pushing too much (both extremes), your daughter will learn to participate in a variety of activities and will become more comfortable in most social environments.

Avoid power struggles. Don't get into a pattern of saying she should become involved and then permit her to persuade you to change your decision. Instead, assume she'll participate and stay positive.

You can use referential speaking as a positive technique for your shy daughter. Adults often talk to each other about how shy these children are, and the children often accept shyness as a label and assume that they can't change. They believe that what the adults are saying about them to each other is always true.

Here's how you can use referential speaking to help your daughter: Say to your spouse when your three-and-a-half-year-old is within hearing, "Did you notice how friendly Rachel is becoming? She doesn't seem to be as shy as she used to be." You could also say to other people, for example grandparents, friends, and relatives, "Have you noticed? Rachel seems to be outgrowing her shyness." This will reinforce her social behavior and help her change her self-image. You will find that positive referential speaking is remarkably effective in helping your daughter develop social confidence.

An example from my personal experience: A mom and her little girl were descending in an elevator with us. My husband waved a friendly hello to the small child, who then clung more tightly to her mother. The mother explained to us that her daughter was very shy. The child clung tighter. I commented to my husband that I thought this girl seemed pretty friendly, and that she wasn't so shy. She moved away from her mother, smiled, and said, "I'm not shy." My husband was impressed. The girl's mother, unfortunately, didn't notice the effect of the change in labeling.

## Dear Dr. Sylvia,

*My very dominant daughter is extremely jealous of the relationship be-tween my husband and me. She will make us feel guilty about wanting to go anywhere together as a couple. It's very frustrating, and we have tried exploring her feelings and explaining ours. What can we do to help her deal with this?*

*Caged Parents*

Dear Caged Parents,

One privilege of parenthood is that you don't have to ask your children for permission for almost anything—especially not to go out together. While it is reasonable to explore your daughter's feelings and even to explain yours, it is not reasonable to assume that you must convince her of your point of view.

It is fairly clear that she perceives herself as having adult rights and status, and you will do her a favor by lifting the burden of too early adulthood from her. Remind her of how fortunate she is to have parents who love each other enough to enjoy each other's company, and assure her you'll be happy to take her along to social events that are intended for whole families. You may even want to explain that when she's old enough to go on dates, you'll return her favor by not insisting on tagging along with her and her companion.

Of course, I don't know your daughter's age, nor do I know if she may have some fears. If the latter is the case, you will want to assure her that you've been careful to select a nice and competent child-care provider for her who will keep her safe and help her with any problems while you're gone.

Your only reason for feeling guilty would come if she keeps you caged. It would not be healthy for your daughter to have so much power over her parents, and it is not good for the two of you (as a couple) to have no adult social life without your daughter.

Once you've decided to go out together and arranged for good child care, you'll find your daughter will easily adjust. She may shed a few tears the first time, but it won't be long before she encourages you to go out and cheerfully anticipates her favorite baby-sitter. You'll soon wonder why you ever worried.

Of course, you should continue to do things that involve all three of you, too.

## *Dear Dr. Sylvia,*

*I have two sons, ages four and one, and I have a concern about my older son. During my conference with his preschool teacher, she told me that when he begins a project at school, he becomes very frustrated and says he "can't do it." He just comes "unglued." I get the impression that if he can't do something perfectly, he doesn't even want to try, and I'm very upset over his attitude. I try to explain to him that his baby brother, who is just learning to walk, keeps falling down, but he keeps getting up and trying again.*

*My husband I are very supportive of him and not negative people. We are always encouraging him. My husband thinks I am overreacting to this situation, but I don't think I am. Is there any way we can help him? I want him to have a good start at school.*

*Very Anxious Mother*

Dear Very Anxious Mother,

You and your husband are both right. Because a preschool teacher has expressed her concern about your son's attitude, you can assume that the problem is real and not an overreaction. Your husband's perception is also correct because your anxiety may truly be complicating the problem for your son.

Your child is exhibiting early signs of perfectionism, which can sometimes lead to underachievement. Firstborn children, particularly if they are very verbal, often get extreme praise and attention from adults. They may internalize the praise as messages of expectation. As preschoolers, it rarely causes them a problem, but since you now have another child, your son may be feeling the "dethronement" or sibling rivalry, which often becomes more obvious when the second child becomes a toddler.

In empowering your son from within so that his power is not only directed toward manipulating you, be sure not to make negative comparisons to his younger siblings. This will only cause him to feel more inadequate and competitive. The increased sibling rivalry may either cause further behavior problems or could move him toward depression as he loses confidence.

Your son's frustration with his imperfection seems to be garnering attention in school and causing extreme anxiety at home. When children become anxious about their performance, too much discussion about the problem seems to become an unconscious power struggle. The more the parent reassures, the more reassurance the child seems to require and the less confidence he seems to develop. Your comments about mistakes and efforts are appropriate, but try not to belabor them. A one-sentence, matter-of-fact statement will be sufficient. That's a "nice" picture instead of a "spectacular" or "magnificent" picture will tell him you're pleased with his drawing without putting pressure on him. Praise him moderately for perseverance, learning from his mistakes, and putting effort into projects.

You can have high hopes that your son will not be an underachiever because you have identified the problem early enough to keep it from becoming more serious.

## Dear Dr. Sylvia,

*I've read your column on helping to build a child's self-esteem in a positive way, but how can children's self-esteem be built in positive ways when they're living in negative ways? I'm incarcerated at a correctional institution. I have a three-year-old stepdaughter, a two-year-old daughter, and a four-month-old son.*

*My children have been around a lot of fighting and violent behavior. Their mother has other people and relatives living with her who don't work. I wrote the caseworker, the director of social services, and the governor. Please, what can I do to stop these kids from going through this? If I were out there, my kids would not be going through this. I feel helpless to try to reach out and help my kids. I'm going to school, and I go to church every Sunday. Doing time is hard for me. Please, for the sake of the children, could you help me or suggest someone who could help them? Thanks for your cooperation in this matter.*

*Helpless Inmate*

Dear Helpless Inmate,

It is unusual for me to receive a letter from an inmate in a correctional institution, but it does seem as if you want something better for your children, despite what you have done to cause your incarceration. Doing time is hard for you, and it is intended to be so. We always hope that it will be unpleasant enough to prevent recurring criminal behavior. Perhaps your letter can give readers hope that incarceration can motivate one to want to improve life in the future and make us all realize that most prisoners have hopes and dreams for a better life.

Going to school and to church will certainly help you prepare yourself for a future day when you will actively become the good father you would like to be. If you are prepared for an honest life and can hold down a good job because you've received a better education, your children will be better off in the future.

Of course, at this time you have little control over your children's home life. If your children's mother visits you, you can talk things through with her and suggest she go for counseling, which is likely to be available free of charge to her because of your imprisonment. Your description of her home life suggests she could surely use help.

You can do some very positive things right now for your children. If you have access to a cassette tape recorder, you can record regular messages to your children so they can hear your voice and your wishes that they be good children. You can reassure them that you're learning and want to have a good life when you are released. You can ask them to send you pictures of themselves (actually their mother will need to do the sending). You can write letters about your love for them and your wish for their forgiveness. Hopefully, their mother will share the letters with them. If you're not sure she'll share the letters with them, you may wish to send them via your own mother, your children's grandmother. Writing is therapeutic for you and will be important for them to see when they're old enough to read.

You are paying the difficult price for whatever harm you've done. Please don't despair. Work hard, study, and plan for the better time ahead. I applaud you for taking an interest in your children's well-being.

### Dear Dr. Sylvia,
*My children get good grades, but have asked me to give them rewards like their friends get. I'm not sure I like that idea.*

*Nonmaterialistic Mom*

Dear Nonmaterialistic Mom,
Achieving children don't require rewards for their good work. Their enjoyment of learning and their good grades have already

proven successful as motivators. Your valuing their accomplishments will help support their continued efforts.

Despite their achievements, these children sometimes ask their parents for rewards. I would suggest one of the following responses, depending on your values:

- I don't mind giving you a reward if you'd like as long as you realize that I understand you'd do the work even if I weren't giving you the reward.
- I think it's better not to use a reward system, but if there's something special you'd like, perhaps we can either get it for you or help you work out a way to earn it.

Most important, shared enthusiasm in learning between parent and child encourages intrinsic motivation and love of learning. This may feel hard after a long day or week at work, but the results are truly rewarding for parents as well as their children.

## Dear Dr. Sylvia,

*My daughter complains a lot about headaches or stomachaches. I've checked with her doctor and there is no physical cause. How can I teach her to cope with discomfort better (without overprotecting her)?*

*Coping Mom*

Dear Coping Mom,

Life has a way of gradually introducing most children to feelings of discomfort, and an encouraging parent can help children to cope with the new feelings without overprotecting them. A hug and some suggestions for ways to cope are usually enough to guide even a very sensitive child to becoming stronger. Here are some examples of ways to teach children coping skills without being overprotective:

**Example:** Your daughter has a headache.

### Overprotection

MOTHER: Poor thing: I'm so sorry you have a headache. I suppose you've inherited them from me. Why don't you lie down on the sofa, and I'll get a cool cloth for your head. I'll stay with you until the pain goes away. I know how awful those headaches feel.

### Teaching Coping Skills and Independence

MOTHER: I'm sorry you have a headache. When I have a headache, I take a pain reliever and rest in a dark room with a cloth over my head. Sometimes it helps me to take a walk out in the fresh air. Which approach would you like to try first? (*Mother then explains about the proper dosage of pain reliever along with appropriate warnings of not taking too much and gives her daughter a hug as she goes to her room to rest.*) I hope you'll feel better soon.

**Example:** Daughter comes home complaining about teasing.

### Overprotection

MOTHER: I wonder why Susan teased you. She really is mean. Your feelings must be hurt. I would suggest you report the problem to the teacher and stay away from her. I hope she gets into real trouble for teasing you. She deserves it for being nasty.

### Teaching Coping Skills

MOTHER: Why do you suppose Susan teased you?
SARAH: I don't know.
MOTHER: Do you think it's something you said or did to hurt her feelings, or do you suppose she was having a problem and took her problem out on you?
SARAH: I don't remember saying anything to hurt her. She just seems angry at everyone.
MOTHER: It sounds as if she may be having a problem. I'd stay away from her until she's more like herself. We're all strong enough to handle a little teasing, although I suspect you may feel a little hurt. Maybe you could talk to her about it when she's feeling better.

The overprotective approach causes your daughter to feel the physical or emotional pain more. She'll enjoy your sympathy but won't learn the independent coping skills that the second approach will teach her. There's no harm done if you overprotect occasionally because you'll be modeling compassion; but too much sympathy may lead your daughter to become oversensitive and dependent instead of coping with struggles on her own.

### Dear Dr. Sylvia,

*My child has been tested through our school and has been labeled "learning disabled," but after hearing you speak, I'm not so sure he isn't a dependent child who has managed to get his parents and teachers believing that we need to provide a great deal of help for him. How can I separate the dyslexia from the dependency?*

*Mystified Mom*

Dear Mystified Mom,

It's so difficult to identify learning disabilities accurately that it's been necessary to invent an operational definition. That definition is almost identical to that of underachievement. Most states conclude that a child achieving significantly below tested abilities in two or more areas has a learning disability. Thus, many underachievers qualify as learning disabled.

When we work with learning-disabled children in the clinic, we help identify techniques to permit them to help themselves without depending on their parents or teachers. For example, if children have trouble reading instructions, we suggest taping the instructions so that they can listen repeatedly and read them simultaneously. Doing so is less dependent than having a parent or teacher read instructions to them. If they have difficulty with handwriting, it is better for them to use a word processor than to dictate to an adult. If their handwriting makes it difficult to write answers to a test, they can dictate their answers into a tape recorder. You can probably invent other creative nondependent techniques, as we do, to match your child's specific disabilities.

Whether your child is truly learning disabled or not, it is important to encourage independence, which will permit him to build self-confidence. Refer to chapter 3 for help in distinguishing the differences between a learning disability and dependency.

Some children are truly disabled but have also become dependent. The key to distinguishing between disability and dependency is the child's response to adult support. If your child performs only with adult support when new material is presented, he is too dependent whether or not there is also a disability.

### Dear Dr. Sylvia,

*My five-year-old son gets very upset when I go to another part of the house and he realizes he can't see me. He starts to yell, "Mama, Mama." I try to reassure him that I'll be right back when I leave for another part of the house. What could be causing this and what can I do about it? The only possible cause I can think of is that some of his friends were telling him about the movie* Home Alone.

*Terrified Tony's Mother*

Dear Terrified Tony's Mother,
You appear to be a good detective. Movies, television, and stories can and do create terrorizing fears for children, and I expect that *Home Alone* has unintentionally frightened more than one child. Undoubtedly, you have already reassured your son that you would not leave him home alone until he was older, but your words have not been as powerful as his imagination and thus have not allayed his fears.

I would suggest the use of a temporary whistle system. At least for a little while, you and he can wear a plastic whistle on a string around your wrist. If he feels afraid, he can whistle to you, and you can return a reassuring whistle signal from wherever you are in the house. Your son will find your new communication to be fun and will soon forget his fears. Although the whistling may be a bit of a nuisance, it will quickly serve to relieve the tension for you and your son.

Whistling has often served to communicate reassurance to children—for example, "Whistle a happy tune, and no one will ever know you're afraid" (from *The King and I*). Your son may enjoy hearing the song and may even learn to whistle without benefit of the plastic or metal implement. Your son will soon learn that whistling away his fears can even help him feel more secure at other risky times.

## Dear Dr. Sylvia,

*Regarding time-outs, what if you take the child to his room, lock the door, and he begins kicking the door and throwing things in his room? Should he be ignored until he stops or should he be stopped?*

*Aggravated*

Dear Aggravated,

Your son who is kicking and throwing things in his room seems very powerful, but the locked-door time-out is especially designed for small children who are in control of their parents. It is the best approach I know for giving the child the security of knowing parents are truly in charge.

Your son should not be physically or verbally restrained. **No** response to his anger is the best response. It may be difficult for you to sit calmly while you hear the tumult inside his room. Eventually, he'll give up and become calm. Then you'll be ready to set the timer for five to ten minutes. When you open the door to let him out, pretend you don't even see the mess. Don't insist he pick it up or another power struggle may ensue. Some kids actually do clean their rooms later. For those who don't, I suggest parents pick things up when the child's in school. The effect of actively ignoring the battle is that it seldom happens twice. Actually you may not even need to lock the door a second time. Your son may learn in that one definite limit-setting experience that you are in charge. You may even be able to give one warning before time-out. The warnings will usually be effective, provided you consistently follow through with time-out if your son doesn't respect your warning.

Some people believe that locking a door on a child for a few minutes is abusive; however, I believe a parent is doing a too powerful child a great favor by letting him or her know who's in charge. Children will be much more secure and respectful. Time-out is the best substitute I know for spanking, beating, or screaming, and the many other desperate measures that many parents use with their strong-willed children. As parents, you should stay as positive as possible with all your children. Brief and absolute time-outs are the least violent, most humane form of setting limits for children who always insist on doing things their way despite their parents' best advice. It is not abusive; it is *responsible*.

## *Dear Dr. Sylvia,*

*What means does a parent use to discipline a strong-willed son who mis-
behaves away from home? What is to be done when he behaves badly in
the supermarket or at the homes of friends or relatives?*

*Feeling Overpowered*

Dear Feeling Overpowered,
Strong-willed children seem to have a special sensitivity to their
parents' vulnerability. It's as if they realize that your limit-setting is
less powerful when you're in public. You will want to prepare
ahead so that you're not caught unprepared. When there is no
time-out room available, small rewards work best.

Before you begin shopping, explain to your son that you know
he really wants to behave, and give him specific guidelines for what
you expect; for example, to stay seated in the cart or stay in the
same aisle as you, not to touch items on the shelves unless you ask
for his help, etc. As you explain how much you appreciate his
shopping company, offer him the opportunity to pick out a small
special treat when you're finished shopping, provided he's behaved
well. You'll need to be very consistent in following through. If he
hasn't earned his treat, his tantrum will only come at the end of
your shopping trip. Then you'll be able to escort him to a time-out
at home immediately afterward. However, don't be surprised if
your treat, in combination with your positive planning, is effective;
it almost always works.

If you're visiting friends or relatives, you may also use the treat
approach. However, if these are close friends with children of their
own, you may ask to borrow their time-out room if necessary. You
are clearly not the only parents with strong-willed children, but
you'll have to assess the appropriateness of your request in each
family situation.

Timing a child out when he gets home is never quite as powerful. A warning to your son that a negative consequence will await
him will be even more effective than telling him exactly what you
intend to do. When he challenges you by asking what you're planning, keep him wondering by explaining that you're giving it some
thought. Your pondering and his wondering are far more effective
than threats of overpunishment, which he realizes you may not
carry out.

A strong-willed child sometimes feels more like a challenge than a joy, but beneath his powerful facade is your wonderful son. If you can manage to stay both positive and firm, you'll reach the "sweet kid" within more frequently.

### Dear Dr. Sylvia,

*Can you give any tips regarding discipline in the car? Time-outs are out, aren't they?*

*Driving Me Crazy*

Dear Driving Me Crazy,
Driving children in cars seems to provide absolute proof of the territoriality of human beings. As soon as children can talk, they seem to begin carving out with their hands their own car territory. Whatever territory one sibling claims, the other seems to covet. When the litigation begins, you, the pilot (or copilot), are bound to be called in to mediate. Because territorial debate seems to come with our species, there's little chance you'll be able to prevent it. Hopefully, however, you can manage to withdraw from the mediating role so that your attention doesn't serve to increase the arguing.

For short trips, when the volume or activity gets too loud for safety, pulling off to the side of the road to await a moment of silence seems reasonably helpful and gives the kids a pause that may shock them into silence. Dropping off an out-of-control child to walk two or three blocks (only if the child is old enough and safe walking is available) may stem your child's misbehavior next time. Specific seating arrangements that separate the least compatible children to front and back seats (or, if you have three children and own a van, to front, middle, and back seats) seems to prevent aggressive activity. Cassette tapes of children's music or books can be helpful. Earphones and individual recorders can permit a variety of selections.

If you're brave enough to drive a long trip, and many families do, you'll want to do some special planning. Bags of surprise activities and games, separately marked for each half day of the trip, provide variety. Games developed to increase observational skills encourage learning and keep kids busy. Some children can look to the right; the others to the left. They can search for and count parks, out-of-state license plates, birds, ponds, rivers, wooded areas, brick buildings, red barns, railroad crossings, buses, taxis, or most anything else you select for a particular route. Map reading can add to the fun of counting miles to destinations.

When the ride is unusually long, and territorial battles become exuberant, permit the children to earn points for every hour that they are nice to each other. They only earn points if all cooperate. Earning five points could result in a special stop for a treat. After five peaceful hours, they'll deserve it, and you'll enjoy it.

### Dear Dr. Sylvia,

*Do you believe in attention deficit disorder? Is it correct that you don't favor the use of Ritalin or other medications for ADD? If not, why not? How do you suggest meeting the attention or the impulsive needs of some children?*

Parent of Overactive Child

Dear Parent of Overactive Child,
I do believe that biological attention deficit disorders are real. I also believe that attention deficit disorders are poorly diagnosed, and that there is considerable overdiagnosis and overmedication of the problem. I worry about the side effects of Ritalin when children are not appropriately monitored, and most of all, I believe that parents are too anxiously looking for a magical cure for problems that need to be dealt with through better parenting strategies. Sometimes there is also teacher pressure to medicate the child.

Each time parents describe their son or daughter as the "ADHD [attention deficit–hyperactivity disorder] child," they are applying a label that takes power and responsibility away from the child. Even if the child is on medication, many behavior strategies can help the child. Parental consistency, although difficult with high-energy children, is critical. Positive teaching strategies that don't label the child a "troublemaker" make a great difference in the classroom. Literally dozens of strategies can help high-energy children to concentrate. Only after these strategies have been tried can parents and doctors know whether the problems exhibited are truly attention disorders.

Intellectually and artistically gifted children are often misdiagnosed as having ADHD. Their high energy teamed with their intensity and a lack of school curriculum challenge can cause them to appear distracted and impulsive. For too many families, Ritalin is the easy way out. Nevertheless, I do believe that some children improve their concentration dramatically with Ritalin or Cylert, and they are clearly appropriate medications. However, medication alone is never the only answer, and medication itself is not diagnostic. Parents do need help in guiding the ADHD or ADD child.

## Dear Dr. Sylvia,

*What suggestions do you have for dealing with a teenager who lies and argues with her parents? Because of her constant lying we have trouble trusting her, so we occasionally check with other parents regarding the plans we have been told about. This always causes major arguments. Any suggestions?*

*Distrustful Mom*

Dear Distrustful Mom,

In a calm frame of mind and not as a punishment for past behavior, explain to your daughter your wish to be able to trust her. Together, negotiate an agreement that provides you with reassurance of her honesty, including a specific time she'll be home and a reasonable consequence for noncompliance. Indicate that you'll become more lenient as she shows you that she can be trusted.

There aren't many privileges you can control during your daughter's teenage years, so you need to be sure the ones you select are within your control. They must also be meaningful and fair to her. Examples include losing telephone privileges for a week, not using the family car on a weekend if she drives, or withdrawal of an allowance if she's younger. Grounding her for an important night out can work, but more than one night becomes more of a punishment for you as parents than for your teenager. They seem to know how to spread their misery around while they're suffering.

When and if your daughter pushes the existing limits, remind her of your disappointment and invoke the consequences. She'll probably try to argue, but don't be tempted to lose your temper or add more punishments. That will only make the problem worse. Instead, remind her that you're not giving up hope on her becoming honest, and encourage her to try again. Always follow through on the agreed-upon consequence, and don't revert to arguing about whether the consequence was right or wrong. As you can guess, this is not going to be easy.

For this approach to be successful, both parents should be in solid agreement on all issues. If one parent makes any effort to side with your teenager against the other parent, the plan is doomed to failure, and the lies will continue ad infinitum. When an adolescent pushes limits by lying, there is a good chance that she believes she can get one parent to side with her against the other parent at least some of the time. Staying united, firm, and positive are critical to changing your daughter's dishonest behaviors.

### Dear Dr. Sylvia,

*What should I do when I tell my sixteen-year-old daughter she can't go out, and then she goes out anyway?*

*Powerless Mother*

Dear Powerless Mother,
If this is a first-time disobedience, it is important that you don't overreact. A long talk is more appropriate than anger or punishments. If she seems angry at you, indicate that you'd like to talk to her when both of you are in a better frame of mind. Your discussion may yield some information as to why she felt it necessary to leave, but don't expect her to change her point of view. She'll try to justify her misbehavior. Although you can be understanding, make it clear that you won't tolerate her misbehavior again. Remind her that there will be a consequence if she ignores your restriction. However, there's no need to tell her what the consequence might be. She may be more vigilant if she is worried about the potential consequence.

If your sixteen-year-old has been leaving home regularly despite your repeated disapproval, you have probably given her more power than you ever intended. You may actually have very few controls over her behavior. In my book *Why Bright Kids Get Poor Grades,* I advise parents not to get into power struggles unless they're reasonably sure they can control the outcome. In other words, you'll have to choose your battles. If there are times she shouldn't be leaving or places she shouldn't go, don't just forbid her with grounding threats or you may find yourself being ignored.

You'll want to inventory the control you have left. Restrictions of clothing, allowance, phone privileges, and perhaps her driver's license or a special trip are often the few choices parents have left if they've already rendered themselves powerless. Actually, your withdrawal of an allowance or the use of the family car on the weekend works pretty well. Try to frame discussion of future consequences positively. Here's an example: "We'd be happy to let you use the family car on Saturday night provided you can follow our guidelines for where or when you can go out; unfortunately, we can't do that if you ignore us when we tell you that you can't do something."

Hopefully this or withholding her allowance will be persuasive. Be sure to follow through on consequences. If you or her dad give in despite her noncompliance, you'll have given her entire control. Actually, parental agreement is absolutely critical to the success of any plan with your daughter.

If she still ignores you after knowing the consequences, you might at least try to get her into family therapy. I suspect that she's not very happy either. She may go along with the idea of therapy only because she wants to blame you for her problems, but a qualified psychologist will be able to sort out the issues and, hopefully, help you to retrieve your legitimate parent power.

### Dear Dr. Sylvia,

*What are your suggestions on how to handle a twelve-year-old who is abusive verbally? She swears and cusses constantly, especially if she's told to do a chore or her homework. I am a recent immigrant from Laos.*

*Angry Mother*

Dear Angry Mother,

Welcome to our country. Other than Native Americans, we are a nation of immigrants.

Verbal abuse by a twelve-year-old is likely to occur when the child feels that she is more powerful than her parent. The power your daughter is using to abuse you can come from several sources.

Often, American-born children serve as interpreters for their immigrant parents, who do not know the language well or speak with an accent. That role gives the children a sense of power and some feelings that they know more than their parents. These children are sometimes ashamed of their parents and their own cultural heritage. It is important for you to encourage pride in your own culture and to let your children know that they need not be ashamed of you.

Each night during or after the evening meal, take time to sit with your daughter and listen to her stories about school and friends. Share stories with her about your childhood in your own country. Although your life was very different from hers now, she'll always remember your stories and will value the time you took to share with her. If you can join together with other Laotian families to celebrate your holidays, language, and culture, your daughter will be able to share with other children of immigrants both her concerns about her parents' differences and the love and learning of her own heritage.

When your daughter is in a calm frame of mind, explain to her that vulgar language is not a badge of honor in your old country or in this one. Explain that intelligent children and adults express themselves in more refined and logical ways. Tell her that you will no longer get into discussions with her when she speaks inappropriately, and that you will simply walk out of the room if her language is vulgar, although you'll be happy to talk with her when she speaks more appropriately. Then follow through by leaving or avoiding her when she uses inappropriate language.

Our country has often been called a melting pot and compared to the melodious blends of a symphony orchestra. Although children should be raised to respect and honor differences, adjusting to this country has always held some special challenges for the immigrant parents of American-born children. I have wished many times that I could reach back to thank my own parents for immigrating to this country, and although your daughter may not have voiced her thanks to you, she will come to appreciate the opportunity you have provided, and she will grow to respect you as she matures. Please ask her to read this letter, and you can tell her that this writer is also a first-generation American.

# IN CHAPTER 2
## YOU'LL LEARN HOW TO

- stay united with your spouse for your children's sake.

- replace competition in your family with cooperation and compromise.

- avoid causing your spouse to feel or act like an ogre or a dummy.

- improve relationships with other family members.

- communicate with child-care providers.

- cope with special parenting issues related to adoption or foster parenting.

- support and discuss differences with teachers and schools.

# CHAPTER 2

---

# UNITED PARENTING

**Y**OU may have heard your grandparents and great-grandparents talking about parenting with a "united front." In today's society that unity between parents has been superseded in some families by competition within the family. The cooperation and leadership that should belong in parenting is often replaced by power struggles between parents. Cross-generational alliances between parents and children against the other parent or parents may sometimes divide families into opposite camps and destroy family unity. Yet unity and cooperation among parents and other adults who guide children have never been more important or more complex.

In our grandparents' day, the two-parent family was typical. However, children in today's society frequently have multiple parents and caregivers. Sometimes they are reared in traditional two-parent families. Sometimes they have one, three, or four parents. Sometimes grandparents or aunts and uncles take on the roles of parents. The statistics on the number of children brought up in single-parent families suggest that it's becoming an increasingly frequent phenomenon. According to a Census Bureau report, only half of this country's children live in traditional two-parent families.[1] Furthermore, in addition to parent figures, nannies, child-care providers, and day-care-center teachers have important impacts on the children they care for.

Regardless of whether children live with one, two, three, or four parents, or whether their caregivers extend to nannies, day-care centers, grandparents, and teachers, it's important that those adults who guide children's lives guide them in a reasonably unified and consistent way. The term *united front* means that even though adults may have some differences in their preferred styles of parenting, the view from the children's perspective should be of similar expectations, efforts, and limits.

Obviously, with the multiple caregivers in children's lives, it's not possible or necessary to have completely consistent expectations, but certainly among those who are the most critical adults, there should be reasonable similarity. If adults are consistent, children will know what's expected of them. They will also understand that they cannot *avoid* doing what feels a little hard or scary or challenging through the protection of another adult. Benjamin Spock, speaking about his new book *A Better World for Our Children,* stated that the best-behaved children are those whose parents are clear about what they want from their children and go about it in a friendly way.[2]

A UNITED FRONT

# PARENT RIVALRY

Competition invades our families. Parenting books rarely discuss the subtle competition that exists between parents. Underlying parent rivalry is the parents' concern about being good parents. Because our society is so competitive, we often believe that being a good parent means being the "better" parent. However, in an effort to prove himself or herself better, sometimes one parent may cause the other to feel that he or she can never be good enough.

Sometimes one parent sees him- or herself as being the better parent by being kind, caring, loving, and understanding. The other parent sees him- or herself as being best based on being respected and expecting a child to take on responsibilities and showing self-discipline. Although each parent sees him- or herself in these ways, he or she doesn't necessarily see the spouse in the way that the spouse describes him- or herself. The parent who sees him- or herself as kind and caring, therefore, may be viewed by the other spouse as being overprotective. The parent who sees him- or herself as being disciplined and responsible is likely to be viewed by the spouse as being rigid and too strict. They don't see each other in the same way as they see themselves, so they unconsciously decide that because their own way is best, they must change the other parent. Each absolutely believes he or she is right and the other parent is wrong. Only after fruitless efforts to change each other do they give up and decide that they must balance out the other parent by becoming more extreme in what they believe. Therefore, the kind, caring parent becomes more protective in order to shelter the children from the parent who expects too much. The expecting parent becomes more demanding to balance out the overprotective parent. The more one expects, the more the other protects. The more the second protects, the more the first expects. They get further and further apart in their expressed expectations. Parents who come to my clinic assure me they must do this to "balance each other out."

If children face parents who have contradictory expectations, and if these children lack the confidence to meet the expectations of one of their parents, they turn to the other parent, who not only unconditionally supports them but inadvertently teaches them "the easy way out." Without recognizing the problem they're causing their children, the kind and caring parents unintentionally protect their children from challenge. When children grow up in such an environment, they develop the habit of avoiding challenge. They fear taking intellectual and psychological risks because they have no united parent support for risk-taking.

Obviously, this balancing act increases in complexity when three or four parents are involved. Each parent is desperately anxious to provide the best parenting to keep their children's love. They may compensate for the other parent(s) in either the expecting or protecting direction. After divorce, parents are more likely to believe they can tempt children to love them by protecting them the most, doing too much for them, or buying them more.

The competitive rituals that take place between parents when the parents have inconsistent expectations are described in my book *Why Bright Kids Get Poor Grades and What You Can Do About It*.[3] They are labeled "ogre and dummy games." One, two, three, or four of these games can take place singly or in combination for any one child and may take place differently for other children in the same family. There are variations of ogre and dummy games that involve stepparents, grandparents, and aunts and uncles, and those that change between childhood and adolescence. Once you have read descriptions of these four rituals you will easily be able to imagine how they could happen in your own home without specific efforts to maintain a united front. Imagine other permutations and combinations of these sabotage rituals that could result from alliance between an adult and a child in opposition to another adult!

**Father Is an Ogre.** In the traditional family where this ritual takes place, the father is viewed by outsiders as successful and powerful, the mother as kind and caring. The parents often appear to be happily married and often are before the children are born. A closer view of the family shows a father who has high expectations for his children. The expectations may or may not actually be too high, but they are always *perceived* as being too high by the mother and the children. The children's perceptions of too high expectations by their father may be realistic, or they may only be based on Mother's interpretation of Father's actions and her overprotection of the children. The children learn to bypass Father's authority by appealing to their kind, sweet mother. Mother manages to convince Dad to change his initial decisions or surreptitiously permits the children to carry out their desired activities anyway.

The ritual becomes more extreme as the children grow older because the father begins to feel powerless over his family. He becomes more authoritarian and irrational as he tries to cope with his frustration. In response to his increasing authoritarianism, Mother feels even more obliged to shelter and defend her children. In her desperation she invents new ways to undermine her husband's power in the belief that she's doing the best thing for her children. She literally encourages her husband to become an "ogre" in her determination to protect her children.

Children tend to emulate a parent who appears powerful and similar to themselves. Girls in this family will tend to be achievement oriented because they see their mother as powerful, while boys will tend to underachieve. They see no effective model in their father, who appears both mean and powerless. They may fear and resent him, but they aren't likely to respect or emulate him, instead opposing and competing with him and choosing goals that are counter to his values. Dad may escape through continual work, which further convinces his sons to avoid being like their "workaholic" father. As children mature, their learned opposition of their father often generalizes to angry opposition to other authority figures as well.

When we look at the history of this marriage, it can usually be described as a traditional-style marriage, with Father serving as the main breadwinner who is expected to make all major decisions. The mother has chosen her husband because she prefers a strong partner. As her husband pursues a meaningful career, she defines her role as being in charge of the children and other household tasks. Although the traditional marriage is not what it used to be and Mother may work outside the home as well, her career or job is typically considered secondary and may only be part-time. Initially, the final word on parenting the children is also Dad's by agreement and by appearances. In reality, however, Mother covertly decides that, in fact, she should be the children's protector and guide. She will let her husband think he's in charge, but her role as "good mother" will always preempt his power. Her primary source of self-confidence is derived from parenting her children, and she sees her investment as being more than her husband's. She simply is sure she knows better than he how to handle their children.

Here are several Father-Is-an-Ogre scenarios, which I've repeatedly heard at my clinic:

## Scenario 1: Sam, Age "Terrible" Two

Mother has arrived home from work. She is, of course, tired but needs to get some information about Sam's day from the caregiver, who is about to leave. Sam is impatient to see his mother and interrupts constantly as the two of them converse. Mother asks two-year-old Sam to wait patiently for just a few minutes, and Sam is crying as tired Father walks in the door. He tells Sam to settle down, and Sam clings to Mother, crying even louder. Dad, furious at walking in the house amidst a brouhaha, picks Sam up and deposits him in his crib, where he screams even louder. Mother quickly dismisses the caregiver and races to Sam's room, removes him from the crib, and hugs and comforts him, apologizing for Dad's impatience and her having to take care of her business with the caregiver. Father turns on the TV in disgust, wondering how a two-year-old can already be so spoiled.

## Scenario 2: Sam, Age Ten, the Underachiever

Mother and Sam are sitting together doing Sam's homework at the kitchen table when Father walks in.

**FATHER:** Why do you need to work with Sam all night? He's smart enough to do his work on his own.
**MOTHER:** Sam needs my help. His math is hard. We'll be done soon.
**FATHER:** (*One hour later*) Are you still working on that math? You're spoon-feeding him. He's not that dumb. You don't have to do it for him. Send him here. I'm sure I can explain it to him.
**SAM:** Mom, you help me. Daddy will only get mad at me.
**MOTHER:** Sam, you better let Dad teach you. He wants to help you.
(*Sam picks up his book and wanders to the other room hesitantly.*)
**FATHER:** (*Looking over material*) Oh, yes. I remember this. Let me show you how to do it. Here's how it's done. Now you do the next one.

*(Sam does one example while Dad watches.)*

**FATHER:** No, Son, you've done that wrong. Don't you understand? I showed you. Try again. It's easy. *(Dad shows him again.)*

*(Sam does it wrong again.)*

**FATHER:** *(In a loud, booming voice)* You're not even trying, Sam. Look, your columns aren't even straight. No wonder you make mistakes. You're just careless. Weren't you listening when I explained?

**SAM:** Dad, I think Mom can help me better. At least she doesn't yell at me. *(Escapes to Mom)* See, Mom, I told you Dad doesn't understand me.

**MOTHER:** I'm sorry, Sam. Here, let me help you. Dad just doesn't know how hard math is for you.

Sam and Mother work together the remainder of the evening while scowling and angry Father continues to watch the game.

These scenarios illustrate a repeated sabotage ritual that eventually frustrates Father and empowers his son against him. The pattern causes the son to compete with his dad for his mother's attention and cements a close mother-son relationship in opposition to Dad. The father feels a sense of powerlessness he doesn't understand. Father may not even be aware of the mother-son protective tête-à-têtes or special purchases that often take place.

These incidents become a continual pattern of mother-son sabotages that Mother thinks of as necessary protections for her child from her husband's wrath. She wishes Dad wouldn't lose his temper so easily and that he'd be more understanding of his son. But, alas, over the years the father-son relationship worsens. Father never learns to talk to his son, and Sam feels no respect for his dad. Instead there is an awesome fear and a determination never to grow up to be as mean as he. By age sixteen, the act has solidified into a persistent ritual.

## Scenario 3: Sam, Age Sixteen, the Musician

### Part 1

Sam had taken violin and piano lessons for about two years at his own request. Although his parents paid for his lessons and instruments, Sam rarely practiced. Mother nagged. Father yelled at Mother and Sam. Finally, both parents gave up.

**Sam:** Mom, you know music is my life. I've just been playing the wrong instruments. I need a guitar. Then I can really become a rock star.

**Mother:** Guitars are expensive, and lessons cost money. I know you love music, but I just don't think I can convince your dad after you quit both piano and violin.

**Sam:** You won't have to pay for lessons. I'll learn it on my own. I'll make a more unique sound without lessons anyway.

**Mother:** What about renting a guitar? Maybe I could convince Dad to rent it for you.

**Sam:** No, renting won't work. The rented ones aren't good enough. I know just the right one to buy. They're a little expensive, but they're worth it. They have a better sound, and look at all you'll save without lessons.

**Mother:** Sam, I understand how important this is to you, but you'll have to ask your dad. He'll really be angry at me if I buy you another instrument.

**Sam:** Okay, but it's a waste of time. He always says no. He just doesn't understand me.

**Mother:** I know, Sam, but try to talk to Dad.

## Part 2

**Sam:** Dad, could I talk to you for a minute?

**Dad:** (*Watching game on TV*) Sam, it's a championship game. Don't you want to watch?

**Sam:** Naw. Remember, I hate sports. Dad, music is my life, and I really want a guitar. I think I could make it big as a rock star.

**Dad:** You're just a lazy dreamer! I'm afraid you'll never amount to anything. Why don't you get a job? You'll never practice anyway. I'm tired of wasting my money. You don't even do your homework. How are you going to have time for a guitar? Absolutely no! (*Returns to TV*)

**Sam:** (*Returns to Mom*) Mom, Dad will never understand me, and I'll never be able to play my music now. He just doesn't understand my generation. Sometimes he acts like he's as old as Grandpa.

**Mom:** Sam, I do have some money put aside for you. If a guitar is what you really want, you can use it for that. But please, Sam, don't play it when Dad is at home, and I'd rather you not mention it to him.

**Sam:** (*Hugs Mom briefly*) Gee, Mom, you're wonderful! Thanks a lot!

What has this kind, sweet mom done? She has literally made her husband into an ogre—and a powerless one at that. Why would Sam want to be like Dad? What son would respect a mean father who doesn't truly have the respect of his own wife?

When Sam was little, he said he was more like his mom. As he got older and it became uncomfortable for him to acknowledge similarity to his mother, he preferred to think he was like neither parent. "I don't really know who I'm like," he says. "I know I'm not like either of my parents." As a matter of fact, Sam doesn't really know what he wants to do, where he wants to go to school, or what he'd like to major in. He just can't seem to find any direction except that "music is my life." But that's all right. Mom'll probably help!

There are several ways in which Mom "tried to help" but inadvertently made Father into an ogre. For example, she pointed out to her son that Dad worked much too hard. She doesn't believe any work is worth all the time away from family. The underlying subtle message to her son is "Don't be like Dad—don't work so hard—life without all that work is more meaningful." By the time the son gets to high school, or possibly earlier, his application of this concept

FATHER IS AN OGRE

and his response to his parents is "I don't see why I should do this work at school. It's really only busywork and has no relevance for me. There's much more to life than just schoolwork anyway."

Mom, does this sound familiar? You gave your son that message. Unfortunately, he no longer listens, even to you, when you now tell him to study hard and do his homework.

Here's another part of the same ogre sabotage ritual: Dad would like his son to take challenging courses and to encourage (not force) him in the direction of his own career. Mother protests that their son has the right to choose his own courses, his own career, and to "do his own thing." Furthermore, she puts down her husband's career as one that requires too much travel or too much time away from home or too much arguing (as in attorney) or does not produce enough salary. The indirect message to their son is "Don't be like your father" and "Don't do the things he recommends." The idea emerges in the words of an adolescent son as "I want to do my own thing." He knows what he's against: his dad, his dad's career, his dad's course choices, and his dad's authority. He must choose something that's different and oppositional to establish his uniqueness. He can't take advice from anyone, except for those who are also doing their own thing—his peers. So he grows long hair or shaves his head, experiments with drugs, plays his music, or maybe he even joins a cult. He says he must "experience living." If he's prevented from accepting his father as a model, then he must find some other person or group that accepts and notices him and provides a model.

At a time in his life when he could be establishing a positive identity, the son invests many years in establishing his identity based only on what he is against. By this time, Mother isn't happy either, yet she unwittingly stole from her son an ideal role model— the man she loved and chose to marry, her successful husband, the boy's successful father. She unintentionally turned her husband into the man against whom her son must rebel—"the bad guy"— instead of a model from whom he could learn, and now neither Mom nor Dad understands their son.

**Mother Is an Ogre.** Sometimes husbands make their wives into ogres. This is the pattern seen most frequently on family TV shows. The family in which this ritual takes place includes a kind, soft-hearted husband who would be viewed by women outside the family as "perfect." He appears generous, loving, warm, and even enjoys discussing feelings. He values his parenting role and considers himself a good, fair father. He rarely loses his temper and frequently discusses differences of opinion with his children. They know they can talk things over with him and that he understands them. Understanding them usually involves seeing things their way. It never occurs to Dad that rivalry exists between him and his wife, although he does see himself as being more fair, more understanding, and the better parent. He wishes his wife wouldn't be so controlling. He acknowledges to me during counseling that he also feels controlled by his wife and, therefore, understands why his children feel the same way.

Of course there should be some discipline in the home. Children should be guided. Because Father is the "good guy," he recommends to his wife that she be in charge of the rules for the children. Mother values self-discipline and clearly sees the need for guidelines for her children. She establishes rules. But here's the catch: Mom makes the rules—and Dad breaks the rules! Here are some examples:

## Scenario 1: Hardworking Crew

Mom walks in the house from work to see Dad relaxing with a drink and the kids intently watching TV. Coats and books are strewn all over the living room. Mom is furious. She clicks off the TV. The kids scream and attempt to turn it back on.

**Mom:** The rule is, children are supposed to have the table set and the salad done before television goes on, and *(to her husband)* Jeff, you were going to heat up the dinner so we could all eat when I got home.

**Jeff:** I know, honey, but I just got home. Can't a man relax for a few minutes without a wife bossing him? You remind me of my mother—nag, nag, nag.

**Lisa and Charlie:** *(In chorus)* Gee, Mom, we just got home from school. We need to relax for a few minutes. We'll do it if you'll just stop nagging. C'mon, Charlie, I guess we'd better pick things up and set the table. Darn, it was such a good show. *(Lisa gets up to start picking things up. Charlie clicks on the TV.)* Charlie, are you coming?

**CHARLIE:** Yeah, I'm coming. I just want to finish watching the show. Stop nagging. You're beginning to sound just like Mom.

**LISA:** (*To Mom in the kitchen*) Gee, Mom, you walk into the house and the trouble begins. It was calm and cool before you got home. What do you want us to put on the table?

# Scenario 2: An Underachiever
## Part 1

Mr. and Mrs. Drew enter my office. Mother looks anxious. Dad seems annoyed to be here. They are here about Michael, their seventeen-year-old son.

**DR. RIMM:** Could you tell me a little about your son's problem?

**MRS. DREW:** Michael's a good kid. He has nice friends and his grades aren't bad. They're just not what they could be or what they used to be. He does most of his homework, except math, but he won't actually study anything. Every time I remind him about college or SATs or study, he becomes furious at me. I can't seem to talk to him at all. It's heartbreaking to see him losing opportunities. He has so much ability.

**DR. RIMM:** Mr. Drew, how do you see Michael's problem?

**MR. DREW:** This is just a waste of time. He hasn't got any problems. He's just not ready to study. It's only high school. He's having fun. He'll grow up. If his mother would just get off his case, he'd be fine. I wouldn't even be here if the wife hadn't dragged me along. Mike's a nice kid. He'll grow up when he gets to college.

**DR. RIMM:** Mr. Drew, how old were you when you got serious about school?

**MR. DREW:** I guess I didn't grow up till college, but then I did fine.

**DR. RIMM:** Do you remember your grade point average in high school?

**MR. DREW:** About a B average.

**DR. RIMM:** What about your son's now?

**MR. DREW:** Well, I think he has about a C- only because of that math for the last two years. I'm sure if his mother would just quit nagging him, he'd do better.

## Part 2

Michael enters my office.

**DR. RIMM:** Hi, Michael. Glad to meet you. I'd like to figure out how I can help you at school.

**Michael:** (*Angry*) Don't bother. This is a waste of time. Just tell my mother to get off my case and ask her to get my math teacher switched. I'll be fine. School is great otherwise. I have lots of friends and my grades are fine.

Michael is completely unrealistic about his failing grades and so is his father at first.

The Mother-Is-an-Ogre ritual fosters underachievement syndrome in both boys and girls. Girls in families where this ritual is taking place underachieve because they see their mother as powerless and an ogre. She delivers the serious school message, and Dad undermines it. The boys and girls in this family are happy to identify with their father. They like being "powerful and easygoing." Unfortunately, the message they receive from Dad doesn't encourage achievement. It's a passive-aggressive message to ignore Mother, to ignore teachers, and to ignore rules. It's a message to stay cool and relaxed, to avoid demands of others, and to procrastinate until you feel ready. The readiness rarely comes—doors of opportunity close.

MOTHER IS AN OGRE

**Daddy Is a Dummy.** This ritual is a slight modification of the ogre play and is found mainly in homes where mothers are psychologists, educators, or have recently taken parenting classes. Their husbands, on the other hand, may be doctors, engineers, truck drivers, or any profession that doesn't include child psychology courses. The main difference, of course, is that the mother has learned the "right" way to bring up the children and the father hasn't, as in the following scenario where Mother decides that it's her responsibility to give Father directions on how to rear their only son, Bryant, correctly:

> Mother and Father have worked out their schedules efficiently to allow for the care of their son. Mother teaches elementary school and begins her day early. Dad teaches at tech school, and his classes are all in the evening. Their parenting shift changes at about four o'clock when Mother returns from work. The family eats a snack together, and Dad goes off to work for the evening.
>
> Although Mother works outside the home, she continues to see her role as parent as her main source of fulfillment. Dad, however, also perceives himself as being a house husband and begins by bragging to his friends about his new parenting role. Mother doesn't exactly understand her feelings, but she feels deprived, perhaps even jealous, of the amount of time Dad devotes to parenting their only son. She also feels guilty about not having as much time for Bryant. In the two hours of family time shared by all, she finds herself cranky and complaining about all the tasks she believes her husband should be doing better. The barrage of complaints seems to escape from her as soon as she enters the house. It sounds like this, with a few variations: "Did you read to Bryant? Are you sure you've given him the proper nutrition? Are you giving him plenty of stimulation? Are you taking him to play group? Did you remember to put his warm jacket on him?"
>
> At first Dad answers with pride and satisfaction. As the questions continue, more of the answers are "No" or "I'll do that tomorrow." It isn't very long before three-year-old Bryant is reporting to Mother what Daddy has forgotten to do. By the time Bryant turns four, Father not only feels thoroughly inadequate and bored, but he decides to take a daytime job and convince his wife that day care would be better for Bryant. "Maybe," he thinks, "women are just better at bringing up children." If he could only put off caring for his son until the boy is a manageable size, he could

probably do better. Perhaps he'll go back to school and get another degree. If he worked on Saturdays, that would surely improve his opportunities for promotion and he could earn more money, and in the long run, he could probably do more for his son.

Dad's conclusion: I'll work hard on my job now and play with Bryant when he's older. I don't think I was cut out to be a house husband.

Mom's conclusion: I wish Bob wouldn't have to work so much, but he doesn't handle Bryant very well anyway, so at least I can get him on the right track through day care.

Bryant's conclusion: Daddy's never home. All Daddy does is work. That's dumb, but Mommy always said he didn't do so well with me. I sure don't want to be like Daddy.

At about this time, Daddy Is a Dummy becomes Father Is an Ogre, and the pattern continues from there.

**Mother Is the Mouse of the House.** The dummy ritual for mothers, which results in rebellious adolescent daughters, begins in a conspiratorial relationship between Father and Emily. It's a special alliance that pairs Father and his perfect little girl with each other

DADDY IS A DUMMY

but, by definition, gives Mom the role of being "not too bright" or somehow "out of it." During early childhood, Daddy never says no to Emily. She has a special way of winding him around her little finger. Mother admires the relationship, but from early on she doesn't quite understand it nor is she really part of it. Father and Emily go off hand in hand, looking with wonder at each other. Emily knows Daddy is easier on her and admits that she can do things when her dad's at home that she would never be allowed to do if Mom were also at home. Specifically, Emily tells me that she can eat treats when Daddy is at home that she wouldn't even ask Mommy if she could have.

Preadolescence arrives, and Mother notices a subtle, and sometimes not-so-subtle, battle taking place between Emily and herself. She's not exactly sure why, but Emily can't seem to take the slightest criticism or even suggestions from her. They seem to argue about almost everything, mainly hairstyles or appropriate clothes. Neither Mother nor Emily understands why the arguments begin. Because they are totally irrational, Mother often loses her temper in frustration. Father, "the great mediator," then emerges from the other room saying, "Now, girls, would you stop your arguing. Let me see if I can help you settle things." Or even worse, Dad says to

MOTHER IS A MOUSE

his wife, "Dear, would you please stop screaming at our daughter. I don't see why you two can't get along. No one else seems to have a problem with Emily. I certainly don't. The school doesn't. Personally, I think it's your problem." He, of course, directs this criticism to his wife (his theoretical partner) all within his daughter's hearing. The arguments continue and increase in quality and quantity. Dad mediates, smooths things over, and helps Emily to feel better. She sits on his lap and snuggles with him as he comforts. Mom just doesn't understand why she loses her temper and feels so out of control with Emily, nor does she understand why it is that they always argue. When I ask Mom during a therapy session what they argue about, Mom says, "I don't know, just anything." When I ask Emily, what they argue about, she responds, "I don't know. We just argue."

Then Emily begins maturing physically. Father notices and does a sudden about-face. He begins to worry about his perfect little girl. He remembers when he was a teenage boy. Dangers lurk in the corridors, in the lavatories, at school dances, and at parties. Father initiates a tirade of cautions about cigarettes, alcohol, drugs, and of course, teenage boys. He must protect his perfect daughter from the evils of teenage boys, but Emily says, "Dad, don't you trust me?"

THE GREAT MEDIATOR

Dad answers that he trusts her, but he isn't so sure about the rest of the world, so he decides it's time for rules.

Rules mean noes, and Emily has never really received a no from her father. Noes feel terrible and irrational to her. She is sure Dad must be going through some sort of midlife crisis or something. She appeals to Mom. She reminds Mom that she was once a teenage girl. Mom is delighted at her new relationship with Emily. She believes that they've stopped arguing because Emily is finally maturing. Now she colludes with Emily and offers to be a support to her. Emily explains her dilemma, and Mom assures her that she'll talk to her father about permission to stay at the party later than he ruled. Mom talks to Dad and convinces him to relent, and Emily has discovered a new manipulation. Now she allies with Mother against Father. When that works, she continues to manipulate. When Mom's alliance doesn't work, she returns to try Dad. First she manipulates Mom against Dad, then she manipulates Dad against Mom. Sometimes Emily has different categories in manipulating each parent: Mom understands about clothes and Dad understands about going to basketball games when homework isn't done.

The complex manipulations continue for several years until Emily is in high school. Suddenly, Mom and Dad recognize that Emily has been manipulating both of them. They decide that it's time for unity; it's time for consistency and compromise; it's time to be on the same team.

Now Emily asks for permission to stay at a party until twelve-thirty. Her father says, "No, twelve." She begs Dad. "Please, Dad, pretty please with sugar on it." Dad persists. Emily retreats to Mom. "Mom, you were a teenage girl once, remember? Can't I stay a little later? All the girls are staying out later."

Mom says no. Dad says no. Now Dad and Mom agree. Emily stands alone against them. They're saying no, and even when she does her best manipulating, she can't change their decision. She feels desperate. She proclaims, "My parents are controlling me. They used to treat me like an adult and now they treat me like a child." She goes to the party and stays out until two-thirty. Her parents are anxious, scared, and worried. When she walks in the door, they can smell the alcohol on her breath. They ground her. First, they ground her for a weekend. In her somewhat drunken state, she says she doesn't care. Then they ground her for a week. She stubbornly announces that doesn't matter. Then they ground her for three weeks. She defies them and says, "You can't ground me." Finally, they ground her for life! When she's grounded for life, she can do most anything and she does. They have completely lost the opportunity to guide Emily. She is immersed in opposition, and she finds many other antiparent friends to support her.

Now Mom and Dad are really anxious. Emily is in with the wrong crowd. They've found cigarettes in her room. How can they trust her? Mom tries to talk to her, but that never worked before. Dad tries to communicate his concerns. That's a little better but not really effective, because he wants her to stop smoking. She won't. She says she is her own person; it's her body, and her parents must stop being so controlling. She says they don't respect her. Her parents read her journal that she leaves out on her desk. They know from the journal that Emily "hates" her parents, her father only a little less than her mother. She's disrespectful, uses four-letter words profusely, ignores their rules, and her formerly A and B grades have dropped to D's and F's. She skips classes and argues with her parents, and her most frequent words are "Stop controlling me" and "You don't understand me." They can no longer con-

GROUNDED FOR LIFE

trol Emily, and they can't understand what has happened to their sweet, perfect little girl. She has joined a group of antiparent, anti-school rebels, and she just can't wait until she can get out of her parents' controlling home.

Emily's parents bring her to my office. She doesn't want to come. She plops herself down in the chair across from me, determined that I won't help her, and says in a disdainful voice, "My mother is stupid. You'd think she was born one hundred years ago. She's controlling. Even Dad knows that. I don't need your help; she does."

"And your father?" I ask, wishing I didn't have to hear the answer.

"He's not much better—well, maybe a little better. Neither of them have a life. I really can't stand them. I can't wait until I get out on my own. I'm counting the days till I'm eighteen."

The rebellious daughter, who had too much power as a small child and whose father unwittingly encouraged her to compete with her mother (who should have been his first love), feels rejected, unloved, and out of control. Girls like Emily take various paths, but they all signal the same sense of lack of power, which they feel mainly because they were overempowered as children.

Some girls express their feelings of rejection by parents in patterns of promiscuous sexual relationships. They say their parents (especially their fathers) don't love them anymore, and they must have love. When they're in a boy's arms, they mistakenly believe that he loves them, and it feels good. When they leave that bed for the next one, they feel rejected and embittered and easily accept the next invitation that looks like love. They're always sure that their new love will not carry HIV and will never leave them, and they feel safe in his arms.

Other girls express silent rebellions; bulimia, anorexia nervosa, depression, and suicide attempts are powerful ways of expressing feelings of loss of control. These illnesses leave parents feeling helpless and blaming each other. Parental fear and guilt put the adolescents or young adults in control of their parents but not in control of themselves. Fathers who conspire with their little girls to put Mother down as the "mouse of the house" can expect to suffer through their girls' adolescence.

When I talk to parents of delightful little girls whose fathers are unwittingly sabotaging their wives, I have great difficulty convincing them of their power and the likely dreadful outcome. Here's the brief description I use that usually gets their attention:

> The wink of the eye between Daddy and his little girl that suggests that Mom is not really "with it" becomes the rolled-back eyes of the preadolescent daughter at her mother. As Dad sees his daughter maturing and suddenly changes his attitude, thus deciding to set rules for his daughter, her rebellion extends to him as well. When teenagers assume that neither their mom nor dad understands them, and that their father is rejecting them, they go from bed to bed in search of a love that feels as intimate as the love they used to feel for Dad.

My description almost always gets a father's attention, but if he still insists that there's nothing wrong with his undermining his wife, I share the story of a sweet, bright young woman whose dad unintentionally sabotaged her mother for years. Now she has dropped out of high school, earned a GED, dropped out of college twice, had two abortions, and finally realized that her relationship with her boyfriend was mainly based on their shared anger at their parents.

This negative pattern doesn't have to take place. **It takes parental support for each other and a united effort at maintaining a positive and firm relationship with a daughter to permit her to respect both her mother and her dad.** Although the mother-is-a-mouse pattern typically begins early, it can easily be changed before a daughter reaches the teenage years and even during adolescence. However, during those precarious teenage years, a daughter who has competed with her mother for her dad's attention and now loses his support may feel as if no one understands her. Staying positive during adolescence becomes difficult for both parents if sabotage of one parent or the other has taken place all during childhood.

**PARENT POINTER**

**How to Avoid Ogre and Dummy Games.** The key to avoiding ogre and dummy games is *respect.* If parents voice and show respect for each other, children will respect their parents. Ogre and dummy games can be corrected simply by parents recognizing or being aware that

they exist. Parents don't usually require therapy to make changes;
however, they do require cooperation and compromise, and they

should not compete with each other for their children's love. **Here
are some suggestions:**

- Make it clear to your children that you value and respect the
  intelligence of your spouse. Don't put your spouse down except in jest and only when it's absolutely clear that you're joking. Use conversations with your children to point out the
  excellent qualities of your husband or wife.
- Be sure to describe your spouse's career in respectful terms so
  that neither of you is feeling as if you're doing work that the
  other doesn't value.
- Don't join in an alliance with your children against your
  spouse in any way that suggests disrespect. Sometimes parents do this subtly, as in, "I agree with you, but I'm not sure I
  can convince your mom (or dad)." If you communicate to
  your children that you value their other parent, it will almost
  always be good for your children, for your spouse, and for
  you. Be particularly careful when your children reach adolescence. Just a few slips may be enough to initiate disrespect.
- Reassure your oppositional children frequently of your mutual support for them. However, be positively firm in not permitting them to manipulate either of you. They'll perceive
  your support of each other as a betrayal and will feel hurt or
  depressed. Because they're in a habit of seeing relationships
  between others as betrayals of commitments to them, you
  should assure them frequently that spouses can respect each
  other and still love their children. This is a difficult reality for
  these youths to cope with, and they may feel emotionally isolated unless they're reassured. These children can easily place
  one of the parents (the "good" one) in the position of mediator unless the parent absolutely refuses to play that role.
- When your children come to you to complain about their father or mother expecting too much of them, they do it because they're hoping that you'll support their easy-way-out
  position and side with them. They're hoping you'll help them
  get out of what the other parent has asked them to do. You'll
  want to respond with kindness while evincing your respect

for your spouse. If the child says, "Mother (or Father) expects too much of me," or, "Mom (or Dad) is always yelling at me," examples of appropriate answers follow: "Your mother expects this of you because she knows you're capable. If she didn't expect it of you, it would mean that she didn't believe you could do it. You should be pleased that your mom expects it; it really means she values you. After you do it, Mom will be proud, and you'll feel good."

Here's another example of an appropriate response I recently heard in my clinic:

The father had asked his son, Josh, to pick up his things in the living room. Josh hadn't done it, and his father, losing his temper, scolded him and reminded him that he ought to do it right away. Sixteen-year-old Josh came to his mom, rolled his eyes disrespectfully with defiance to Dad, and complained, "Dad's yelling at me again." Mom recalled that when she and Josh used to play ogre games, she would have protected her son. This time, however, after one appointment at my clinic, she knew better and said, "Dad wouldn't have had to yell at you if you had picked things up the first time." The boy was shocked for a moment, but immediately turned to do the job. In this new response, Mother clearly supported Dad, and Josh knew what he was expected to do and did it.

This kind of response, whether related to their father or mother, gives children a message of confidence. Most of all, it provides the united expectations that permit your children to build self-confidence through achievement.

## WHY DO WE SABOTAGE?

A mother and father sat before me in the clinic looking puzzled and said, "I guess we sabotaged each other. No wonder we're powerless with that kid. It's like shooting yourself in the foot!"

Why do we do it? Why do we sabotage our spouses? Is it a need to compete with each other? Do we want to be the better parent? All are probably at least partially accurate.

What about that wonderful sense of intimacy we feel when we're baring our souls to our very closest genetic relations, our children? Are we so desperate for closeness that we value that intimacy before the closeness of our spouse? Is our disappointment in the loneliness of our marital relationship sending us desperately in search of intimacy to our children?

We all know that adolescents establish closeness by talking negatively about other kids, that unions build solidarity by confirming that administrators are bad guys, and that nations build patriotism in the face of enemies. Whether our alliances with our children against our spouses are attempts to deal with our personal loneliness, to establish our expertise as parents, to feel good about ourselves as being sensitive to our children's needs, to build solidarity with our children, or all of the above, these alliances surely cause problems for our children. They also adversely affect our marriages and our children's future marriages. In these insecure times of prevalent divorce, are we perpetrating infidelity to our spouse in the name of good parenting? These are some hard and heavy questions to think about the next time you confide in your child about your spouse's problems. Remember, although you may believe you are only being honest, you are actually committing sabotage.

Abraham Lincoln addressed our nation as he faced the hard decisions that led to the Civil War and concluded, "A house divided against itself cannot stand." Perhaps this important observation about our country has even more applicability within our families.

## ABUSE: WHEN THERE CAN'T BE A UNITED FRONT

In some homes a parent cannot support the children's other parent. Children must be protected from verbal, sexual, or physical abuse, or alcohol or drug abuse. You cannot and must not whitewash or ignore abuse. You must take an advocacy and sheltering role for your children. Children who are living in an environment where there can't be a united front are going to suffer from their alliance with an adult against another adult. However, that's much less harmful than the suffering that comes from abuse by a parent. **Your first step in dealing with an abusive situation is to provide protection for your children.** Second, **make it clear to the abuser**

PARENT
POINTERS

**that your children will be protected. Their safety comes first.** Once you've found shelter, you'll want to explain to your children why you've taken this protective position.

When there has been physical abuse of either a parent or children, be careful not to make the abuser appear meaner and more powerful than he or she really is. Continual discussion about the abuse won't help the children or the situation. After you've explained the abuse and listened to the children's concerns about it, it's best that you go on from there. Be willing to listen if they wish to talk, but don't assume you should rediscuss, reexplain, reexcuse, or recondemn the abuser. **Continual talk may encourage more feelings of anxiety, fear, and powerlessness. You and the children will require some professional counseling.**

PARENT POINTER

An important problem for parents is diagnosing the difference between real abuse, borderline abuse, and nonabuse. It is obviously wrong for a parent to physically or sexually abuse a child. But parents may disagree about what they consider abuse. Take, for example, spanking. I never recommend spanking, and it's certainly not the best form of punishment, but parents do have the right to spank children. However, if one parent tries to use spanking for discipline and the other parent feels this is abusive, the spanking is likely to be counterproductive.

Suppose Father spanks, and Mother tells him, within the children's hearing, he has no right to spank. The children act even worse because they know that Mother is defending their position against Dad. It makes the children more powerful and determined to act out. It causes the father to feel more frustrated and powerless and, therefore, to spank more. In this situation, you can see that abuse wasn't intended and shouldn't be so interpreted. If the mother feels that spanking is inappropriate, she should defer expressing her judgment about the spanking because it doesn't qualify as abuse. She should discuss her differences with her husband out of the children's hearing. If she intervenes to defend her children against their dad's spanking, she may cause further problems.

Verbal abuse is also hard to define. What if a child does something careless, and the parent calls the child an "idiot"? We all know that parents shouldn't call children idiots. Yet probably thousands of parents have called their children that or similar negative names in occasional anger or frustration.

How do you deal with that kind of situation? If one parent considers it verbal abuse to call the child an idiot and the other one considers it just a way of describing a child's dumb behavior, the best way to resolve the difference is with humor. If that doesn't work, and if the child comes to the parent and says, "Mom shouldn't have called me an idiot," Dad should simply say, "You really acted pretty dumb. You mother doesn't really think you're an idiot. Next time think about what you're doing. I guess we all act like idiots sometimes." In that way, you let the child know she need not take the label of stupidity seriously. On the other hand, you also remind the child that you expect her to think before she acts. Your statement doesn't, however, show disrespect for the other parent.

I wouldn't categorize the *occasional* inappropriate name-calling as abuse. Calling a child an idiot, dumb, or stupid once in a while won't destroy her. Children are resilient enough to handle a few put-downs. However, a **parent who continually uses terms that make children feel stupid may cause them major confidence problems in the future. It's something that parents should definitely not habitually do.**

Whenever you disapprove of the way your partner has treated your child, it's better not to take the child's position but to talk the problem through with the offending parent. It will be less harmful to the child. **Maintain the united front if parental discussion can assure you of improvement in the future. In real abuse, don't enable the abuser. Protect your children.**

PARENT
POINTER

PARENT
POINTER

# WHEN PARENTS LOVE THEIR CHILDREN BUT NOT EACH OTHER

The ogre and dummy games that take place in a family during or after divorce, or in a newly blended family where there are stepparents, become much more complex and are somewhat more difficult to cope with. Although many children in our society experience their parents' divorce, it continues to be traumatic regardless of their ages. It can't necessarily be assumed that divorce is more traumatic than living with unhappily married parents. That comparison would be difficult to prove. If you are going through a divorce, there are ways to help your children adjust and to lessen the trauma they feel.

The key to a child's good adjustment to a divorce is the mother and father's after-divorce relationship. The children feel love for both parents despite the fact that their parents don't love and perhaps even hate each other. The parents, in turn, may both love the children and may be afraid that they'll lose their children's love. Children often feel caught in the middle and may worry that if they express love to one parent, the other parent will no longer love them and vice versa. Even more extreme, they may feel they are making a parent happy and even taking care of that parent by expressing dislike or distrust for the other parent. They may feel pressured into playing the role of adult as they fear their parent requires their help. They may actually feel as if they are trapped into lying or losing a parent's love.

As you help your children cope with divorce, **give them assurance that they'll be loved and that they may continue to love the other parent.** They should receive positive descriptions *of* both parents, *from* both parents. Sometimes that may be difficult in the anger of divorce. Here's an example:

PARENT
POINTER

> The mother of a teenage girl and a preadolescent boy went through a traumatic divorce after her husband had an affair with another woman during a "midlife crisis." The father decided that he was in love with that woman and wanted a divorce. The mother, who had earlier thought that she had an excellent marriage, naturally felt rejected and angry. During the several separations that preceded the divorce, she tried to explain to her children, most particularly her daughter, that their father's behavior was "childish and immature" since she could not rationally explain it. This seemed only fair and honest so as to prevent her daughter from assuming the mother was at fault. The daughter agreed with her mother that her father was behaving childishly.
>
> Later, in counseling, the daughter shared with me the things that her dad allowed her to do of which her mother wouldn't approve, such as going to heavy-metal concerts and wearing inappropriate T-shirts. Her mother had blamed her dad for allowing her daughter these experiences, but her daughter had asked her dad for them without telling her mother that she had asked. Before the divorce even became final, the teenage daughter had begun manipulating both her mother and father. Although

the dad wasn't intending to hurt his daughter, in an effort to keep her love, he was giving her a "sabotage" message that said she could ignore her mother's limits and even that he thought those limits were "goody-goody." Not only was this girl feeling caught between her parents, but she was learning to manipulate each of them in ways that eventually made her feel insecure and angry. If her parents had continued this pattern, she would have become a rebellious and depressed teenager; fortunately, both parents were willing to acknowledge the risks to their daughter, and the manipulating subsided.

Here's another example:

A father called in to my public radio program to ask me how he could improve his children's visitations with him. It took them days to warm up and be pleasant to him, and then, of course, it was time for them to return to their mother. He told me he believed their bad attitudes were caused by his former wife's "setting them up" not to like him. He wanted to know if I had any suggestions.

I advised this dad to say nice things about his former wife in the first few minutes of the children's visit, even if he felt like choking on his comments. A few nice statements would put the children at ease and not cause them to feel like traitors to their mother.

PARENT POINTER

**Although it is difficult to say nice things about your former spouse (or even your present spouse), do it anyway.** It encourages children to feel good about both of you. They can then relax and enjoy being with either one of you without feeling guilty of betrayal. It works.

Children tend to manipulate their parents after divorce, often unintentionally. They do what seems to work for them at this time of insecurity. Parents are vulnerable because they are competing for their children's love and are afraid of losing their children to the other parent.

PARENT POINTER

After divorce, **emphasize positive, achieving aspects of the other parent so that he or she can be a constructive role model for your children.** Children will begin to see that parent as a role model, especially if they identify with him or her. The more you emphasize the negative characteristics of the other parent, the more helpless your children will feel to do anything about their own negative characteristics, which may be similar. **If it's difficult to find positive characteristics about the other parent, don't say anything at all.** At least you decrease the likelihood of your children's copying the parent's unpleasant characteristics.

Children who live with and visit parents in separate homes should have two locations where they can receive love, learn to work and make an effort, and play and have fun. That kind of arrangement provides a real sense of consistency and security for them despite divorce. Of course, it also requires good communication between parents, and that's not usually easy. Having one home that is all work compared to the other that is fun and games during visitation turns the work parent into an ogre and the visitation parent into "the easy way out." Here's an interesting case study:

PARENT
POINTER

James, a ninth-grader and the older of two boys, lived with his mom, who had been divorced for approximately three years. He was positive, responsible, and an achiever in school. When I asked him about his visitations with his father, he said it was a lot like staying at a hotel. He had few responsibilities. He didn't have to pick up or clean. They went out to eat. I then asked him if he enjoyed that easy lifestyle, assuming that he did. To my surprise, he responded by saying no. He really rather enjoyed being at home with his mom. He described the difference between the homes as "my father is liquid, my mother is solid." He felt better about the responsible kind of lifestyle that he was handling at home than he did about the "fun and games" visitations with his dad.

It's important to mention that although neither the mother nor father was remarried, the mother had several family friends in the neighborhood who provided good male role models for James and permitted him to join with their families for activities. He also considered his band teacher to be an inspiration to him.

It's equally important to know that Mike, his younger brother, was underachieving and loved his dad's "hotel" way of life. Mike is doing fine now, but it required some changes and some new friends as role models. Dad lost interest in both boys soon after their therapy began.

PARENT
POINTER

**Continue to treat your children as children, especially after a divorce.** Too often the oldest child becomes a parent's confidant and is given adult status. Although the child enjoys the power of being an equal adult, if the parent tries to set limits at a later date, the child won't accept child status. He may become rebellious with the very parent who had originally awarded him the adult status. Remember the V of Love. Power given is not easily taken away.

PARENT
POINTER

Although both parents should assure their children of their love (if both continue to be available), **it's unnecessary and even harmful to assure them that you'll always love them more than anyone else.** Parents do give that message frequently to their children. It is likely to result in the children's feeling unloved, rejected, and distrustful when the parent chooses to remarry. Children who have been assured of being in first place aren't willing to share their parent's love with another adult or with future stepsiblings. Children who have the power of a spouse are likely to exhibit anger and aggression when they feel displaced by a parent's new adult friend.

PARENT
POINTER

**Don't feel guilty about divorce.** No one is perfect. Guilt has never helped improve parenting. You're human and doing as well as you can under the circumstances. Time will heal the feelings of hurt and will put problems into perspective for your children. **Get**

PARENT
POINTER

**some counseling for yourself and your children to help you through the trauma of your divorce.** Your children will want a safe person to talk to, and it will help them to avoid feeling caught in the middle, particularly if both parents agree to the counseling. Figure 2.1 is a summary of suggestions for single parents, whether divorced or in other circumstances.

PARENT
POINTER

Some final words about divorce and single parenting: Neither is easy for children or their parents. **If there is even a 5 percent chance that your marriage may improve by counseling, make the attempt.** All marriages go through crises, and many marriages improve with outside help and problem solving. Many parents have assured me that they have appreciated this advice, which helped them keep their marriage together. Don't give up on your marriage if there's any hope of improving it. Children will benefit when the marriage stays together effectively, and most children suffer through divorce.

Figure 2.1

# Suggestions for Single Parents

As a single parent, are you destined to have an underachieving child? Of course not, but your job is more difficult. Here are some simple rules to guide you—simple only in that they're few and straightforward. In reality, they're terribly difficult for single parents to negotiate. Pat yourself on the back for each successful day. You deserve it.

- Find a career direction for your life to give you a sense of purpose and to build your personal self-confidence. Making your children your only purpose gives them power and causes them pressure that will be too stressful for them to manage.
- Find some adult social outlets for yourself. Don't feel guilty about enjoying yourself as an adult away from your children.
- Find a reliable baby-sitter or day-care facility for your children. Consistency in caregivers and surroundings is important for young children.
- Treat your child as a child, not a toy to be played with or an adult to be depended upon. *Do not* share your bed with your child (except during thunderstorms). That is an adult status that you should reserve for a spouse.
- Don't tell your children you will love them more than anyone else forever, or a new partner will cause them to believe you deceived them.
- If your children come home from a visitation and are unruly, don't blame that poor behavior on the other parent. Instead, tell them you're pleased they had a nice time, and if you can manage a nice comment about the other parent, they'll settle down more easily. They need to know they can love you both.
- Take time (you have little) to enjoy your children's achievements and encourage them to take responsibilities.

Below are three special rules for single mothers who are parenting boys:

- Boys should have an older male as a model. Find effective role models for your boys. Uncles, grandfathers, teachers, Boy Scout leaders, and Big Brothers may all be helpful to your sons in learning to be comfortable with their masculinity.
- If you don't view your children's natural father as an effective role model, absolutely don't tell your boys how much they look like and remind you of their father, especially when you are angry.

continued on next page

Figure 2.1 (continued)

## Suggestions for Single Parents

· Avoid power struggles with your children's father. If their father mistreats you and shows open disrespect toward you, your sons are likely to imitate this powerful but disrespectful behavior.

These rules will sound simplistic to some of you and impossible to others. They may be difficult for a single parent to live by, but they are effective for parenting your children in a single-parent household. Remember, many successful and happy children have been brought up in single-parent families.

SOURCE: *Why Bright Kids Get Poor Grades and What You Can do About It* by S. B. Rimm (New York: Crown Publishing Group, 1995).

# ADOPTION AND FOSTER PARENTING: CAN THERE BE A UNITED FRONT?

There are special difficulties in maintaining a united front when children have been adopted or if they are in foster placement.

**Adoption.** Many children are adopted into loving homes, and adoptive parents become the real and only parents to these children. Sometimes adoption takes place when children are so young that no bonding has taken place between them and their birth parents, thus allowing adoptive parents and children alike to experience bonding that is similar to that between children and their birth parents. At other times, adoption takes place when children are older, often after they have experienced early trauma in war-torn countries, in the homes of alcohol or drug abusers, or in a variety of temporary foster placements.

With some adoptions, parents have never met and have little knowledge about the birth parents or the child's preadoption history. With others, the adoptive parents not only know the birth parents but have developed a relationship with them, which they may all have agreed to maintain. However, maintaining a united front among so many parents can be fraught with problems, especially during the child's adolescence.

If your children were adopted, whether at birth or later, but are no longer part of their birth parents' lives, you can tell your children honestly that you know little about their parents. If your children question whether their parents loved them, you can explain as truthfully as possible, but without sharing information that would hurt your children. Here are a few examples of responses you could give depending on the circumstances:

- Your parents really didn't get to know you; if they did, they surely would have loved you.
- Your parents loved you so much but knew they wouldn't be able to raise you as they would have liked, so they gave us this privilege of raising you.
- Your parents were too sick to take care of a baby, so they knew they needed help.
- Your parents died soon after you were born (only if it's true), and rescue workers (or the orphanage) searched for families to take in children. We were so happy to get you.

If your children were adopted from another country or culture, you may wish to continue some traditions out of respect for their heritage. However, too much emphasis on their birth heritage can cause them to feel alienated from you; after all, they really are your children to lead, to love, and to teach.

If your children's birth parent(s) continue to be important in their lives, it may cause some problems or rivalry as the children grow up. When they are babies, it is easier to share communication with their other parents and help those parents adjust to their loss. As the children mature, however, your values may be different from those of the birth parents, and unity in parenting messages may be entirely impossible. Although birth parents may have voluntarily given up legal rights, genetic similarities may tempt them to believe they should have input into parenting their children. Even occasional visits may suggest to adolescents that life could have been more carefree in the home of their birth parents. At times when parents must be firm about discipline, teenagers may look to their birth mother or father for the easy way out. I have heard too many adolescents tell me their "real" mother or dad wouldn't have expected so much from them when actually their adoptive parents expect only reasonable responsibility. A continued alliance between birth parents and adoptive parents after adoption is difficult to continue and often puts the adoptive parents in the roles of ogres. Even when I remind these children that their "real" parents are their adoptive parents, the easy way out they imagine tempts them.

It is too hard on children to ask them to choose between the parents who gave birth to them and the parents who raised them. It is unfair to parents who adopt to limit their power in raising their children. No research indicates that open adoptions are more effective than closed adoptions over time, and I see little likelihood that so many unrelated parents could stay united through their child's adolescence.

Adopted children sometimes seek to find their own birth parents when there has not been an open adoption. This is natural, but **adulthood seems early enough for that discovery, and it is unlikely to pose problems by that time.**

**Foster Parenting.** Foster parents provide a temporary loving environment when parent(s) are not able to parent their children for a variety of psychological or physical reasons. Foster placement is mainly intended to be a "holding place" to keep children feeling safe and secure while decisions are being made about their future. Sometimes they will return to live with their birth parents, while at other times foster homes are transitions either to adoption or the children's adulthood. Foster parents are often special people who are willing to open their homes and their hearts to children, although they understand the temporary nature of the arrangement. It may be very difficult indeed to keep a united front with birth parents, who sometimes have inadequate parenting skills.

Foster parents who invest in teaching their foster children about limits and respect may feel frustrated when these children visit their own parent(s) and are given license to ignore these limits. Foster parents may even try to teach the children's parents in caring ways how to improve their parenting skills while their children look on. **If foster parents correct, criticize, and disagree with the children's parents in front of the children, it sets the stage for parental sabotage.** Continued communication to birth parents about their parenting skills, if done when children are present, suggests the inadequacy of the parents and only causes feelings of insecurity for them and their children. Children need desperately to have confidence in the adults who are responsible for them, and when other adults correct their parents in front of them, it causes them to question their parents' adequacy and causes problems for everyone. Children who see their parent(s) as powerless and inadequate will not obey them even when they attempt to set limits appropriately. It is too easy for children to get into an alliance with foster parents against birth parents or vice versa, and birth parent(s) can have difficulty establishing adequacy or power. Also, if professionals who are arranging foster care, such as social workers, correct parents in front of their children, they, too, steal from them the power they require to be good parents.

Although kids would not be upset if their parents obtain some advice, it needs to be given as though those parents are truly competent so that children can continue to have confidence in them. This can be difficult for foster parents or child-care workers because they often have little or no confidence in the children's birth parents. **Foster parents and child-care professionals should meet privately with the birth parents to impart their wisdom and give them parenting advice.**

PARENT
POINTER

Also, foster parents may be required to do some acting when communicating expectations to the children in order to empower birth parents to take charge. Words such as "your mother knows what's best for you, so be sure to listen to her" are appropriate but may seem risky to foster parents who don't actually believe that a birth parent has the experience or knowledge to guide the children well. Yes, maintaining a united front between foster parents and real parents is a high priority, but it is extremely difficult under these circumstances.

## MAINTAINING A UNITED FRONT WITH RELATIVES

Occasionally, I'll see children whose behavior, achievement, or school learning has been more adversely affected by differences between grandparents and parents, or aunts and uncles and parents, than by differences between parents themselves. The differences can be dramatic and traumatic, particularly when children are brought up in households where other adults are serving as caretakers.

**Grandparents.** Sometimes the power struggles that used to take place between Grandmother and Mother affect how the grandmother treats her grandchild. It seems almost as if Grandmother is trying to get even with her child. In effect, it may provide an easy way out for a grandchild if Grandmother and Grandchild form an alliance against Mother. Figure 2.2 includes some recommendations for grandparenting.

There's a disturbing little joke that says the reason grandchildren and grandparents get along so well is that they have a common enemy—parents. That would be funny if it weren't so sad. Relationships between grandchildren and their grandparents can be built as a beautiful alliance based on special learning, fun, and experiences. No parents should fall victim to being the enemy. Once grandparents are alerted to the damage they can do as well as the beneficial support they can provide, almost all of them choose the supportive role. Here's an example from my clinic work:

Sixteen-year-old Stephanie was very rebellious with her parents. She had made heavy drinking and sex with her boyfriend a regular part of her weekend partying. Her parents had lost control of their daughter and were frustrated and angry. Grounding was no longer effective; Stephanie went out anyway.

Her parents confronted her at 2 A.M. after a typical Saturday-night drinking orgy. They were greeted by a stream of four-letter words, which they were only too accustomed to hearing, and their daughter, in her fury, left home for the safety of her grandparents' home.

Stephanie arrived at her grandparents' house in tears and anger, exclaiming how terrible her parents were and begging for shelter. She claimed her parents no longer loved her and asked if she could live with them. The grandparents obviously knew only part of the story and wanted to be supportive of this grandchild whom they loved so much. They called the parents, saying they'd keep Stephanie overnight, and reassured Stephanie that they'd settle "this thing" between her and her parents, implying that the parents needed their guidance.

At the request of the parents, the grandparents came to see me at my

## Figure 2.2

# Do's and Don'ts of Grandparenting

- *DO love your grandchild as much as you'd like.* You can't love them too much. If you don't express your love, it is a sad loss for you and your grandchildren.
- *DO stay in close touch.* Telephone your grandchildren directly, or when you're calling their parents, be sure to also talk with the grandchildren. Write letters and send pictures and encourage the children to do the same. Save the children's letters for them. They will appreciate them when they are grown. If your grandchildren live nearby, arrange regular visits for doing something special. Introduce them to cultural opportunities that their parents may not have time for or just spend time with them.
- *DO give special gifts for enriched learning.* Now may be a time in your life when you are able to purchase a set of encyclopedias for your grandchildren that would be too expensive for the parents of young children to afford. Your grandchildren will remember that you're the one who gave them that special gift, and their parents will appreciate your help. If the children's parents can't manage the cost of a computer or a special camp experience, you may be able to help with those opportunities also. If your finances are limited, sharing some interesting books or toys from your own childhood may provide in-depth enrichment.
- *DO share stories about your own childhood.* Encourage your grandchildren to tape-record your stories. They will have them forever and will always be able to hear your voice. They will appreciate the past and have a better sense of history. Encourage their questions and observations.
- *DO play competitive games with your grandchildren.* Children may be very competitive, so be sure not to let them always win. They should learn to cope with both winning and losing. Children often recall playing cards, checkers, or chess with Grandma or Grandpa. Games are also a nice way for informal communication to just "happen."
- *DO projects with your grandchildren.* For example, if you play music, knit, crochet, quilt, or sew, or do woodworking or art, share these interests with your grandchildren. Sharing skills can have a great impact on them. It will make the children feel closer to you, and they will learn to appreciate your talents. Furthermore, they will always remember that a particular skill was taught to them by their grandparents.
- *DO read to your grandchildren.* Encouraging children to love books is always valuable for them. You may wish to share books from your childhood or from their parents' childhoods. Listen to your grandchildren read to you, but only if they enjoy reading aloud. Forcing them to read aloud may cause them to feel pressured.

continued on next page

Figure 2.2 (continued)

## Do's and Don'ts of Grandparenting

•*DO listen to your grandchildren.* Let them talk to you and tell you stories. Be an attentive audience. Children often love to talk, and other children may not be as interested.

- *DO say positive things about your grandchildren's parents.* If the children believe that you respect their mom and dad, it will help the parents maintain their children's respect. This will be good for your grandchildren and for you. They will respect you, too.
- *DO give your grandchildren a clear message about education.* Tell them how important school and learning are. Ask your grandchildren about their grades and how they're doing, but even more important, ask them about what they're learning in school. Your interest in their learning encourages their interest in their learning.

Here are the DON'TS:

- *DON'T spoil your grandchildren by giving them too many material possessions.* It makes grandparents feel good to give, but it's not good for children to be given too much. They won't appreciate what they have and will only want more. Each time you walk in the door, they'll expect gifts.
- *DON'T sabotage your grandchildren's parent.* Don't secretly tell the children, for example, "Well, Dad is punishing you, but now that your dad is gone, I'll let you watch TV even though he said you couldn't." Sabotaging parents is the most damaging thing that grandparents can do. Children sometimes believe that they're equal to adults, and siding with them against their parents is likely to encourage opposition and rebelliousness.
- *DON'T impose your value system on your children's parenting style.* There may be differences in philosophy between a grandparent and a parent, but the grandparent must defer to the parent's wishes. Grandparents should share some (not too much) information based on their many years of parenting, but must leave it up to the parents whether to follow that advice. Sometimes giving your children a parenting book, newspaper article, or tape works best, but again, giving your children too many newspaper clippings may only make them angry and cause them to feel as if you're trying to control them.
- *DON'T do too much for your grandchildren.* Encourage their independence.
- *DON'T tell a grandchild that he or she is your favorite.* Don't say they're the

Figure 2.2

smartest, the most creative, the best, or the most special. It may make them feel good, but another grandchild may learn about that message, too. By comparison, the other children will feel less favored. Don't call them kings or princesses. They'll internalize these words as pressures and expectations and may expect too much of themselves or become dependent on praise and attention.

· *DON'T talk about your grandchildren in negative ways to their parents when the grandchildren might overhear it (referential speaking).* The grandparents and parents may say, "He's just a mess," "She's so disorganized," "He's so shy," or, "She's afraid to do anything," and the child may hear this and feel negatively labeled. It's always better to talk positively, but do avoid the extremes.

SOURCE: *Keys to Parenting the Gifted Child* by S. B. Rimm (Hauppauge, N.Y.: Barron's Educational Series, 1994).

clinic. They were not the first grandparents who had visited me to complain about the way their grandchildren were being parented, and of course, I listened first to their concerns. They believed their granddaughter's parents were not being sufficiently loving or understanding and wanted them to ease up on Stephanie. Stephanie had convinced her grandparents that her parents loved each other too much and her not enough because she couldn't get her dad to side with her against her mother. The grandparents wanted me to straighten out Stephanie's parents, particularly her mother, who was also their daughter.

I explained to those kind, caring grandparents that I had asked Stephanie's parents to stay united, and all her parents wanted for their daughter was that she lead a positive life, that she study in school, that she not drink illegally and to excess, that she save her sexual relationships until she was mature enough to handle them, and that she use reasonable, respectful language. I asked how they would feel about Stephanie's activities if she became pregnant or got into an alcohol-related automobile accident, and I urged them to be supportive of Stephanie's parents. If they could only remind Stephanie how much they and her parents loved her, Stephanie, in a more sober state, would have a better chance of moving forward. They were loving, smart grandparents and meant no harm. They understood immediately the kind of support Stephanie really needed and that united they could have a much more positive impact on Stephanie. They returned to Stephanie to give her the encouragement she needed. Although it did not entirely heal wounds between mother and daughter, at least these grandparents didn't further destroy the relationship.

**Aunts and Uncles.** Aunts and uncles, particularly those who don't have their own children, sometimes provide an easy way out for their nieces and nephews regarding parents' expectations. In some ways, they may be continuing former sibling rivalries through the children. Telling the children that their mother or father was always a "goody-goody" may cause Auntie or Uncle to feel like a cool friend to a kid, but it destroys parental power. Aunts and uncles can have delightful relationships with their nieces and nephews provided they convey the importance of school and parents and don't put their siblings down.

If you have sisters or brothers who are sabotaging your parenting power, be firm and clear with them. Let them know how you feel and what your expectations are for your children. **If they continue to undermine your parental authority, ask them not to visit.** They're doing harm to the children they love. For the most

PARENT
POINTER

GRANDMOTHER SABOTAGE

part, however, once they're aware of the importance of a united family front for children, they'll be willing to put aside the competitive feelings that they may have toward you and recognize what valuable and loving relatives they can be to your children. Many children have close, caring relationships with aunts and uncles. Here's an example:

> Sonja's aunt Maria lived next door. Maria was the youngest of her family and was not yet married, although all her older siblings had families. She also had a family reputation of being a bit outlandish, the rebel of the family. Her dress, her partying lifestyle, and her liberal attitudes about most everything were well-known to the family. The adult siblings were close and loved each other despite very different philosophies about life.
>
> Sonja, a fourth-grader, had a close relationship with Aunt Maria. She'd often visit, talk, and watch TV with her. Recently Sonja had become disrespectful to her teacher as well as to her father. I questioned the parents during counseling about their parenting style to identify the source of the child's overempowerment. Her mother called it a case of "early adolescence." The parents seemed united with each other and were also supportive of Sonja's teacher.
>
> Sonja gave me the clue when she described her aunt Maria as the only one who really understood her. A friendly session with a loving Aunt Maria helped her to understand how her niece was misusing her aunt's understanding messages. Aunt Maria never meant to sabotage, but she was accustomed to a free and easy lifestyle and was definitely not as respectful of authority as she would have been if she were a mother.

## MAINTAINING A UNITED FRONT WITH CHILD-CARE GIVERS, NANNIES, AND OTHER IMPORTANT PEOPLE

The adults you select to provide child care while you work are extremely important in your children's lives. Select as carefully as you can afford to and ask about prospective caregivers' values on discipline, praise, television, activity, eating, language, money, education, and religion. They will obviously not always agree with your child-rearing approaches; they may even have some good ideas that you can use that might be more effective than what you have in mind. If you have a choice, select a caregiver whose values coincide with yours or who is willing to accept your values for guiding your children. If two parents are involved, the values you emphasize should reflect both your perspectives. However, no matter how carefully you choose, differences will emerge.

Continuous communication with your caregiver, outside your children's hearing, will be absolutely necessary to keep a united front. Here's a case example:

> Vicki was a day nanny for the four children of the Townsend family. She sent the children off to school in the morning and stayed with them until both parents returned at night. Mother returned a little earlier than Dad, but Vicki helped with the children's meals before she went home for the evening. Alex, the eleven-year-old, had recently become disrespectful to both his mother and Vicki, and Vicki felt extremely frustrated at her loss of control over a boy she had not had problems with earlier. Unbeknownst to either his mother or the nanny, Alex's dad had been undermining Vicki's authority. Each time Alex complained confidentially to his dad about Vicki's being too strict, his dad agreed that Vicki had a lot to learn about child care. He even mentioned confidentially to Alex that they were searching for a new nanny. Overempowered, Alex took on his nanny; undersupported, the nanny was helpless to guide him.

PARENT POINTER

Child-care providers get power to guide their children from you. **They need help, support, and clear messages about the priorities you have for your children or your children will not be respectful toward them.** United with you, they can make an important difference for your children in a home where they are critical parent surrogates. Choose your caregivers carefully and stay united.

## SIBLING RIVALRY

As you come to understand parent rivalry, it will make it easier to understand sibling rivalry. Sisters and brothers can love each other and still feel that their intelligence, beauty, athletic prowess, musical success, good behavior, and so on are valued only in comparison with that of their siblings. In our competitive society, it is difficult to prevent competition from invading the family. Ideally, we wish that family relationships could provide a cooperative shelter from competition.

A parental united front will help to minimize sibling competition because children will be less likely to take sides with one parent against the other. However, sibling rivalry is not likely to ever be eliminated, nor should it be. If there are no brother-sister struggles in your family, it's likely that one child is giving orders and the other accepting them. Children should have differences and should be assertive enough to express and even argue about those differences. Thus, some sibling quarrels and fighting are a healthy indication that none of the children are completely submissive. Part of your children's experience involves learning to solve problems when there are differences. However, if you're wondering if sibling rivalry is too extreme in your family, see figure 2.3.

An important guideline for parents who must cope with sibling squabbles is to try not to meddle or ferret out which child is to blame. Parents should first attempt to ignore their children's arguments so that the children can work them out themselves. It is often more effective for parents to time themselves out, preferably in Bermuda (this suggestion is courtesy of Michael Cornale, codirector of Family Achievement Clinic, Wisconsin), rather than to time-out their children. Paying attention to the argument usually rewards the fighting. Each child tries to get the parents on his or her side. **Your mediation is likely to increase the arguing as well as the actual rivalry.**

**Set a limit for your arguing children's reasonable noise level or aggressive behavior. Reserve the option of separating them for fifteen minutes or half an hour.** Any two different rooms will do, but don't give them their choice of rooms or they'll fight about those. They don't necessarily require an official time-out, only some separation. Of course, they will want to be back together again as soon as possible, but hopefully not for another argument.

In addition to withdrawing attention from the arguments, try to build positive and cooperative relationships. A token reward system can be used temporarily to reinforce their cooperative behavior. That works particularly well when children are required to spend a great amount of time together; for example, during summer vacation or a long car ride. Dividing the day into two or three

PARENT
POINTER

PARENT
POINTER

## Figure 2.3

# What Is Extreme Rivalry?

To help you determine whether your children are fighting more than is emotionally healthy, ask yourself these questions: Do your children seem to enjoy each other and express warmth and affection for each other at times when they are not fighting? If they do, they are normal. If they don't, you may want to look further for some family problems that can be corrected. Here are some examples of correctable family problems:

- Do you consider either child the "goody-goody" or "perfect"—the one who never causes problems?
- Is one of the children a scapegoat for the rest of the family—the one being blamed by everyone?
- Do you and your spouse argue a lot in front of the children so they see it as a model of how to communicate?
- Do you take sides with one child while your spouse sides with the other?

Any of these four patterns can cause long-lasting negative effects on your children, and sibling rivalry may be worse than typical. Of course, you can change these patterns.

Source: *How to Stop Underachievement Newsletter* 5, no. 3 (1995), by S. B. Rimm (Watertown, Wis: Educational Assessment Service).

sections, you can give children a point for each period of cooperative behavior. Early morning to noon might be one section of the day; afternoon to evening meal could be a second section; and evening meal to bedtime could be a third section. Siblings receive a group point if both children are being nice to each other. This will encourage their cooperation. The goal is to accumulate a small number of points (10–15) toward an activity in which both children can participate, like going out for pizza, going to a movie, or renting a special video. You'll know that your system is effective when one child hits or teases and the other one says it's not a bother because he or she knows it's all in fun. That's a real confirmation of the children's cooperation; reward your children with one point.

SIBLING WARFARE

No token reward system works for long, but this will be effective at particularly stressful times.

Another approach to building cooperative sibling behavior is using surprise plannings. **When one parent gets the children to-gether to plan a surprise for the other parent or for another child, then the children get involved in cooperative planning and feel closer.** An alliance with a positive goal builds unity. The secrets of gift giving, surprises, and parties seem to unite brothers and sisters and diminish arguing. Planning something special for Grandma, Grandpa, Aunt, Uncle, a neighbor, or friend encourages the sense of togetherness that comes from joint efforts. Collecting food for the hungry or doing something for a sick neighbor teaches both cooperation and kindness. Parents can use cooperative strategies often to build a sense of sibling solidarity within their family.

Sibling rivalry almost always affects children's achievement. Children tend to assume that their achievement appears more impressive if their brothers' and sisters' performance is not as good. Some parents try to help their children with their feelings of competition by giving each child a special "best" place in the family; thus they often label the first child "the scholar," the second child

PARENT POINTER

"the creative one," the third "the athlete," the fourth child "the social one," and so on. Parents don't realize that in effect they are setting up competitive and limiting expectations for their children that often exacerbate rivalries. The creative ones don't believe they can be scholars or athletes, the athletes see themselves only in that role, and the social ones are determined to provide the best drinking parties. **Children need to be reminded that although their individuality is valued, they can have a "whole smart family," all of whose members can think creatively, participate in athletics, and have a reasonable social life without being best in any of their pursuits.** Explain to your children that achievement in any domain by one child doesn't limit achievement by the others.

PARENT
POINTER

Children should be encouraged to admit any feelings of jealousy. Most children have them. They will learn to handle these feelings better by accepting the challenge of openly admiring their sisters or brothers. That helps everyone and minimizes the put-downs. Explain to older siblings that younger children usually down deep think their older siblings are wonderful. They want to be just like them.

If your children put each other down, don't take sides at the time. However, you should communicate privately your concerns to the one who is doing the putting down. **There's a much better chance of improved behavior if you don't criticize the child in front of siblings.**

PARENT
POINTER

As parents of achieving or underachieving children, your attention should be directed at effort and positive performances so you don't find yourself reinforcing your children's lack of achievement by your attention. Don't appoint your achiever as tutor for your underachiever. It will only serve as a daily put-down for the underachiever. Children typically say they appreciate the help, but it makes them feel dumb.

Mainly, **be patient and avoid taking sides.** Don't even try to treat children equally, only fairly. To encourage you to have hope when your children argue, let me assure you that the two children in our family who did the most arguing, Eric and Sara, are delightfully close as young adults. I wish I had known that would be the case as they were growing up.

PARENT
POINTER

# RIVALRY BETWEEN PARENT AND SAME-GENDER CHILD

Considering how much competition exists in our society, one can assume that there are many possible combinations of rivalry. Competition between father and son or mother and daughter are legendary. Despite that assumption, I find only minimal rivalry between child and adult if ogre and dummy patterns do not occur in the family. Instead, there is an alliance between child and parent, with the child viewing the parent as a role model. Of course, games and sports provide an avenue for appropriate competition between adults and children, but they seem to act more as an outlet rather than leading to more destructive competition.

As an adolescent moves into young adulthood, there is normal jockeying for power to establish his or her new status as an adult, which often causes some competitive feelings. When young adults select careers that are similar to their parents' or share business relationships, competition may complicate the relationship if the young adult has not separated from the parent first in order to gain experience elsewhere. **If a parent is willing to step aside and relinquish some power in order to encourage the sons' or daughters' new skills and experience, transitions and sharing of professions will go more smoothly.** Many mother-daughter or father-son duos have learned to manage potential feelings of competition to cooperate in similar businesses or professions.

PARENT
POINTER

# THE PARENT-TEACHER UNITED FRONT

Remember, most teachers became teachers because they wanted to teach children. They usually care about and wish to make a positive difference for them, although you may feel that you can prove this isn't the case with some of the teachers who have taught your children. A small percentage of teachers feel and act burned-out, may not want to teach anymore, never really wanted to teach, or thought teaching would be something different from what they're experiencing. Despite your occasional negative experiences, I would nevertheless maintain that most teachers care about teaching children well.

Parent-teacher conflicts emerge mainly because of differing philosophies about how children should be taught. Some parents believe their philosophies are better than those held by their children's teachers. The parents may be right—it is possible that their approaches might be better for their children. However, the teachers may also be right. It's equally possible that their approaches work more effectively. The real problem occurs when teachers and parents disagree on how children should be taught, because a mismatch of philosophies can destroy the united parent-teacher front.

If educational philosophies between teachers and parents differ in directions that encourage children to do more than the teacher expects, it probably won't cause any problems for children. They'll continue to receive a message of achievement. However, if the philosophy of the parents differs from the teacher's so that it provides an easy way out for children, or if it describes the teacher's philosophy as inappropriate, irrelevant, or boring, it provides an excuse for children not to accomplish what the teacher expects. Although the parents may make appropriate points in their analysis of the teacher's philosophy, the **parents should not share their opinions about teachers with their children if there is the risk of subtly permitting them to avoid school responsibility.**

PARENT
POINTER

Consider that your children are sitting in the classroom and are faced with assignments, some of which are interesting, some not so interesting, some tiresome, and some repetitive. If they've received the message from you that these aren't worthwhile projects, why would your children consider it important to fulfill the teacher's expectations? They know they can come home and find a sympathetic ear in their mother or father, who basically agrees that the assignment was inappropriate to their interest or intelligence, their use of time, or for some other reason. If you want your children to achieve in school, **give your children clear messages of respect for teachers.** Let them know that teachers are devoted to children and to making a difference for our society through education. If you give them that message about respect for educators, it will go a long way toward encouraging them to feel positive

PARENT
POINTER

about their teachers and about school. It will likely make a great difference in their entire attitude about school learning and achievement.

**Children should hear how much you value their teachers.** This is no small issue, because in my experience many parents do just the opposite. If you suggest to children that teachers are "not too bright" or only "go into teaching because they're not capable of doing anything else" or "don't deserve the salaries that taxpayers pay them," those comments might as well be messages to children not to perform well in school. If they aren't expected to respect their teachers, they won't.

Sometimes teachers who are also parents give negative messages about their fellow professionals. Their children are listening. Subtle statements that make it appear that you don't respect teachers or administrators can cause problems. Here are some examples:

Matt, a fifth-grader, considered himself a debater. His parents proclaimed that, indeed, he would make a fine lawyer. He exercised his arguing skills specifically with teachers and not only provoked arguments but persevered beyond reason and respect. In his arguments, he attempted to put his teachers down. At home, Matt had a good relationship with both his parents, except that he continually argued with his mother in that same haughty tone of voice.

In counseling, it became clear that his father had remarked that teachers were "not very bright." His mother was an active leader in the PTA. Her activities were referred to by his dad as "busywork." His father, in describing the teachers' and his mother's activity as essentially unintelligent, was implying that Matt was more intelligent than his teachers and his mom. This encouraged Matt to try to prove that neither his teachers nor his mother were as smart as he; thus the arguing and the resulting underachievement continued.

Here's an example of a positive communication with a teacher:

Susan, a third-grader, complained to her mother and dad repeatedly that her teacher didn't like her. The parents were anxious about their daughter, who was less and less willing to go to school. She complained about illnesses and made excuses for avoiding school. The parents handled the difficult situation with responsible communication. At conference time they explained to the teacher what they were hearing from their child. They told the teacher that they assumed the teacher didn't dislike their daughter but only wanted to let her know what their child was saying.

Within one week, Susan's attitude changed. Her teacher gave Susan a little extra temporary, positive attention, which seemed to be sufficient to make her feel approved of again. The avoidance and anxiety disappeared, and the problem was solved in a respectful, positive way. The parents never agreed with the child about the teacher's supposed dislike. They never even told their daughter about their conversation with the teacher. They simply communicated their concerns in an adult, respectful way, and the problem disappeared.

Here's another example of a radio question about a parent-teacher difference:

A single mother called me in desperation because her sixth-grade son was not doing his homework. She explained that her son's teacher had called him "lazy" in front of the whole class. She wondered how she could motivate her son if his teacher didn't like him and acted so inappropriately. Here's the way I believe she could respond to her son: "Of course, I don't think your teacher should call you lazy, and I know you can be a very hard worker. Nevertheless, no teacher would call a child who was doing his work lazy, so you must be goofing off or daydreaming in class. I suggest you work very hard in class, and I can guarantee your teacher won't ever call you lazy again. Once your teacher sees what good work you're doing, she'll be pleased and consider you one of her better students. You'll feel better about yourself as well."

I also suggested ways to set up a study time for her son and arrange supportive daily or weekly communications with the teacher. See chapter 3 for details.

PARENT
POINTER

**If your children complain to you about a teacher, and you don't respond at all, they will assume you agree with them and accept your "no comment" as confirmation of their conclusions.** You should say something positive about their teachers or reframe what they have said to let them know you expect them to respect the teacher and work hard in the classroom.

**Selecting Your Children's Teachers.** If you were able to select your children's teachers, it would be more likely that you and those teachers would be united in an educational philosophy for your children. That doesn't necessarily mean that you would select the teachers that teach your children best. For example, sometimes parents who are oversolicitous and facilitate their child's dependency would select a teacher who is also oversolicitous and encourages dependency. That teacher may be totally inappropriate for that child, but there would be much less opposition between you and that teacher. Because opposition between parent and teacher can cause more harm than oversolicitousness, your child would probably continue to benefit by the choice.

**If your child has had a negative school year, you should informally investigate whether you, as parents, can recommend or select a teacher for your child.** Schools vary a great deal in their policies about honoring parents' requests for teachers. Some have formal policies while others have informal guidelines. You aren't likely to be able to specifically select a teacher, but many schools will permit you to suggest the teacher that you would prefer. The principal may assure you that he or she will try to accommodate your wishes. Principals can't guarantee you your choice because if many parents select the same teacher, it would obviously cause the principal major problems.

PARENT POINTER

In some schools, the child's present teacher may make a recommendation for the following year. In that case, you may want to discuss with the teacher your preferences. Again, the teacher won't be able to provide a guarantee, but it may be worthwhile for you to initiate the discussion.

Most schools don't advertise their policy of permitting parents to request teachers. There's a good reason for that. If they announced the policy, parents might feel obligated to select a teacher for their children. The principal might feel pressured to honor their requests. This could cause an impossible situation for the school. **You should subtly investigate the informal or formal policies in your school.** If you're privileged to make requests, don't advertise it to the parents of your children's friends or they, too, may ask for the very same teacher. That will result in too many requests having to be honored. When you ask for a teacher, don't put down the

PARENT POINTER

other teachers in any way. Recognize the principal's responsibility for placing all children in the best-matched classrooms.

**Changing Your Children's School.** A united front between you and your children's teachers is so important that if the philosophy of the entire school differs from yours, you may wish to at least consider changing your children's school. **Changing schools should never by done lightly. You will never agree with all the teachers in any school.** During the time you're considering a change, don't discuss the change with your children. Discussion, either directly or indirectly, within their hearing, could cause them to resist your exploration or to assume you don't like their teachers. If they assume their problems are really due to their teachers, they may halt their efforts at school, thus making it even more difficult to determine if a change of school is necessary.

PARENT
POINTER

Another risk of changing schools is the children's possible assumption that when they don't like their school or teachers, they can misbehave to effect change. Nevertheless, the value of being able to support your children's school outweighs the risks involved in making a school change.

Of course, many of you can't make a choice even if you would like to. Therefore, you need to be supportive of your children's teachers while becoming an active but respectful advocate for educational change within your community. Taking a strong, positive position will not only be effective in improving the education of the children in your community but will show for your children the importance of education and the important positive power that their parents have.

# EXCEPTIONS TO THE PARENT-TEACHER UNITED FRONT

At times, regardless of how hard you try, you feel as though you just can't maintain a united front between you and your child's teacher. There may be curriculum issues and general philosophies of education with which you disagree, a sense that your child and a teacher are in a power struggle, or an attitude about discipline that you feel is inappropriate for your child. Your first priority is to show respect and humility when expressing your concern to that teacher. **Don't accuse the teacher of being wrong.** Ask the teacher questions about what you're hearing from your child rather than assuming that your child's information is accurate. Don't report the problem to the principal unless your initial efforts with the teacher don't work and there is potential harm for your child or other children in the class.

PARENT POINTER

**Curriculum Differences.** In cases of intellectually gifted children, there may be dramatic differences in philosophies among teachers. Some believe that gifted children should do all of the assigned work even if it is not challenging or an appropriate learning experience. In gifted education, this is called busywork. Children who already know the material or who could learn it with much briefer assignments may turn off to what they view as irrelevant work. As parents with a good understanding of your child's capabilities, you may side with your child against the teacher's inappropriate curriculum. I recommend that you communicate to the teacher the child's concerns without assuming that the teacher is wrong. **If there's a gifted coordinator or gifted consultant in the district, a meeting between the teacher and the consultant to talk about your child's special abilities may be productive.**

PARENT POINTER

Although you may have taken all the appropriate steps, some teachers don't believe in educating gifted children differently. Even these tactful approaches may not effect change in your children's curriculum. Next, tell your children that although you realize they could learn better or faster, they should complete the teacher's requirements as best they can. Suggest that they do them quickly and efficiently and use the extra time to do independent reading or learning projects at school or at home with you. Let them know that you're interested in sharing learning with them. That way, you won't provide children with an easy way out. You do, however, show them you recognize that not all teachers agree on the way gifted children should be taught. You haven't indicated disrespect for their teachers. You've shifted the responsibility for learning to your children by expecting them to take further initiative in their education even when it's not appropriately provided by their school.

PARENT
POINTER

**You, as parents, should take a proactive stance in the school district to provide gifted children with the appropriate curriculum.** Plan to be positive, patient, and persevering. Meanwhile, don't undermine your children's respect for school. Even if they're doing busywork, they will learn reasonable conformity and the necessity of jumping the educational hurdles that they will face as they continue through high school and college.

Some requirements in our schools simply are not appropriate for all children. Nevertheless, they'll probably not be harmful. A little extra practice or drill, despite the fact that children know the information, can even be helpful. Most children are resilient enough to cope with some boredom.

PARENT
POINTER

**If you find the curriculum totally inappropriate for your children, you can't ignore the issues.** Although you should continue to give messages of respect to your children about their teachers, you can take your concerns to higher administrative levels. Some educators are so overconcerned about children staying with their age-mates, they may forget that learning is the main objective of schools.[4] If the curriculum is too challenging or not challenging enough, children may learn to underachieve.[5]

**Physical or Verbal Abuse.** Sometimes a more extreme exception to a united parent-teacher front is required. If parents believe that a teacher is being abusive to children, whether it's physical or verbal abuse, their responsibility is to protect their children. Classroom abuse is wrong, and all children deserve a safe classroom.

Again, the first step is to meet with the teacher without taking a confrontational approach. Relate what's been reported by your child in the classroom and tell the teacher of your concern. Give the teacher a chance to either change or defend the behavior. If the reports continue, the second step is to contact the principal or the teacher's immediate supervisor. Even in severe cases, you should not intentionally give your children permission to misbehave or challenge that teacher. Your message to your child should be that there's little danger of their being physically or verbally abused by their teacher if they behave appropriately in the classroom and pay attention to their work. In no way give your child permission to be disrespectful to a teacher.

**If the abuse is genuine, you must be a strong advocate for safe classrooms. Join forces with other parents who voice similar concerns.** Be an advocate for children, but remember, be positive, patient, and persevering, and don't center your life and that of your children around constantly discussing the issue.

**Sexual Abuse.** Children are often too frightened to report sexual abuse by teachers. They may only hint to you that a teacher is making them "feel funny" or that a teacher gets uncomfortably close to them. **The suggestion of strange behavior demands you immediately follow up to discuss and clarify.** Explain to your children their right not to stay in a student-teacher relationship that feels uncomfortable, and **encourage them to report any further suspicions to you immediately. Don't overreact but do bypass the teacher and tell the principal of your concerns.**

If your children have been physically or sexually abused by a teacher, you must handle this difficult situation carefully. Your children may be asked to testify in court. You and they may feel justifiably indignant about how the school administration or the courts are treating the abuse. Although you and your children will be coping with a difficult emotional problem, **don't make the mistake of permitting the problem to monopolize your lives.** As the abuse and the children become the center of attention, you will find yourself in an alliance with them against the court or the school. Despite the good cause, children can be overempowered by the advocacy battle. As they hear parents continually talking to neighbors, teachers, and each other about the abuse, your children may begin to focus all their attention on the incident. Assure your children that you will support them in their testimony and that you will persevere in your attempts to provide safe classrooms. **Help them to understand that they are not to blame for the problem. Let them know you will be their advocates,** but they should go on with their activities.

Here's an example that illustrates the high risk of getting children overly involved:

Katy said she wanted to drop fifth-grade band. When her mother asked her why, she said that her band teacher made her "feel funny" in band

PARENT POINTER
PARENT POINTER
PARENT POINTER
PARENT POINTER
PARENT POINTER

class by coming too close to her. Based on that description, the mother permitted her to drop out of the band program.

A year later, after testimony by several students, it was determined that the band teacher had been sexually abusing several girls in his class by touching them inappropriately.

Katy and her parents became advocates for the teacher's dismissal. Police hearings and court testimony followed, and the teacher was transferred to another school and required to undergo therapy. He was not dismissed from the school district.

Katy and her parents were indignant. It was the topic of constant home discussion, as were the many plans for attendance at school board meetings and protests. Although I supported Katy's parents' concern for school safety, I believed that the issue was becoming overwhelming for their daughter. Katy's entire attention was now centering on the issue, and she was deriving a great deal of power and attention from it. She was at high risk for depression, underachievement, and oppositional behavior in school after the court case was over, regardless of the result.

Fortunately, my advice to the parents came in sufficient time so they could gradually ease out Katy from involvement in their efforts. Katy's first response to this exclusion, even though she was assured the problem would be taken care of, was a temporary depression. The parents were prepared and were able to help Katy move beyond the abuse case. Had they not, Katy, with her parents, would have become intensely involved in an adult oppositional struggle that may have caused her more adjustment problems than the uneasy feelings that she had felt around her band teacher.

# THE TEACHER-PARENT UNITED FRONT

Although most of this section has been directed to you, as parents, it's equally important that teachers give a message of support for you. If teachers aren't supportive of parents and aren't saying positive things to children about them, they may render parents powerless to follow through at home on teachers' suggestions or recommendations. **Teachers should be especially careful not to talk to other teachers negatively about parents.** That may easily happen when parents volunteer in schools. If children hear about the opposition between teachers and their parents, it may have an adverse effect on the parent-child-school relationship. When teachers express respect for parents, it facilitates children's learning in school and at home.

## QUESTIONS AND ANSWERS

### *Dear Dr. Sylvia,*

*I have three sons, ages nineteen, twelve, and ten. The oldest has recently moved out. We have always had the problem of my sons manipulating me and my husband. My husband would always lose his temper, and I always came to the rescue. What can I do to change this pattern of manipulation with my two younger sons?*

*Protective Mom*

Dear Protective Mom,

I usually describe this classic situation, in which Father feels more and more powerless, as Father Is an Ogre. It occurs when Dad loses his temper and the kids go to Mom to complain about Dad, thus escaping any responsibilities that Dad places on them, and blaming all their problems on Dad's temper. It can become a vicious pattern, but it can be changed when the parents become aware of how they're being unconsciously manipulated.

When your sons run to you to complain about Dad, reframe their complaints about the situation. For example:

> Your husband asked your son to mow the lawn, and your son didn't do it. When your son comes to you to complain that Dad came home and scolded him for not mowing the lawn, instead of saying, "Oh, I'm sorry. Your dad's just having a bad day," thus giving your son permission to avoid responsibility, you should say, "Your dad is upset because he knows you really can do the job, and he's disappointed that you didn't do it. Why don't you go out there now and show him that you can do the job. After all, you wouldn't want your father to think you are irresponsible. If you had done the job immediately, Dad wouldn't have had to yell."

There are some fathers (and mothers) who do set standards too high and never seem satisfied with their children's work. Parents should come to a compromise about their standards. When parents are united, everyone wins.

### Dear Dr. Sylvia,

*I have a five-and-a-half-year-old daughter who has recently been continuously very angry, even saying she hates me, and is a behavior problem. We also have a three-year-old and a new baby. I try to talk with my daughter and reassure her that I love her but not her behavior. We used to have a very special mother-daughter relationship. The problem is only at home; they haven't noticed anything at school. Also, she goes to her dad, who rescues her after I become upset when she is misbehaving and gets upset with me when I yell at her.*

*Sabotaged Mom*

Dear Sabotaged Mom,

Your daughter has been dethroned twice by younger siblings, but her anger stems only partially from losing the number one position in the family. Her loving dad is causing much more of the problem than either of you suspect. Unconsciously, your daughter has learned that when you lose your temper, her father and she become closer. This relationship is clearly based on protection from an enemy, and she feels even closer to him if she blames you for scolding her. Unfortunately, your husband's unintentional sabotage can cause your daughter major lifelong relationship problems and can diminish the likelihood of your ever having a good relationship with her.

As to your efforts to separate her from her behavior, save your persuasive talk for when she is older and can make that separation. What you need most now is a little fun time alone with your daughter and a husband who doesn't give your daughter more power and status than he gives his wife. It's important that he support you, or your daughter will unintentionally—but effectively—trap you into continually losing your temper.

### Dear Dr. Sylvia,

*I have an eight-year-old grandson in third grade. He is in a regular class, but has a learning disability. He keeps up well.*

*My daughter gets fully involved in his schoolwork. She is constantly in fear of his being sent to a special school, so she makes sure his homework is done and sits and works with him. He is also on a football team, and this interferes with his homework. My daughter and her husband fight over this. He (the husband) feels strongly about the football, but the child can't finish his homework on those nights when he has football or does it way beyond his bedtime.*

*The entire situation is causing a real rift between the parents. What advice do you have for them?*

*Observant Grandmother*

Dear Observant Grandmother,

Although your grandson's first priority should be his learning, even learning-disabled third-graders can usually manage homework and sports. Furthermore, participation in sports is good for children's self-confidence.

The real problem for your grandson lies in his parents' disagreements. He may assume that his dad doesn't care about school at all, so he will most likely fight his mother's overinvolvement in his schoolwork. Most children with learning disabilities can perform their schoolwork independently, although they may need to make some adjustments in their work habits.

Your daughter and her husband may have to compromise in their expectations of your grandson. Otherwise the rift you observe between the parents will cause your grandson to feel that he can't please either parent. This is likely to result in underachievement, anxiety, and defiant behavior. Although you can't take sides with either parent, you may wish to refer your children to chapter 2, "United Parenting." If you can convince your children to compromise, your grandson's life will be happier and healthier. Compromise is a small price to pay for an important long-term goal—your grandson's future success.

## Dear Dr. Sylvia,

*After I married my husband, I adopted his two children, ages seven and eleven. In the past year or so, I have become their main parent. My husband is involved in his own things and doesn't seem to want to spend any of his time with his family. The kids then come to me and say, "How come Dad doesn't want to do anything with us?" I've tried to encourage him. I've even made plans for him to spend time with his kids, but it doesn't seem to be working. How can I get my husband more involved with his children?*

*Put-upon Wife*

Dear Put-upon Wife,

It sounds as if your husband thinks he married a free nanny instead of a wife. Even if he has a more traditional view of marriage, there is no reason for neglecting his children.

You seem hesitant about confronting your husband about this serious problem. Set a time when the children are not at home or they're asleep to talk with him about responsibilities. You should explain your need for time away from the children as well as their need for time alone with their dad. Each of you could also create some time with one child alone and some time each day when Dad can be entirely in charge. You have a right to an explanation and to refuse to accept his involvement in his own things as an excuse; hopefully, your husband's sense of fairness will help him hear your message. Too many fathers regret too late not finding time for their children. Do your husband a favor and insist he take on his fair share of parenting. He may soon find he enjoys it more than he expected.

## *Dear Dr. Sylvia,*

*My husband travels frequently, so the role of main caregiver and disciplinarian for our thirteen-year-old son falls to me. Our son sees me as a policeman and his dad as a fun-loving buddy. I feel sad about this situation and feel that I have been handed a role that I don't want or like, but I don't know how to change this. Do you have any suggestions?*

*Alone and Frustrated*

Dear Alone and Frustrated,

There are many traveling dads, and these days, there are even some traveling moms. A frequent travel schedule complicates parenting roles and responsibilities. You and your husband need to creatively organize your lives to include some discipline and fun from both of you with your son. Telephones, daily notes, and lists help make the enterprise doable. When Dad calls from an airport, he can ask your son whether he's done his homework. He can also remind him that he expects him to be respectful toward you. Furthermore, he can make some (not all) special weekend events dependent on good behavior that week.

While your spouse is traveling, be sure not to undermine your own power or your husband's. For example, don't let your son hear you say you can't handle him alone, or he'll assume you're powerless and won't listen to you. Don't threaten him with his dad's punishments if you know your husband won't follow through with them. Be absolutely sure to give yourself a night out without your son. You needn't feel guilty about leaving him alone occasionally so you can have some fun. And last, but not least, try to plan for some family fun together during the week.

If your husband does not participate in parenting while he travels, you may wish to remind him that children of such absent parents frequently become underachievers in school and have discipline problems at home and school. United parenting is always important. It's always much harder to stay united when one parent travels, but not only can it work well, it can also lead to a better marriage and more successful and happy children.

## Dear Dr. Sylvia,

*I am seventeen years old, and I have not spoken to my father for over a year because he says that we can't have a relationship based only on talking on the phone.*

*You see, my parents got divorced when I was young, and my sister and I were shared by our parents every other week with "moving" days being on Thursdays. The times at each house were enjoyable, but since I am a girl, I felt more of a need to be with my mother because there are some things a father and daughter just cannot talk about. So, last year I moved into my mother's house for good.*

*During those alternating weeks of my life, I was forced to put my life on hold and pack up my belongings and move to another house. My bedrooms didn't have many toys because I knew I would be leaving for the other. I was faced with different disciplinary methods and rules at each house. Then, when I got older, I was faced with problems such as trying to keep my friends updated on my whereabouts during that week. Even in my teenage years, I was still faced with having a bare bedroom and different rules concerning curfew and dating.*

*I just wanted to let you know that even though the parents may be happy, it is not always in the child's best interest to be in two houses. I am not alone. Friends of mine who have grown up in "joint housing" have sacrificed relationships with one parent because this living relationship never works out in the end.*

*Divided Daughter*

Dear Divided Daughter,

Your feelings of continuous dislocation are precisely the reason I encourage parents who are divorcing to permit children to live mainly with one parent while visiting the other parent. I usually suggest that the school week not be divided so that children can maintain their school routines without interruption.

It is understandable that a teenage girl would want to be able to communicate with her mother about female issues. On the other hand, developing a good relationship with your dad will help you understand a male point of view and can become the basis for your understanding of how to relate to young men.

Your dad must undoubtedly feel the pain of being rejected by his daughter whom he loves. Perhaps now that you have been permitted to make a choice and feel the security and comfort of your own room in your own house, you could reach out to your dad and at least arrange regular visits with him. With time and discussion, he'll surely understand your feelings better. Perhaps you'll also be able to forgive him for arranging with your mother a schedule that unintentionally caused you to feel confused and without a real home. Consider that your parents made the decision because both of them wanted to be good parents for you.

## Dear Dr. Sylvia,

*I'm forty-one years old and recently remarried. I have a six-year-old boy who lives with his mother, and my current wife has an eight-year-old boy who lives with us. I want to be a better part-time dad to my son on our weekends and a good stepdad to my wife's son. We are planning on having another child, and I don't want to make the same mistakes with a new child. I feel completely inadequate as a parent.*

*I have not disciplined my son the way I should have because I was scared of pushing him away and making him not want to be with me. I*

*know this is wrong. I just found out my son is in all likelihood moving to
another state. I am committed to being a good father regardless of where
he is and will participate in his life. I'm in need of some guidance.*

*Divided Dad*

Dear Divided Dad,
Fathering can be complex when there are "yours, mine, and ours"
children. Once your new child is born, you will have all three categories. For your wife's child, who will live with you, try not to play
the heavy role at first. Bonding with him and helping him to develop
trust in you should be your first priority. Plan some one-to-one projects that will encourage a close relationship. On the other hand, be
sure to support your wife's discipline of her son. Gradually, you, too,
can take on the discipline that should come from both of you.

For your own son, it is time for you to be supportive of your former wife. Make it clear to your son that, although you are no longer
married to his mother, both you and she want the same good things
from him, and that you expect him to be well behaved at home and
to study hard in school. When he comes to visit you, certainly continue some fun activities, but be sure he has a few household
chores, and definitely ask him about school and study. It's also important for your son not to feel rejected when the new baby is born.
Your reliability is most critical. Make every effort not to cancel
when he expects you to pick him up for visits.

Gradually the two boys will get to know each other. Because
both boys are "onlys," expect some uncomfortable sibling rivalry
until they adjust. They will both need some time alone with you
before and after the new baby comes.

With your new baby, it should be a bit easier. Remember to be
supportive of and united with your wife, just as with your other
child. If you are both clear and consistent with your son about your
expectations, he will benefit from it.

## Dear Dr. Sylvia,

*What do I do when I don't like my ex-husband, and my seven-year-old
talks constantly about his dad's house, hobbies, etc.? Also, what can I do
to help my son grow up balanced in two households?*

*Resentful Divorced Mother*

Dear Resentful Divorced Mother,

It must feel awful to hear your son admiring his father and sharing with you their interests together. Although I understand your anger, his open discussion indicates that both you and your husband are managing your divorce well. If your son felt torn, he would tell you only the negative things about his dad or nothing at all for fear it would upset you. Seven-year-olds like to please adults, so he must believe you want to hear about his dad. I congratulate you on being a good sport, listening, and not tearing down his dad. It's the kindest behavior you could show despite your resentful feelings, and I would encourage you to continue to try to be tolerant of your son's good feelings about his dad.

You can help your son to grow up balanced in two households by sharing your own interests with him. Outdoor activities, books, music, games, or hobbies that you can share can provide quality time for the two of you. It is often difficult for single moms to find the time to play after a working day or a week, but investment in work and play together provide the bonding that will keep you close. A little fun time goes a long way in cementing your relationship. Your son can continue to love both his mother and father even though they no longer love each other.

## Dear Dr. Sylvia,

*How can I become a friend to my stepchildren? I've been married for two years. Besides my six-year-old daughter, I have twin stepsons, age fifteen, and a stepdaughter, age thirteen, who have different mothers and live in different states. My husband was never married to either of the women.*

*The boys spent the summer with us a few years ago. We haven't seen them since. We see my stepdaughter a little more often. I explained to the stepchildren that I am not, nor am I trying to be, their mother. I just want to be their friend, and they were always welcome in our home.*

*There is some hostility. My stepdaughter will not acknowledge my position. She never talks to me when she calls here. My six-year-old daughter is very receptive to her half sister and brothers, but they treat her like an alien. I have sent my stepdaughter things that she never acknowledges to me. She communicates through her father but is appreciative of my gifts.*

*My husband is paying dearly for child support, but the boys never call our home; their father always calls them. My stepdaughter's mother will not let us see her. I just don't know where to go from here. Can you help me?*

*Determined Stepmother*

Dear Determined Stepmother,
Although your efforts seem to merit a more positive response from your stepchildren, yours is a difficult task. Your stepdaughter may resent you because she sees you as a rival for her dad's attention. Your stepsons have apparently not accepted their dad either, so it isn't likely they'll accept you. Although it is true that your husband's children should appreciate his financial support, you've not mentioned whether he spent much time with the children when they were growing up. If he didn't, they may feel alienated now.

Blending families usually takes time, and if you are not in the same city, and you don't see the children often, it will simply take extra time. You can continue to send them occasional gifts and letters.

When your husband talks on the phone, you can listen in and talk on an extension until they become accustomed to your being part of the family. When your husband visits them, you and your daughter can go along, but let him have a little time alone with his children as well. Finally, since your daughter is the youngest, the older children may be able to take care of her a little when you visit and will thus get to know her better.

Keep in mind that most teenagers don't have the easiest time relating to new adults in the family. Most important, feel good about your efforts and expect that it may take a little longer. It is possible that they will never fully accept you, but at least you will know that you've tried.

## Dear Dr. Sylvia,

*Our teenagers don't know that my wife and I have decided to divorce. What should we keep in mind when talking to them about this, and are there some things we should be prepared for?*

*Soon-to-Divorce Dad*

Dear Soon-to-Divorce Dad,

Be prepared to discover that your teenagers may know more about your intended divorce than you expect. Although younger children are occasionally oblivious to an oncoming breakup, adolescents rarely miss the continuing conflicts, even when parents keep overt arguing to a minimum.

Whether or not your teenagers have sensed problems, the actual divorce announcement may have a shocking effect. They may cry, be angry, or try to convince you to stay together. On the other hand, they could be silent or even agree that the divorce is appropriate. Responses vary with individuals and families. Although knowing this may not prepare you for exactly what will happen, it helps to be ready for everything.

Regardless of your adolescents' overt responses, it's important to recognize that your announcement will be traumatic. They will need your support and further communication. It is best if you and your wife, together, tell them. It's also important that neither of you blame the other. Here's an example of how you can tell your children:

> Mom and I have tried very hard to make our marriage work, but it is only getting worse instead of better. We have lots of details to work out, and we know this is really going to be hard for you, but we want you to know that we both love you and always will. We also want you to know that you can ask us questions, and we'll try to answer them as best we can. Sometimes we just won't be able to explain some issues because they are too private, but we'll both try our best to help you through this.

Tears and hugs are likely to interrupt or follow your discussion. Be sure to allow time for questions. You'll want to assure your children that they are not the cause of the problem, and although life may be tense in the beginning, it will be normal again after the arrangements are worked out.

Try to help your teenagers to continue with their normal routines, but leave plenty of time for them to talk and ask questions. Absolutely do *not* share your intimacies with them, and don't expect them to understand all of the adult issues. Try not to get them on your side against their mother, and be sensitive and respectful when you refer to her. Your worries about their insecurities may tempt you to tell them you will always love them more than anyone else. That's likely to be a promise you can't keep, and when and if you remarry, they may feel rejected or deceived.

At best, divorces are difficult for children. However, sometimes divorce is better for them than a bad marriage, and indeed, sometimes it is the more courageous choice.

### Dear Dr. Sylvia,

*When my son picks up his daughter from her mother's house (they are divorced), the daughter says, "I hate you, Daddy, and I don't want to go home with you!" What can my son do?*

*Grieving Grandma*

Dear Grieving Grandma,

When your granddaughter proclaims her anger at your son, the prognosis for building an immediate positive relationship is not good. However, your granddaughter is not completely lost to either of you if you and he are willing to persevere.

Your son's best response to his daughter should reflect both his disappointment in her feelings and a loving commitment to her. Here's an example: "I'm sorry you feel that way, but I do love you, and with time, I hope your feelings toward me will change."

Sometimes dads have trouble expressing anything but anger at former wives, who they assume are encouraging hatred toward them. This only causes their children to be more angry and confused. The best way for your son to form an alliance with his daughter is to remain firm and fair, to involve her in interesting work and play, and to describe her mother in positive and respectful ways. Although being kind in his description of her mother is difficult after divorce, negative messages of anger about her mother will only encourage your granddaughter to be more defiant toward her dad.

### Dear Dr. Sylvia,

*How can foster parents prepare themselves and their birth children for the arrival, disruption, behavior, and departures of foster children?*

*United Foster Parents Association of Greater Milwaukee*

Dear Foster Parents,

Foster children require a temporary place to be loved and cared for. They also need to learn about limits and respect for others, especially if they are teenagers. Adults who become foster parents have accepted a major responsibility, mainly because they want to make a positive difference for children.

To prepare your birth children for the arrival of foster children, teach them about sharing and kindness. Your children will probably have to share personal space and possessions. They need to be assured from the outset that you'll value that sharing, but you will not require them to share everything. They may decide they would like to keep some possessions for their own use. You should also let your birth children know that you'll give them some private time, during which they can talk with you about their concerns. You should also extend these privileges to your foster children.

State explicitly to your foster children what responsibilities you expect them to fulfill. They may not be as compliant as your birth children initially, so you should help your children understand that they need to allow their foster siblings time for adjustment.

A first priority for you as foster parents is to understand and accept the temporary nature of your role. Providing your foster children with security while maintaining an appropriate bridge to their own home is not easy. Whether they are teenagers or young children, they may feel anger or disrespect toward their parents. In talking with your foster children, do not discuss their parents in a way that emphasizes inadequacy, unfairness, immaturity, or any other negative characteristics, even if they possess them. Negative descriptions of their parents or correcting the parents in front of the foster children will cause the children to feel more powerful than their parents and may exacerbate their anger at the situation. Explaining to children that most adults face some difficulties in life, and reassuring the children that their parent(s) love them and will be back to take care of them, are the best general ways to facilitate a bridge back to these parents. If their parents don't ever want them back, help tide them through this difficult period, explaining that you care very much about them and assuring the children that permanent, loving parents will be found for them.

Of course, a variety of circumstances lead to the need for foster parenting, so no single response applies to all cases. You should know that your contribution to caring for these children is appreciated and important.

### Dear Dr. Sylvia,

*I have a very sweet five-year-old boy. The last time I saw his biological father, I was only seven weeks pregnant. This man has never indicated an interest in seeing his son. He lives about two hundred miles away.*

*Two years ago, I met and married a man who adopted my son. We have since had another child. Our family is now very close, and my husband is a wonderful parent. My son has never asked about his biological father, but I know one day he will. I know my son has memories of our life before my new marriage. I think his father's leaving may have been a blessing in disguise.*

*I am content to wait until my son brings up the subject himself. Is this right? What do I say when he does ask about his biological father? How do I explain that this man just disappeared as soon as I became pregnant? How do I keep him from feeling bad that his biological father doesn't seem to care about him? I don't want my son to feel deprived or hurt.*

*Contented, but Uncertain*

Dear Contented, but Uncertain,
You may be correct in assuming that your son's father's departure was a "blessing," since apparently he was entirely uninterested in parenting. Your family life sounds very positive now, and both your children have the advantages of good family life.

Your son is unlikely to question you about his birth father now. He's much more likely to by age nine or ten. However, if he doesn't ask by then, you certainly should initiate the conversation, albeit briefly and matter-of-factly. If you don't initiate it, he may hear it indirectly and may resent your having kept it a secret.

Provided your son develops a good relationship with his adoptive father, he is unlikely to feel deprived. Because your husband left before your son was even born, his departure can accurately be attributed to unreadiness for parenting rather than personal rejection. As to feelings of deprivation, they can become realistic concerns because normal sibling rivalry could cause your son to have feelings that his adoptive father cares more about his brother than himself, whether or not that's actually true.

I can also envision some potential adolescent problems when his adoptive dad tries to set reasonable limits and your son wishes to attribute the noes to his not being his "real" father. Your son may ask you to meet his birth father then in hopes that he may be more permissive (or, from your son's perspective, more understanding). I would recommend that you postpone any personal meetings until your son has graduated from high school to prevent any adolescent easy-way-out manipulations, but at that time he should be allowed to know his birth dad if he's interested. Some children bond instantly with their birth parent; but often, one visit with their parent fulfills their burning curiosity, and they part with no developing relationship.

One last suggestion. If your son questions you about his dad suddenly, and you feel unprepared to answer him at that moment, indicate to him that you've been meaning to talk to him about his dad, but you'd like to choose a more appropriate time. Soon afterward, find a little private time to talk briefly with him and answer any questions he may have. Spare the adult details, and talk to him only at the level appropriate to his age.

### Dear Dr. Sylvia,

*I have a twelve-year-old granddaughter who fits your description of an underachiever. I feel sorry for her because she's always getting into trouble at home. She's stubborn and has excuses for everything she doesn't want to do. She constantly argues and disagrees. She does poorly in school. Punishing her doesn't help. She's good in school as far as her behavior goes. I guess part of it may be she's shy. Please help me to help her.*

*Perceptive Grandmother*

Dear Perceptive Grandmother,

Although your granddaughter does not seem shy at home, she may indeed be shy at school. Even more likely, she may lack confidence in her academic ability. Her arguing and excuses may only be cover-ups for her feelings of inadequacy. Punishments don't usually help feelings of incompetence.

It's not unusual for children who underachieve to seek the protection of a parent or grandparent who feels sorry for them, so it is most important that you are supportive of your granddaughter's parents' expectations. Be sure *not* to take her side in any arguments against her parents in the name of her shyness, or she may use your sympathy to take an easy way out. It's also important that your granddaughter's parents are in agreement about their expectations of her so she doesn't use her dad's power to protect her from her mother or vice versa.

Her parents can help her to set up daily independent study time at a desk or table and arrange to get weekly reports from school about work completion. If they'd like, they can provide a small reward or an allowance that is based on her completing her weekly work on time. It's better not to reward good grades, since that may cause her to avoid doing her work for fear she won't be able to accomplish the grades—instead, encourage good work habits that will lead to better grades.

Firmness, patience, and persistence, but most of all, united, positive adults, will help your underachieving granddaughter build confidence and reverse her underachievement.

### Dear Dr. Sylvia,

*What should we be looking for in child care or preschool for our three-year-old son?*

*Loving Parents*

Dear Loving Parents,

I'm not certain if you're looking for part-time child care as an opportunity for your son or need full-time care because you work outside your home. The criteria are quite similar except that consistency and communication between home and school are even more critical if your son will spend a fair amount of his day away from home. Communication will make you feel more secure about the environment that is being provided for your son and permit you to share in your son's developmental milestones despite your not being able to be with him some of the time. Exchanging a daily journal with your caregiver facilitates communication, and good

day-care providers will understand how important that shared ac-
count is for you. You should visit and observe at a child-care facility or preschool that you are considering for your son. A list of
criteria for you to consider follows:

- **Warm, Positive Atmosphere.** Child-care providers should
  be loving toward all the children. If staff members seem to be
  targeting some children who are troublemakers in their conversations with others, consider that your child could become one of those children. If instead they emphasize more
  positive approaches to problem solving, you can rely on a
  supportive environment.
- **Stability of Staff.** Schools that have a history of continuous staff turnover may either not be selecting staff well or
  not training them sufficiently. You can best obtain information on the school's stability from other parents who have
  had children at the school for a while. High staff turnover
  can cause inconsistency in teaching approaches and programs.
- **Classroom Organization and Control.** Reasonable organization and structure are critical to your child's early learning
  of responsibility and self-discipline. Routines that teach children good manners, cleanup responsibilities, consideration
  for others, and respect for teachers in charge provide good
  preparation for school and life. Disorganized, out-of-control
  class environments will cause feelings of insecurity.
- **Fostering the Love of Books.** Most day-care centers and
  preschools foster the love of books, which is a prerequisite
  for the love of learning. Several story hours a day should not
  be replaced by a convenient television set, and television
  should either make up a small part of children's learning in
  preschool or not be present at all.
- **Opportunities for Creative Expression and Curiosity.**
  Toys and equipment should include painting and drawing
  supplies, small and large building blocks, and toys for imaginative play, as well as sturdy outdoor equipment. Opportunities for children to explore, create, invent, feel, and touch
  foster a creative environment in the classroom.

- **Music, Dance, and Movement.** Creative movement provides opportunities for the development of children's love of music and rhythm. Dance or some form of movement to music should be part of almost every preschool day.
- **Outdoor Play and Explorations.** The exploration of nature and the environment may be limited at urban centers, but learning about weather, animals, and nature can be carried out at parks and playgrounds and is important for children.
- **Academic Preparation.** Preschool should provide some academic preparation, but not too much. Children's readiness should be considered, and a holistic approach is important for children to develop appropriately.
- **Value Systems.** Religious points of view and beliefs about honesty, respect, animal-life conservation, and so on should be a reasonable match with your values.
- **Freedom to Choose Within Limits.** School curriculums should not be the same for the whole class, nor should children be permitted to make all of the choices. Rigid preschool lessons will not tap individual differences, but complete freedom to choose may cause children to ignore or neglect some of the more boring skills they will require for kindergarten. A school that permits children to make all the choices empowers preschoolers too much. They will assume school will always be that way and balk at later school environments that feel restrictive by comparison.

Firsthand observations of a preschool class in session, using a checklist, and making notes will help you to evaluate a prospective preschool. An interview with the teacher and telephone calls to other parents will assist you in gathering other information. Between these criteria and your personal priorities, you should be able to arrive at a decision that is best for your child.

## Dear Dr. Sylvia,

*I have two boys, ages four and seven. The younger boy follows the older one around constantly. My older son does not like it, and they are becoming more aggressive toward each other. How do I stop this?*

*Trying to Remain Impartial*

Dear Trying to Remain Impartial,

If there are two boys in a family, the younger one almost always follows the older one around. Our younger son, Eric, used to tell us that his older brother, David, "knew everything." Younger brothers are typically in awe of their older brothers, and just as typically, older brothers refer to their younger siblings as pests. This behavior is also not uncommon in sisters.

It's a good idea to preserve some quiet time alone for each of your children. Your younger son may fight this, but it's actually good for any child's independence and imagination to occupy himself without depending on a sibling or friend. For your older son, it will provide some needed privacy.

In a one-to-one conversation, tell your firstborn how much his brother admires him and looks to him as a model. Encourage him to take a little time each day to play with his little brother and teach him some new skills. The learning experiences could revolve around sports, games, or schoolwork. This will provide some extra status to your older son.

Be sure not to be overprotective of the younger brother. The protection you offer him will only serve to encourage tattling, crying, and teasing on his part and anger and frustration on the part of the older brother. Instead, separate them for ten minutes when the volume gets too loud or the interactions become too aggressive. Don't ever try to determine who started the ruckus.

Encouraging your sons to plan activities and surprises together gives them joint goals. As your children grow, few days will pass without some altercations, but if you don't intervene too often, they're more likely to become friends in adulthood.

### Dear Dr. Sylvia,

*What do you do with a three-year-old boy who turned from a sweetie to a bully—picking on and physically being mean to his seven-year-old sister?*

*Confused Parents*

Dear Confused Parents,

It's somewhat unusual and early for a three-year-old to become angry and mean to an older sister. A few logical reasons explain why this might be taking place; perhaps one or more applies to your children.

Sometimes younger brothers feel angry because their older sisters receive lots of praise and attention. If they did, too, as babies, as they become more actively involved in exploring limits they may find themselves receiving more corrections than praise. They may feel inadequate compared to their older sisters and feel angry, although they don't understand their own anger.

Sometimes older sisters, in their efforts to keep their "good girl" status in the family, unconsciously point out to their parents all of their brothers' flaws. The worse they make their brothers appear, the better they feel about themselves. Little brothers may feel angered by their sisters' subtle put-downs.

Sometimes older sisters take on a mothering role toward their younger brothers. As these little boys grow older, they may resent the double mothering and display their anger at their sisters.

Here are some tips to help you reduce your son's anger toward your daughter:

- You and your spouse each need some one-to-one time with each of your children. Separating the children for individual attention provides some noncompetitive relief for both of them.
- Look for opportunities to comment to your spouse within your children's hearing range about how kind your daughter is to your son and vice versa. That indirect praise is effective for encouraging children's positive qualities.
- Provide a private place for your daughter to work and play without her brother's interruptions. When she has friends visiting her, either of you could try to give your son some one-to-one time so that he doesn't interfere with his sister's guests.
- Time-out is the most effective way to handle your son's aggressive behavior. Be sure the time-out is immediate. Escort him to his room, preferably before you've lost your temper, for ten minutes of quiet. Encourage him to handle his anger by punching a pillow or a punching bag.
- Encourage your daughter's kindness toward her younger brother by helping her to plan surprises for him. Encourage

her to read to him and teach him skills. She'll soon become
the big sister he'll appreciate, respect, and love.

### Dear Dr. Sylvia,

*I have twin sons who are the youngest of four boys. One is very dominant
and independent and one is very submissive. I find myself always correcting the dominant one and cuddling the submissive one. I try not to get
them in those roles, but how can I stop doing this?*

*Feeling Trapped*

Dear Feeling Trapped,
Parents often observe their twins in such a dominant-dependent relationship. Actually, even two same-gender, close-aged children often take on these opposite roles. Your older sons may also exhibit
similar patterns, although theirs is probably less extreme. Furthermore, the patterns seem to perpetuate themselves, or at least parents tend to feel trapped into perpetuating them.

Your more dominant son needs opportunities for positive leadership so he can direct his energy and power appropriately. Help
him get involved in some new interests and activities independent
of his brother. Some separation from each other will diminish the
competition and will neutralize your son's dominance. Because his
friends will be less likely to accept this bossiness, it is likely to be
tempered toward more reasonable leadership.

Of course, your more dependent son will especially benefit
from some separation from his overpowering brother. Separate
father/son trips or activities will be helpful in building his confidence. Although you should continue to be affectionate to
both your sons, avoid overcoddling the more passive one. When
your submissive son seeks out your protection and affection,
too much support may serve as a vote of no confidence. It is like
saying to him, "You need me more than your brother does,"
causing feelings of inadequacy. Encouraging independent interests and active involvement is even more critical for this dependent son.

As you try to balance your parenting among your four boys, expect some frustration. Don't be surprised to find that a growing
confidence in one may cause the other to lose confidence. Con-

tinue some whole-family activities while providing work and play opportunities in one-on-one, parent-child relationships.

Although it is challenging and overwhelming to raise four boys in a family, I have met some wonderful families who have struggled with similar situations. Celebrate your sons' individuality as well as their teamwork, and you can look forward to someday adding four lovely daughters-in-law to balance things out and deliver you from an all-masculine perspective.

## Dear Dr. Sylvia,

*My thirteen-year-old, eighth-grade daughter raises her hand in science to answer questions the teachers asks the class. The teacher tells her to put it down. She can only answer once during class. She thinks the teacher is abrupt with her and makes her do things that she does not make other students do—for example, erase lines made around diagrams other students have made on the board. She is starting to lose interest in science. Should I talk to her teacher? What should I say? My daughter is a straight-A student and loves to learn and read.*

*Mother at a Loss*

Dear Mother at a Loss,
There is surely something strange taking place in your daughter's science class. You may wish to question and listen to your daughter a little more before going in to speak to her teacher. Ask her why she thinks the teacher is treating her differently and if other students may be feeling the same way. Be careful not to suggest that the problem is either the teacher's or your daughter's fault. After you have gathered a few more concrete examples of your daughter's perceptions, arrange a conference with her teacher.

Listen to the teacher's observations of your daughter's progress before you explain your worries. The teacher's description may contain the answers before you ask; for example, your daughter may wish to monopolize class discussion. Verbally bright children sometimes talk too much because they feel smart while they're talking. The teacher may be holding her to a higher standard because she views your daughter as capable of doing more. It is also possible that your daughter is a perfectionist and doesn't accept normal criticism well.

If the teacher's description of your daughter yields no clues to the problem, explain to the teacher that you're sure she is very fair to all her students, but your daughter seems to be having a difficult time adjusting to her class. At that point, ask if she could observe your daughter during the next weeks to help you determine what the problems may be or how the teacher can help.

Don't mention your discussion with the teacher to your daughter. However, if she discovers you've talked to the teacher, respond to her honestly. In the weeks that follow, continue to listen to your daughter's concerns, but attempt to put them in perspective. For example, if she talks too much, you could explain that making only one contribution will encourage her to think through her responses and give a good one. Perhaps the teacher expects her to do especially excellent work to provide her with the challenge she needs.

Of course, you and the teacher may not agree philosophically, but try to discuss the teacher with your daughter in the best terms possible. If the teacher senses your support, she is likely to be more concerned about your daughter. If your daughter realizes that you listen and care but expect her to be respectful of her teacher, it is more likely that she'll adjust to her teacher's different style. On the other hand, if you take her side against the teacher, she is likely to become disrespectful and assume you agree with her negative evaluation of the teacher.

## Dear Dr. Sylvia,

*My child has never been a discipline problem at school and has a B+ average. Her teacher uses group punishment; that is, the good kids are punished along with the offenders. I do not criticize the teacher in my daughter's presence, but it annoys me when I hear that she's had to miss a recess or stay after school when she's done nothing wrong. It clouds her otherwise good attitude about school. Should I complain to the teacher? What is your opinion of group punishment?*

*Good Kid's Mom*

Dear Good Kid's Mom,

We all remember a teacher who used group punishment as a form of discipline. If we were the good kids, we hated it because it never seemed fair, and if we were the troublemakers, we hated it, too. For the troublemakers, it actually holds mixed blessings. While kids get angry at the troublemakers, the troublemakers seem to gain both attention and power.

I don't recommend group punishment as a teaching tool. I didn't like it when I was a child, and I still don't think it's fair. Nevertheless, teachers use it because they often find it effective for some of their most troublesome students, and teachers obviously find themselves frustrated when they can't get kids to behave.

I think you can commiserate with your daughter and explain your agreement with her problem. You might also explain that adults are often subjected to many unfair and unnecessary laws because of the illegal and inappropriate behaviors of others. There is little we or she can do about the problem except to do our best to lead honest and respectful lives in the world and in the classroom. Tell her you're pleased that the class is not being punished for her behavior, and that is most important to you.

You're not completely helpless to change the problem for other children, but I would wait until this school year is over so that a complaint can't be attributed specifically to you and won't negatively affect your daughter. Make an appointment with the principal and explain that you are aware of the teacher's other good qualities, but you would like the principal to know that your daughter found the group punishment quite disturbing. The principal's role is to supervise teachers. He or she will undoubtedly find an appropriate opportunity to recommend a better form of discipline for the future.

As to your daughter, she is undoubtedly resilient enough to survive the varieties of personalities that will lead her in future classrooms. If she is truly disturbed by the situation, you could also suggest she write her teacher a polite letter about her feelings or encourage her to express her feelings to her teacher in private after school. Suggest she use "I" language, as in "I feel discouraged when I get punished for something I didn't do." Emphasize that she explain her position in private—definitely not in front of the class.

That would only result in a no-win situation for her and her teacher. Her teacher may actually be more responsive to your daughter than to you or other adults.

### Dear Dr. Sylvia,

*I'm writing to you in hopes that you could let me know which is the lesser of two evils: making a fourth-grader stick it out for a whole year with a "bad" teacher or switching to a private school.*

*I won't list all of the teacher's evils except to say that she runs a class with a combination of intimidation, yelling, and embarrassment. She has been moved around to various grades/schools within the district, but can't be fired. Other children who have had her suffered headaches, etc.*

*My son is sweet, shy, and sensitive. He does well in school but especially thrives when he doesn't feel threatened. I have asked that he not be placed with this teacher next year. If he is, how do I go about deciding what to do?*

*Mom in Turmoil*

Dear Mom in Turmoil,
You are in a dilemma that many parents face at least once. Although most teachers are indeed dedicated to their work and to children, a small fraction fall far below an excellent standard. They may have taught for many years, and there may not be any way to change their poor teaching. Good principals try first to help them to improve and finally try to tempt them toward early retirement. This teacher may be too determined for the first and too young for the second. She may even believe she is doing a fine job.

Intimidation, yelling, and humiliation are all poor teaching techniques, but this teacher probably doesn't resort to them often enough to be genuinely abusive. If she did, they would have been documented, and the teacher would no longer be in the school, regardless of her long experience. However, this type of teacher may cause tension headaches and stomachaches for sensitive children. All children thrive better without feelings of being threatened.

To make a decision, look ahead beyond the upcoming school year. If your son is put in this negative teacher's class for this grade, will the teachers that follow after this difficult year be mainly positive, or do they, too, have reputations for being negative? What about the principal of the school? Is he or she a good leader? Consider overall curriculum, class teacher-student ratios, peer groups, facilities, values taught, and extracurricular activities.

Evaluate the alternative, private school that you are considering. Are all the teachers in that school reputed to be excellent? Use the same criteria to evaluate the private school that you have for the public school. Consider, also, how the tuition may affect your budget and the enrichment activities you as parents might offer to your children.

After you've compared the overall future educational opportunities of the two schools, you'll be in a much better position to make the best decision for your son. Children shouldn't be moved from school to school based on one negative teacher, but if the prognosis for the future is negative, this may be the year to move him.

If you decide to keep your son in his present school, you may find he is more resilient than you thought. A year with a less predictable teacher might actually help him become stronger. Most important, if you decide not to change, don't let your son hear you describing your worries about his teacher to others, nor should you commiserate with him about the problem. Both will only cause him to feel more anxiety.

Instead, be matter-of-fact about the teacher difference. Let him know that you believe he'll learn to handle her style of discipline, and remind him that because he's a good worker, her scoldings are not likely to be directed at him. Negative teachers hardly ever choose sweet, sensitive, and shy children as recipients of their ire. Be sure to tell your son of any positive information you've heard about the teacher.

Fortunately, you have a choice. Make it objectively and fairly with a concern for your son's overall education instead of his temporary escape. Many parents have no choice. Let me assure them and you that most of us have survived at least one school year when a teacher's approach to discipline was less than ideal. In retrospect, that bad year may not hold the most positive memories for us, yet most of us would acknowledge that we not only survived, but that we also managed to learn in spite of poor teaching.

# IN CHAPTER 3
## YOU'LL LEARN HOW TO

- guide your children toward good study habits.

- teach your children how to study for specific subjects.

- help children improve test-taking skills and cope with test anxiety.

- prevent practice in the arts from being unpleasant.

- encourage pleasant and independent morning, mealtime, and bedtime routines.

- improve family communication and fun.

CHAPTER 3
___

# TEACHING HABITS THAT ENCOURAGE LEARNING

C HILDREN with good habits automatically tend to achieve better in school and for the rest of their lives. However, bad habits can interfere with learning, and changing those bad habits can be challenging. Although some children have no difficulty changing their bad habits, others seem to fight habitual behavior of any kind with a consistency that is itself almost a habit.

I teach a few important habits and routines in my clinic that encourage independent achievement. Teaching them to your children will increase their educational effectiveness and decrease your nagging.

## HOMEWORK AND STUDY

Schools vary in their expectations regarding homework and study, and children vary even more in their response to school expectations. Achieving children study mainly at a desk or table in a quiet place, although some listen to music. However, underachievers exhibit a great many troublesome study habits. Many believe that they can only study lying on their bed or on the floor with a headset or the television on. They consider "study" to be reading something over once quickly; they consider intense study to be reading the material over twice in that same position. Other underachievers do homework only after being nagged, scolded, reminded, and supervised—even then, they protest and expend only minimum effort. A third group of children sit with a parent nightly, certain that they can't complete their assignments without that parent's help and supervision. Finally, some underachievers simply don't do homework or study at all. Some even refuse to bring their books home.

If you are the parents of children in one of these groups, you may wonder how your children fell into such bad habits and why other children have better habits. The next section will assist you in helping your children develop better study approaches. To parents of children who already have good study habits, read on nevertheless. There are also some helpful suggestions for them.

**A Time and a Place.** Good study habits begin with an appropriate time and place for study. A good time for study will have to fit with individual children's other activities as well as their parents' schedules. Study time may need to be quite flexible in many families where parents are not at home when children come home from school; however, some general rules can guide you in setting a proper time and place.

Children's history of responsibility with schoolwork should determine if parents should set their time for study. If children accomplish homework independently and study in a timely manner, there's no need for you to specify a time for study. On the other hand, if your children haven't been studying enough, you should help them structure their time. The amount of time will vary with their grade and school requirements. Elementary-school children should study from fifteen minutes to one hour; middle-school children, one to two hours; and high school students, one and one-half hours to three hours per evening. In some highly academic high schools, more than three hours may be required.

PARENT
POINTER
For children unaccustomed to spending time studying, I recommend you **use a timer and hold them to the specific amount of time initially agreed upon.** If children say they have completed all of their homework and have only filled a fraction of their allotted study time, they may use the remainder of the scheduled time for review, organizing notes, or doing extra reading for future book re-

ports or for pleasure. Of course, breaks are appropriate, but timers should be reset after breaks. Quite a few kids like to include their breaks into the prescribed study times and extend them to exceed the work time. **Remind your kids that the timer and prescriptive study times are only a temporary measure to help them manage their study time independently.** Inform them that when their achievement habits improve, you'll be more flexible and allow them to set their own study schedule. For children who love to read, permitting them to do pleasure reading during study time may be counterproductive. Writing or math study could complete their study time.

PARENT POINTER

There should be a break immediately after school for children to have a snack and some physical and social activity. Children often believe they should use that break to watch television. However, television will put them into a passive mode, and they're unlikely to want to leave television to begin studying. Moving your child from television to study may involve a massive power struggle. **It's better to insist that television follow study and homework.** It's likely that your children will say, "But I need to relax after school." They may have heard something similar from their parents. Assure them that they will get to relax. Exercise is both relaxing and energizing, and more appropriate after a day of sitting. Certainly, having time to chat or clown around or play are appropriate for after school—but not television.

PARENT POINTER

I usually explain the advantages of postponing watching TV by describing my own TV habits: "I know it's hard to get myself away from an interesting program once it begins, so I get my work done before I sit down to watch." By my using myself as an example, my clinic children are less likely to feel put down by my request that they postpone TV and video games.

In determining the right time for study, not only should there be an opportunity for an active break after school, but **there should be something to look forward to after study.** If possible, at least part of the children's study time should take place prior to the evening meal, leaving time after study for play or television. Children often tire after dinner; if the study time is set late in the evening, study is not likely to be as efficient, and there would not be time after study for play. When study time is late, children often sit at their desks daydreaming or half-dozing. With only bedtime to

PARENT POINTER

follow, they aren't motivated toward efficiency. Homework or study may become an excuse to stay up late if it is scheduled just prior to bedtime. (For some reason unknown to adults, few children seem to enjoy going to sleep.) They often look for ways to stay up as long as adults are awake.

Having a designated study place is equally important for providing an atmosphere in which children learn efficiently. **A desk in a kid's own room with a sign, STUDENT AT WORK, posted on the door is ideal.** Many kids have desks, although they may be cluttered with junk. If kids don't have their own rooms, there are other good alternatives. The kitchen, dining room, or basement are reasonable places as long as no one else is in the same room and they're out of listening and viewing range of the TV while they're studying.

Studying together as a family or studying at the local public libraries may also be acceptable study alternatives if a family prefers them. Occasionally I recommend that a parent and child work together at a table, each doing his or her own work. However, parents should be cautious not to permit a dependent relationship in which children ask for more help than they actually require. Research on high-achieving Asian-American children often finds that the family works nightly on individual projects together at a kitchen or dining room table.

Classical conditioning research demonstrates the importance of having an appropriate place for children to study. I often describe to children in my clinic Pavlov's research on the conditioning of dogs to persuade them to study at a desk or table in a quiet atmosphere. The story I tell them, and suggest that you tell your own children, points out how conditioning affects unconscious involuntary behaviors. See figure 3.1.

Children who prefer studying in the dining room with siblings, or those who prefer background noise, often explain that they can't concentrate or study at a desk. After explaining classical conditioning to them, I point out that they have been conditioned to relax when they are socializing with family members or watching television; therefore, under such conditions it is easier to relax but more difficult for them to concentrate on studying. When children assert that they study better while lying on their beds, I ask them what

PARENT
POINTER

Figure 3.1

# How to Tell Your Children Why Time and Place Will Improve Their Study

A physiologist by the name of Ivan Pavlov was doing research with dogs to determine how much they salivated when eating. While the experiment was taking place, Pavlov's assistant observed a serious problem. The dogs began salivating when the caretakers entered the room *before* they received their food. Pavlov's assistant believed that the research was therefore spoiled. Pavlov, a creative scientist, recognized what we call in science a *serendipitous* finding. He discovered some important principles that are now known as the laws of classical conditioning. When two stimuli are paired together over time, the second begins to cause the same response as the first. In other words, because the caretaker always brought the food, the dogs associated the caretaker with food and, therefore, began salivating at the sight of the caretaker (even before they had the.food).

In the same way, when you sit in the same position for daily studying, your automatic responses will be conditioned to concentrate when you assume your study position. This will make it easier for you to automatically concentrate and make good use of your study time.

they associate with doing so. Their response is usually sleep or rest. I point out that their conditioning for sleep doesn't encourage their active involvement in study. They're conditioned to rest or fall asleep when lying on their beds. Children are only reporting their comfort levels, not their efficiency. Furthermore, I remind them that music and social conversation are not permitted by either high school teachers or college professors while taking exams, and that I've never heard of SATs or ACTs given while music is played. I ask them to condition themselves to sit in an upright position so they can be actively involved with the material, have good light, take good notes, and concentrate on the material until it becomes a habit. I point out to them that adults who were good students in college often went to a study carrel in the library, a library table, or a quiet place in a room where everyone was studying and where there wasn't any socializing.

Sometimes it's difficult to convince children to accept an appropriate time and place, but the story of Pavlov's dogs usually gets them started. You should be firm and insist they try it consistently for at least two weeks. Once an appropriate study place and time becomes habitual you'll find you no longer have to nag your children. They'll automatically go to their desks in their rooms to do their homework, and their concentration and efficiency will be improved. Parents with whom I've worked report the home atmosphere improves when the whole family changes its study habits and nagging disappears.

If you're beginning a new study routine with your children, a contract may be helpful. Some sample study contracts can be found in figure 3.2.

**How Parents Can Help (but Not Too Much).** There's another advantage to separating your children from you and their siblings during study. Children who are too dependent, and likely to ask questions before they've tried to solve problems on their own, are less likely to ask those questions if their parents are not in the same room with them. To encourage independence in learning, it is important for your children to take the initiative to work out their homework difficulties on their own. **Don't sit with your children nightly doing homework.** It's their responsibility to do their homework and your responsibility to take an interest or monitor *when appropriate*. You should answer questions only after they have made a determined effort to work on the material independently.

PARENT POINTER

You'll be required to take a more active role, at least temporarily, with children who have had a history of underachievement or dependence. First you should help your children set up strategies for independent work, then monitor their work regularly to be certain that they're completing quality homework. Of course, younger children require more supervision than adolescents. See figure 3.3 for a study plan to encourage independent homework.

PARENT POINTER

**Be careful not to do too much for your children. Ask them to review material at least three times before they ask for help.** If they don't understand the instructions or material, you may explain an example or two. Then permit them to complete the next example to be sure they understand. You may suggest strategies for completing the work, or you may help break it into manageable steps if

## Figure 3.2

# How Study Contracts Work

Rosa, a ninth-grader, habitually forgot her homework. She rarely studied and never studied independently. She always insisted on her mother's help. I pointed out the importance of developing her independence and of promptly handing in assignments. I also explained that I knew she had some bad habits that would not be easy for her to change. We set up some positive and negative consequences that would help her to change those habits. She was delighted with the reward system we offered her but angry about possible punishments. After some reassurance about the temporary nature of our plan and my explanation that she would never be penalized as long as she handed in her work, we agreed to the following contract:

> Rosa, her mother and father, and Dr. Rimm agree that Rosa will do homework and study at her desk in her room for at least two hours a night, five nights a week. She will show one of her parents her completed work daily. If her teacher reports there are no missing assignments on Friday, she will earn 10 points. When she has accumulated 100 points, she may choose a friend to go with her to the theme park for a day. If there are missing assignments, she will not be allowed to go to the Friday-night basketball game with her friends. If she makes up all assignments by game time, she may go to the game; however, the 10 points do not accrue unless the work was done on time.
>
> *Rosa*
> *Mom*
> *Dad*
> *Dr. Rimm*

Although Rosa missed two basketball games, she earned her day at the theme park in twelve weeks. At that point, a new contract was negotiated. The times that Rosa did not complete her assignments, she tried to argue with her parents to convince them of the importance of the basketball games and that almost all assignments were completed. Her parents didn't argue. They simply reminded her of their agreement. She went stomping off to her room, slamming the door behind her, but she didn't go to the game.

That first time was harder for Rosa's parents than for her, but the clear limits were effective. Notice that no extensive punishment was required, and her parents did not increase the punishment despite Rosa's angry behavior.

continued on next page

Figure 3.2 (continued)

## How Study Contracts Work

Jacob, a fourth-grader, argued nightly with his mom about doing his homework. His parents were eager to change this battle into a smooth routine. Here's their contract:

Jacob, Mom, and Dad agree that Jacob will work on his homework between 6:30 and 7:00 each night, five nights a week. He'll work independently at his desk before he watches TV, and there will be no radio, music, or TV on in his room during study time. After his work is completed, Dad will review it. When Jacob's work is completed well, Jacob and Dad will work on model rockets together. Mom and Dad will only remind Jacob once to study, or he will take the initiative independently.

*Jacob*
*Mom*
*Dad*

they feel overwhelmed. You could even recommend a different study or learning approach.

PARENT POINTER

**After you've guided them, be sure your children go back to their desks in their rooms to complete the assignments.** When they've finished their work, they should bring it to you to review. Do an overall review of their work. If it's carelessly done, simply insist they go back and redo it. If your children have misunderstood and the homework is incorrectly done, patiently go over one or two more examples. Then send them back to complete it correctly.

There's no reason to correct every example; that's the teacher's responsibility. If for the most part it is of good quality and looks

PARENT POINTER

correct, it is ready to turn in. **Your message to your children should be that they've done good work, and now it's time to take a break for some fun.**

You may wonder which parent should help your children. Mothers are often assigned to schoolwork supervision; however, ei-

PARENT POINTER

ther mothers or fathers can help their children. **For boys, it's especially helpful if fathers take the major responsibility for**

Figure 3.3

# Study Plan to Encourage Independent Homework

**DAD:** Richard, I've talked to your teacher, and he assures me that you have very good ability. Now that I know that, I want you to get in the habit of doing schoolwork on your own.

**RICHARD:** Gee, Dad, I just need Mom's help. Can't she just help me a little bit? (*A few tears*) I just can't do it without her.

**DAD:** No, neither Mom nor I can help you because we really want you to prove to yourself that you can do it, but we have some good ideas that will make it fun. (*Richard has a sad face, but is listening.*) We'll start by moving Grandpop's old desk up to your room so you can have your own study space. (*Richard has a faint smile of interest.*) Then we'll set up a study time. Your teacher suggested that one hour a day for a sixth-grader would be about right; so we'll start with that. Of course, that's only for five days. You get two days free of homework. They could be either Friday and Saturday or Saturday and Sunday. If your work seems to be very good and you don't need that much time, we can cut it down. Of course, if you don't finish your work in an hour, you will have to work longer than that. That study time will take place in your room, at your new desk, before watching any TV or playing TV games and with no radio or stereo on.

**RICHARD:** Dad, that definitely won't work. I have to watch cartoons when I get home to relax and unwind after school.

**DAD:** Son, cartoon watching will have to wait. I like to watch TV to relax, too, but when I sit down to TV, it's really hard to get up to do any work. So I wait to watch TV until after I've finished my work. You'll have to do the same thing. I don't mind if you have a snack or sit around or go outside for fifteen minutes, but by 4:15 I expect you to be in your room working, and absolutely no TV until you're done and I've checked your work.* That way you'll be all done with your study time before dinner, and we can shoot some baskets after dinner and watch TV when it gets dark.

**RICHARD:** I know this just won't work. I think I should watch TV for half an hour before homework.

**DAD:** Richard, part of this new homework plan is that you are going to earn some fun things for doing your homework on your own. It's not that we're paying you for homework, but we thought it might help you to make a game of it at first. Now you'll need to think of something you might want to save for.

**RICHARD:** (*Full smile*) Gee, Dad, that sounds neat. What kind of things can I save for, and how do I get the prize?

---

*For more information about TV locks, please see resources list in the back of this book.
SOURCE: *Why Bright Kids Get Poor Grades* by S. B. Rimm (New York: Crown Publishing Group, 1995).

helping or monitoring their schoolwork, particularly if they are
not performing well in school. That doesn't mean that mothers
can't help occasionally for some subjects. If Mom is the only person
who monitors her son's schoolwork, it becomes important for Dad,
if he's available, to communicate clearly to his son the importance
of schoolwork. **He should tell his son that he'll be checking with
Mom regularly to be sure he's doing his work.** Boys seem to have
problems if only their mothers take responsibility for supervising
schoolwork. They assume it's not masculine to be concerned about
education. As they mature, they see education as less relevant because their dads haven't shown an active interest.

**PARENT POINTER**

**Work with children on special projects.** They can be enjoyable family learning experiences. However, even for those, it is important for you to be the "guide on the side" rather than get so
heavily involved that when the project is complete, it's not clear to
your children whether you or they completed the project.

**PARENT POINTER**

If your children have already developed independent habits,
you won't have to remind them about doing homework or studying and should only share with them those materials that they wish
to share with you. **Show interest, but don't impose;** for example,
reading a story they've written or checking for errors in a first or
second draft of a composition might be an appropriate assist if they
request it. Discussing ideas with your children is also suitable.
Quizzing them in spelling or Spanish after they've studied it is a
fine show of support for their study. **Teaching them strategies for
study is certainly helpful;** sharing your interest is always appropriate.

**PARENT POINTER**

**PARENT POINTER**

## MOTIVATING CHILDREN TO STUDY MORE

After you explain to your children why they should study more efficiently, you may find that your children still do not wish to
change their bad habits. They may continue to provide you with all
kinds of reasons why their old ways work better. I suggest that you
ask them to experiment with good study habits in one or more subjects. Encourage them to select a priority subject to which they can
make their commitment for the experiment. **Convince them to**

**PARENT POINTER**

**add fifteen minutes a day to their study time of that subject.** If they add fifteen efficient minutes to what they would normally do, their grade in that subject should increase by at least one level. They can expect to go from F to D, D to C, C to B, or B to A. If your children do this using the study techniques described in this section or a technique taught by their teacher, they should find that they can raise their grade. Remember, we're trying to teach them the relationship between their personal effort and their grade. They really don't believe that efficient study techniques apply to them, nor do they think that study will improve their grade. Convincing them to try one subject may be sufficient to tempt them to adopt more effective study practices in other subjects. This approach works very well for improving the quality of their work once they've learned to get all their assignments in on time. Sometimes students who have tried this approach raise their grades two or three levels. Even they are surprised by the power of their study.

Studying more than one needs to is called overlearning. You can explain to your children that research finds that when one overlearns material, it improves the recall of that material and is therefore likely to improve test grades. Of course, in reality the fifteen minutes of their additional time may not be overlearning so much as sufficient study. Either way, it's bound to improve their grade a little, and hopefully, they'll be pleased to see they can improve their grade. Some children, out of fear that extra studying and using new techniques won't really help them, are more resistant than others. The case of Alice will give you insight into that underlying fear:

> Alice, a sophomore, was completing all her homework and putting extra time into studying for tests. Her B and C grades now matched her high-average ability. However, Alice's test grades in Spanish were D's and F's. It was not difficult to convince Alice to put more time into study, but it seemed impossible to persuade her to study effectively. Even for her final exam, she avoided using the techniques I had recommended. She was completely honest in admitting that she ignored my advice. Finally, I asked Alice, "Is it possible that you don't want to improve your Spanish grade?" Alice's answer unveiled her underlying fear of not being smart enough. She responded hesitantly, but insightfully, "Suppose I do study the right way and I still get a D?"

# HOW-TO-STUDY HINTS

I suggested earlier that you give children some direction and strategies for study. Following are some study hints that may be helpful
to you as you guide your children. Remember that their study must
be effective for them to develop a sense of accomplishment. If they
have inefficient or poor study habits or don't know how to study,
they're likely to assume that study doesn't make a difference. I've already emphasized the importance of setting a time and place for
your children to study, and you know that it will be difficult to convince them to take on the responsibility of real study. Now all you
need are some study techniques to share with your children.

Many books about study habits are more complete than this
chapter, but I've included a few tips that seem to make a difference
for children who come to my clinic.

**Using All Senses.** We know that children vary in their learning styles.
Some children learn more efficiently visually; others are more effective listeners and prefer auditory learning; and still others learn
best by tactile senses or through hands-on activities. Stories that involve feelings or emotions enhance learning for most children. Using all four styles can encourage your children to utilize their

strengths to learn. **For visual learners, writing, copying, drawing, or collecting pictures will reinforce their memory. Looking
at the teacher directly (eye contact) will also help visual learners. For auditory learners, listening to and talking on tapes and
oral repetition will assist in improving their memory. Kines-
thetic children will learn better by manipulating counters,
markers, or flash cards. Teaching children to make up stories,
rhymes, or mnemonic devices will assist all of them in involving their feelings to improve their memories.** Teach your children to discover what works best for them. Using as many senses as
possible for studying will help.

I often tell teachers stories of my fourth-grade teacher, Miss
Shoobridge, a white-haired lady who was close to retirement. She
was my favorite teacher. I recall that she spoke in a quiet voice so we
had to listen carefully to hear her. She always shared wonderful pictures from her travels, as well as beautiful nature pictures from the
Audubon Society. We also learned to use maps and globes. I loved

to touch the continents when it was my turn to go to the map. What I remember most from her class are the stories she shared with us. She was so "human," and not just a teacher. She had a real life outside the classroom, something I never imagined that teachers did. She shared feelings and touched my emotions.

How can it be that after exposure to so many teachers in so many grades and in so many subjects, I can recall so clearly what Miss Shoobridge taught me? Perhaps it was her use of all the senses that strengthened my recall. Her stories and pictures of her travels and experiences reinforced my memory of explorers, continents, national parks, birds, and animals. I remember her description of Ponce de León and his search for the fountain of youth, even the question that I asked her: "Why would anyone want to look for a fountain of youth?" (It seemed so silly to me then.) As well as her answer: "Someday you'll understand, Sylvia." Yes, Miss Shoobridge, I do understand.

As you teach your children to remember information, **encourage them to use all their senses and their emotions.** You may become as effective as Miss Shoobridge was for me. After all, parents are teachers, too.

PARENT
POINTER

I UNDERSTAND NOW, MISS SHOOBRIDGE

**Memorization.** Memory is extremely important for children's success on tests, yet children know little about how to memorize material. Some children seem to automatically learn, and other children have intuitively sorted out memory techniques. Some psychological concepts can help all children to understand and use their memory better. Try the explanation in figure 3.4, which I use to explain to children about short-term and long-term memory. I emphasize the importance of their active involvement in studying.

Figure 3.4

# Memory

Short-term memory is a temporary storage area for information. For example, if I gave you a telephone number and you immediately dialed the number, then had a conversation with someone, you would no longer remember the number after you'd hung up. It's as if the number had gone in one ear and out the other. It didn't make any permanent traces or lines on your brain, and the number is literally gone from your memory. If information isn't moved from short-term memory to long-term memory, it can't be retrieved unless it's very meaningful or you have an extraordinary memory. Thus, when you read something over once or twice, unless the material is especially interesting to you, you can't remember it for use on your test.

All of us can recall times when we've sat with a book in front of us and read the material. Then, after we put the book down, we had no recall of what we'd read. The feeling you have when you take a test after that kind of perusal of material is best described as, "What's wrong with my memory? Why do other kids do better?"

Long-term memory provides much more permanent storage. The information that you move into long-term memory makes traces or lines on your brain, which can be retrieved and recalled for testing. To move material from short-term memory to long-term memory, you have to (1) make it meaningful, (2) organize it, and (3) rehearse or practice it. All these strategies will cause that information, boring or otherwise, to move to long-term memory for retrieval for your test.

If you study the same amount of time but study the right way so that the information is moved to long-term memory, you'll have the sense of confidence that comes when you feel smart when taking your test. If you study the wrong way, you're likely to feel dumb because you think your poor performance is due to your poor memory. We'd all rather feel smart, right?

The more actively they're involved, the more likely the information will be moved into long-term memory storage.

Some study hints for specific subjects can lead to improved overall memory. These hints are included in the next sections, which I've addressed directly to your children. As parents, you may read these to them or copy the pages to share with your children.

**Note Taking.** When you take notes from a class lecture, whether it be social studies, science, or English, leave a wide margin at the side of the paper. During study time at home, review your notes and write summary statements or key vocabulary words in those wide margins. Reviewing notes the same day you've taken them will help you to correct notes you may not have understood or those you've written down too quickly. You may want to reorganize them. Before a test, read the key words or sentences and recall from memory the notes you made in lectures or read the written notes and recall the key words. Either talk aloud to yourself or write summary statements as you study.

**Studying from Textbooks.** Here are some suggestions for studying social studies, science, literature, or other subjects that you must read:

- After reading each paragraph, write down a summary sentence of the paragraph in your notebook. You can use that summary sentence for later study.
- Use a stopwatch or set an alarm for every five to ten minutes. Summarize what you have learned out loud or in writing. The stopwatch will help you to concentrate better.
- At test time, make up a test question from each summary sentence. Your questions should be the same type that your teacher usually uses, whether multiple-choice, matching, true-false, or essay. This will be excellent preparation for your tests.
- If your teacher expects you to recall definitions on your tests, write key words and their definitions as you study. When you review for your test, quiz yourself using those key words. Don't just study them orally, because the tests aren't given orally. Study in the same way the test is given. Write the key

words and write their definitions. Then check back to see whether your definitions are correct.

- If you've made up essay-test questions, select a few of the most important essay questions to answer. Write out the essays for the best practice. Although your teacher's questions may be different, they will probably incorporate much of the same information. Furthermore, it will teach you to think like your teacher and become a better test taker.

**Learning Math Facts.** If you're in elementary grades, you're often required to study addition, subtraction, multiplication, and division tables. For some children this is a simple task. However, even for some bright children, this task is challenging. It may be that anxiety or tension interferes with your memory or you find the memorization boring. The best way to study the facts is in written form and to review the same tests many times so you have rehearsed the process in writing. Time yourself on the same test over and over again, always trying to beat your own time. The more you time yourself at home, the less tense you'll feel in school. You'll finally be master of those basic facts, and the tension you feel will disappear.

**Studying for Math Tests.** Save all your past homework to prepare for your math tests. Then redo at least one homework problem from each assignment from scratch and match your new answers to those that were already corrected on your homework. Doing the hardest problem from each assignment will usually be enough to review for an exam. Just reading or looking over examples is not enough to prepare for your math test. You must get *actively* involved, actually doing the problems. Some high schools and most colleges typically provide practice problems before exams. You can use your own homework in the same way.

**Spelling.** When you study spelling, you should do so in writing rather than orally, unless you're practicing for an oral spelling bee. If spelling bees are given in your classroom, you should study both orally and in writing. The old-fashioned method of folding a paper vertically into four columns is still helpful for studying spelling. Copy the word first from your book, then cover it up and write it in the next column, check back, cover it up, write it in the third column, then check back again, and covering up all three columns, write it the fourth time and check back. This method will make you a superspeller. Check carefully so you don't repeat mistakes. Having a parent quiz you orally for spelling is not effective for written spelling tests. Oral quizzing won't hurt you and may be done if you and your parents enjoy it, but only after you've written your spelling words. When you've completed your study, ask your parents to give you a practice test in writing. If you make any mistakes, practice those words again in writing. You're about to become an expert speller.

**Foreign Languages.** Teachers often ask you to prepare flash cards to study foreign-language vocabulary. Although flash cards are helpful, the teacher's testing approach should determine how you study. For the most part, students are either asked to write vocabulary words or write definitions. Therefore, flash cards are a good way to collect the vocabulary for study. Instead of practicing flash cards orally, you should use them to write the appropriate vocabulary words or the appropriate definitions or translations. That's especially important for improving foreign-language spelling. Many students lose points on tests because they've spelled words incorrectly or left off accent marks. They feel frustrated because they knew the words but didn't get credit because of their spelling. That happens mainly because they've studied orally and haven't studied in the way that helps them memorize correct spelling. Here's a real case example:

> Jordan, a college junior, had decided to major in Russian. This decision came only after much vacillation and uncertainty. Now that he was absolutely certain of his direction, he discovered that although he enjoyed his Russian studies, his grades were not sufficiently high to permit his admission into the Russian major program. He had only one semester to achieve the necessary grade point average.
>
> We discussed how much time he was putting into his studies and what methods he was using to study the language. He was using flash cards for memorization, but spelling errors on exams were lowering his grades. Jordan implemented the "studying in writing" plan I recommended for foreign languages and came in only once more to see me. His confident smile paired with a notebook filled with pages of written vocabulary made it

clear that we had little else to discuss. Jordan would easily be admitted to the Russian program.

**Finding Ideas.** You may feel frustrated when you are asked to write a composition or do a social studies or science project and find it difficult to get started. You may wait until the last minute and sometimes even avoid doing the assignments because you feel so overwhelmed. Students often tell me that they have spent lots of time thinking of how to get started but haven't been able to come up with a good idea. Sometimes they even ask their parents for topics. Parents frequently respond with suggestions that they feel are appropriate. However, you may not like your parents' ideas and may even feel angry at them because they can't seem to help you. Even if your parents give you a good idea, because the idea was theirs, not yours, you don't want to use it. So, although your parents are really trying to be helpful, you find yourself feeling helpless and frustrated.

Students who are seeking good ideas criticize themselves continuously. They can't find ideas that they think are good enough, so they avoid getting started. Some children tell me that this happens

THE ROOTS OF PROCRASTINATION

especially in their strongest subject. For example, if they think they're good creative writers or very good in social studies or science, they feel particularly afraid to complete a project in that area. They're afraid the project won't be as good as it should be considering it's their known area of expertise. They're feeling pressure. An example of a plan you may use for coming up with ideas for special projects is in figure 3.5. Other systems procrastinators may find useful are included in figures 3.6 and 3.7.

**Organizational Skills.** Disorganization is a frequent symptom of underachievement syndrome. Most underachievers appear to be disorganized. For some, the disorganization shows itself in messy desks, messy papers, and messy rooms. Others seem unable to plan their time and thus hand assignments in late or not at all. Concomitant with the disorganization patterns are excuses that may not be entirely honest, such as "I forgot," "I didn't know I had any homework," "I didn't know today was the deadline," or "I thought I had already completed the assignment." Although some students will admit that such statements are excuses, others will swear that the statements are honest. They seem like declarations of opposition to organization and commitments to nonconformity.

Two main parenting styles seem to foster disorganization patterns. One style advocates a disorganized lifestyle. The parents value disorganization as synonymous with freedom and creativity and assert openly that they prefer a disorganized lifestyle. Their children emulate them and never learn organizational techniques. Disorganization feels natural, right, and creative and remains a preferred approach to daily life for the whole family.

Although it is true that many creative people appear from the outside to live in disordered environments, that appearance is, in a sense, an illusion. Although creative people aren't usually rigid and do tolerate ambiguity well, their real skill is in organizing chaos. They're frequently very detail-oriented in their final product. Modeling organizational strategies and allowing time for organizational tasks will be helpful to your children. Reasonable strategies won't deter creativity and will enhance children's effective learning in school.

The second parenting style is much more common and more difficult to identify. In this family situation, one parent uses disor-

Figure 3.5

# Idea-Finding Plan for a Science Project

1. Gather up your science book from school and science books around the house. Take them up to your desk in your room.
2. Get pencils and pad.
3. Leaf through books, and daydream a bit about ideas you see.
4. Write down any possible project ideas: they can be silly; they can be hard; they can be impossible; they can seem dumb.
5. Don't criticize any of your ideas; just keep writing.
6. Try combining ideas.
7. Borrow ideas from books or pictures or other kids.
8. Remember, don't criticize any ideas.
9. If you run out of ideas from books, look around the room; you may see some more. Look out the window to find more ideas. *Anything* can be on your list.
10. Write down at least thirty ideas before you stop.
11. Now go back and look over the list.
12. Cross out the ones that don't interest you or seem truly impossible.
13. Leave four or five ideas on your list that look pretty good. Try combining some of your ideas.
14. Now come up with plans for those four or five ideas.
15. Bring your plans to Dad and Mom and have a little meeting. They can hear all about your plans and help you if you need a little. I know you'll be able to find ideas this way because I've tried it, and it really works.
16. Set a schedule for the completion of your projects. Be sure to include some extra time.
17. Make a list of the parts of your assignment and check off each item as you finish it.

Children who are taught techniques for idea production begin to incorporate these approaches into their general thinking and develop the confidence that dissipates passivity and perfectionism. Encourage these techniques by teaching them and by personally modeling them. Incorporate them into your own problem-solving approaches.

SOURCE: *Why Bright Kids Get Poor Grades and What You Can Do About It* by S. B. Rimm (New York: Crown Publishing Group, 1995).

Figure 3.6

# Tips for Procrastinators

- Allow more time than you think a project will take; for example, if you think a writing assignment or report will take two hours, give yourself three or even four hours to do it.
- Set realistic goals, but don't set them in stone. Stay flexible.
- Break down big and intimidating projects into smaller, more doable ones.
- Remove distractions from your workplace. Keep food, TV, magazines, games, and other temptations out of your way.
- Keep a list of backup projects, things you mean to do when you have time. Once you've made tips 1–9 part of your life, you will have the time to do them!
- Plan to have fun without feeling guilty. Start with the things you enjoy most, the things you usually save for last and don't get around to at all. Then add the things you're supposed to do.
- Reward yourself after each accomplishment, large or small.
- Begin your day with your most difficult task. The rest of the day will seem easy by comparison.
- Make a conscious effort to realize that your paper, project, or whatever can't be perfect. Accepting this helps deflate fear of a failure.
- Keep a diary of your progress. List the things you accomplish each day. Read it over from time to time and feel proud of what you've done.

SOURCE: "10 Tips for Procrastinators," excerpt from *Perfectionism: What's Bad About Being Too Good* by Miriam Adderholdt-Elliott (Minneapolis, Minn.: Free Spirit Publishing, Inc., 1987).

ganization as a passive-aggressive power play in an oppositional marriage. One parent is typically a perfectionist, or very well organized, and apparently the more powerful parent. The second parent can't assertively or rationally deal with his or her sense of powerlessness, so he or she uses passive-aggressive techniques like forgetting things, not preparing things on time, not accomplishing requested tasks, and ignoring responsibilities. Although this spouse feels powerless, he or she may be viewed as powerful by one or more of the children. Those children will emulate the passive-aggressive parent in opposing the demanding, more structured parent. Disorganization relative to schoolwork becomes a weapon for them. Here's an example:

---

Figure 3.7

# How to Plan a Long-Term Assignment and Fight Procrastination

- Determine how many study days remain between today and the due date for the assignments; for example, fifteen days.
- Divide the assignment into fifteen parts (or the number of days remaining). Students may need help in dividing the assignment, but here's an example:
    - 5 days—library research and note cards
    - 1 day—organizing note cards
    - 2 days—forming an outline, three sections to outline
    - 3 days—writing one section a day
    - 2 days—revisions and changes
    - 1 day—preparing final draft
    - 1 day—extra day in case needed
- Students should now describe each part of the assignment in their assignment notebook for each day it is to be accomplished.
- One or two extra days should be left over should any part of the assignment take longer than expected.

Source: *Why Bright Kids Get Poor Grades and What You Can Do About It* by S.B. Rimm (New York: Crown Publishing Group, 1995).

---

Molly was a senior in high school and had underachieved for years. She had made sufficient progress to be accepted into college, but both her parents were worried about her organizational skills. When I asked her if she was more like her mom or her dad, she cheerfully acknowledged she was more like her dad. Mom was always trying to organize him, too, but he knew what he was doing, and despite the mess in her room, she also believed she knew where everything was. However, she didn't and neither did her dad. He admitted his problem; Molly didn't and only copied his behavior.

PARENT
POINTER

Living with a small amount of chaos or ambiguity can be healthy and can contribute to creativity and a noncompulsive lifestyle. Conversely, rigidity and perfectionism can interfere with school and life achievement. **Reasonable structure and organization are**

**necessary to school and life accomplishment,** but moderation is more effective than extremes. **Parents should take the initiative to model and teach reasonable organizational techniques as they relate to home and school responsibilities.**

PARENT POINTER

**Children should always be advised to adopt techniques for remembering assignments. Let your children choose the organizational technique they prefer,** but talk through the process with them. Help them plan organizational strategies by asking these questions:

PARENT POINTER

- Where will you write your assignments?
- Where will you store papers to be completed?
- Where will you place your work that is already completed?
- How will you remember which books and papers should come home?
- How will you remember which books and papers should go back to school?
- How will you carry books and papers to and from school?

If children help to choose or invent the strategies, they often get more personally involved in their good habits. **Set an example by making lists for your own organizational purposes,** and advise children to adapt or make up their own methods for reinforcing their memory of school responsibilities. Figures 3.8 and 3.9 give some techniques to help your child become organized and to remember assignments.

PARENT POINTER

## ANXIETIES AND DISABILITIES

Your children may have deficits in basic skills that are cause for real concern. When a child has a deficit in a particular skill, the teacher often asks the parents to help children practice, which is almost always disastrous. All parents who work with their children in a deficient area feel considerable anxiety, which they can easily convey to their children. I was first alerted to this by a fourth-grade boy who said, "How come my mom gets so tense when I read to her?" Insisting that a child read aloud to a parent can be a daily lesson in reading anxiety. A parent teaching a child who is having problems with math may provide a daily lesson in math anxiety. These par-

---

Figure 3.8

# Sample Contract for Organization

David, his mom, and Dr. Rimm have agreed to the following organizational plan:

- Folders that are labeled for subjects; one side for unfinished work, the other side for completed papers.
- Folders reviewed and cleaned out once a week.
- Hanging organizer for locker.
- Braided bracelet for reminders of after-school responsibilities.
- Bring *all* folders home every night.

*David*
*Mom*
*Dr. Rimm*

---

ents unintentionally convey their own anxiety to their children. Taking anxiety out of learning is a high priority.

PARENT POINTER

**Writing (Pencil) Anxieties.** For children with writing anxieties, word-processing and "speeding" exercises enhance confidence (see figure 3.10). **Using fine-line markers is better than ballpoint pens.** Children don't have to apply as much pressure and find they can write faster and more smoothly.

Children have repeatedly shown dramatic improvement through the use of computers. Children may use simple word-processing programs as early as the first grade and should be encouraged to do as much written work on the computer as possible. Don't require them to learn keyboarding first, and don't require them to write a rough draft by hand—those will only serve as hurdles. **Let them go directly to the computer and "hunt and peck" any way they prefer.** Word processors give children a wonderful sense of control over their writing, particularly since many children nowadays have been comfortable with computers from their preschool years.

PARENT POINTER

Once children have learned to use the word processor, they may wish to write a family or class newsletter. Interviewing family members or writing funny stories and putting them into newsletter form

Figure 3.9

# Suggestions for Helping Students Remember Assignments

- Don't use small assignment notebooks. They almost always get lost.
- Assignment notebooks can be full-size spiral notebooks. Each day's assignments can be on a fresh page. The page is torn out when all assignments are complete. The advantages are (1) the notebook is less likely to be lost because of size, (2) the child derives satisfaction from tearing out completed pages and showing them to parents or teachers, (3) the new assignments are always on the top page. One disadvantage is that it's somewhat wasteful of paper.
- Teachers sometimes prepare special assignment forms for children to be placed in their loose-leaf notebook. They should assign time at the end of the day for children to copy assignments in the appropriate place and gather necessary books.
- Some children find it helpful to use double-sided folders for each subject. Unfinished work goes on one side. Completed work is saved in the other side. On the weekend, children review their folder, save what they need, and toss the rest.
- Children can create their own assignment-reminder strategies. Some children are very inventive, and when they invest themselves in their own devices, they're more likely to remain committed.
- Assignment notebooks that students consider cool are more apt to be used.

will increase your children's writing skills, decrease their anxiety, and encourage them to love writing.

**Creative Writing. Children who have difficulty writing a story should be encouraged to talk through the story first by talking to themselves or to a cassette recorder.** Once they have told the story, they can move easily to writing a rough draft of it. Of course, they will need further drafts to improve the story before handing it to their teachers.

PARENT
POINTER

**Reading Anxieties.** Children with reading anxiety rush through reading and guess at words based on initial consonants and context clues. They don't have the confidence to sound out words phonet-

THE TEACHER ASKED ME TO HELP

ically. The recommendations in figure 3.11 will help these children at home and school. These recommendations will do no harm even if your child is dyslexic.

**Math and Spatial Disabilities.** A small number of students who come to my clinic seem to exhibit spatial disabilities. They seem to have difficulty remembering visual images and understanding how they fit together. Low scores in Block Design and Object Assembly on the WISC-III *(Weschler Intelligence Scales for Children—3rd Edition)* are characteristic of these children. Schoolwork that seems especially difficult for such children includes telling time, using money, geometry, math story problems, reading maps and geography, math-related science, and interpreting diagrams.

I recommend the following games and activities to enhance spatial skills: puzzles, Legos, blocks, TV games, tangrams, cards (War, Go Fish, etc.), Concentration, dominoes, checkers, chess, Chinese checkers, Monopoly, money games, and board games. They can be played at home or at school. However, don't be surprised if your children with spatial disabilities aren't fond of these activities. They tend to find them difficult, so a few minutes a day may be all you

## Figure 3.10

# Speeding

Many dependent children write slowly. It is impossible to determine the chicken/egg relationship here—whether slow writing encourages parental attention to dependency or dependent children write slower because they are less confident. Nevertheless, increasing writing speed is a goal worth pursuing. This can be accomplished using a personal self-competition model and can be applied to copying written material or to doing math facts. The necessary materials include a digital watch and multiple sheets of the same math facts or written material to copy. Children copy the first material and set a baseline time that can be recorded on an old calendar. The next day they write the same material again and mark their time. For each time they beat their earlier time, they can earn points or stickers. Writing the same material every day may get boring, but they will soon find that they can write much faster. The selections they choose for writing should be shorter or longer depending on their age and skill level and can be varied every week or two.

The same approach can be used for helping kids learn math facts. Begin with easier facts and do the same page for a whole week. Many dependent children become tense during timed tests. They will become much more relaxed about timed tests if timing themselves becomes a daily habit.

can expect. Try to keep them fun so the children's anxiety doesn't increase. Recent research has found that exposure to music and studying the musical keyboard during preschool years also improves spatial skills.

A diagnostic tutor in mathematics can tell you whether your child has difficulty understanding mathematics or if the problem is caused by anxiety or carelessness. If the problem is anxiety, goal-directed tutoring in mathematics can probably relieve it. Once these children have proven that they can catch up in skills, they will have built up sufficient confidence to go on independently. Tutoring should be temporary for these students, or they will become dependent on one-to-one instruction. Tutoring shouldn't be done by parents or siblings, although in a few cases an older brother or sister may be helpful. The tutoring should stop as soon as children feel caught up, but they should be encouraged to let you know if they still want occasional help.

Figure 3.11

# Tips to Reduce Reading Anxiety

Reading is a first-priority subject for comfortable learning in the classroom. If children struggle with learning to read, the rest of the educational process will be considerably more difficult. Here are some special recommendations for children with reading problems that will help parents and teachers guide children toward self-confidence and independence despite their difficulties.

- Family reading should begin in infancy and extend throughout life. There are no age limits on family reading. Reading together either aloud or silently creates an atmosphere in which children are more likely to love books.
- Children should not be made to read aloud to their parents, because the parents' anxieties about their children's reading may be conveyed to the children. Most parents feel tense when poor readers read aloud to them. Children may, of course, read aloud if they choose to do so.
- Parents should read aloud to their children as long as the children enjoy it (eighth grade is not too old).
- Children should be permitted to stay up half an hour later at night if they're in their beds reading to themselves (children don't usually like to sleep; it's adults who do).
- Encourage children to read whatever they like (within reason) before bedtime. Don't insist they read grade-level material. Comics, cartoons, sports magazines, easy material, and books they have read multiple times are all good. If they love reading, they will expand their interests as their reading improves.
- Encourage children to read stories while listening to tapes of the stories. Don't hover over them to be sure they're actually reading; they will eventually read.
- Be an example by keeping a book around that your children see you enjoying. Newspapers and magazines will also serve well.
- Encourage children to read to their younger siblings, provided those siblings aren't better readers than they are. They can read to younger children in school as well.
- Visit and browse through libraries with your children.
- When shopping, stop by bookstores and browse and purchase books.
- Monitor TV watching and limit video games. If limiting these becomes a power struggle, you may find using a TV plug lock* effective.
- If your child is having serious reading problems, ask your school psychologist or a private clinic to evaluate him or her for a reading disability. You may also want to have your child evaluated for a reading disability called scotopic sensitivity syndrome,* a biological disorder that is typically inherited. Scotopic sensitivity is helped dramatically by colored lenses.

Figure 3.11

## Tips to Reduce Reading Anxiety

- Don't read homework instructions to your children. If they don't understand, encourage them to read the instructions to themselves several times. Also suggest that they "whisper"-read them.
- If your children continue to require assistance in understanding assignments because of reading problems, tape-record the instructions and let them listen while they're reading them.
- Textbooks in such areas as social studies or science should be made available to poor readers on cassette tapes for simultaneous listening while reading.
- Don't unintentionally label poor readers negatively by talking about their problems to other adults within their hearing.
- Don't take responsibility for poor readers. Identify a means by which they can carry on activities independently by use of audio equipment instead of people.
- Encourage poor readers to become actively involved in drama and forensics. Mastery of verbal material will help build their confidence.
- Be patient and supportive. If your children continue to read without undue pressure, they will eventually master and learn to love reading.

*For more information about TV plug locks or scotopic sensitivity syndrome, see the resources list in the back of this book.
SOURCE: *How to Stop Underachievement Newsletter* 5, no. 1 (1994), by S. B. Rimm (Watertown, Wis.: Educational Assessment Service, Inc.).

**Learning Disabilities.** Some children actually have learning disabilities. Figure 3.12 will help you determine if your children are truly learning disabled or just dependent underachievers.

A general principle for guiding learning-disabled children is to find them techniques to compensate for their disability without depending on others. Word processors and tape recorders are appropriate for children with writing disabilities. Shortened assignments are appropriate where extensive writing could be a laborious task. Teachers may be helpful with adjustments to new methods. Permitting children to dictate materials or stories to a teacher or parent is inappropriate except in the case of very young children, because it encourages their dependence on someone else to complete assignments. Dictating tests to children or their dictating answers to teach-

Figure 3.12

# Ways to Discriminate between Dependence and Disability

| Dependence | Disability |
|---|---|
| 1. Child asks for explanations regularly despite differences in subject matter. | Child asks for explanations in particular subjects that are difficult. |
| 2. Child asks for explanation of instructions regardless of style used, either auditory or visual. | Child asks for explanations of instructions only when given in one instruction style, either auditory or visual, but not both. |
| 3. Child's questions are not specific to material but appear to be mainly to gain adult attention. | Child's questions are specific to material, and once process is explained, child works effficiently. |
| 4. Child is disorganized or slow in assignments but becomes much more efficient when a meaningful reward is presented as motivation. | Child's disorganization or slow pace continues despite motivating rewards. |
| 5. Child works only when an adult is nearby at school and/or at home. | Child works independently once process is clearly explained. |
| 6. Individually administered measures of ability indicate that the child is capable of learning the material. Individual tests improve with tester encouragement and support. Group measures may not indicate good abilities or skills. | Both individual and group measures indicate lack of specific abilities or skills. Tester encouragement has no significant effect on scores. |
| 7. Child exhibits "poor me" body language (tears, helplessness, pouting, copying) regularly when new work is presented. Teacher or adult attention eases the symptoms. | Child exhibits "poor me" body language only with instructions or assignments in specific disability areas and accepts challenges in areas of strength. |

Figure 3.12

# Ways to Discriminate Between Dependence and Disability

| DEPENDENCE | DISABILITY |
|---|---|
| 8. Parents report whining, complaining, attention getting, temper tantrums, and poor sportsmanship at home. | Although parents may find similar symptoms at home, they tend to be more sporadic than regular, particularly the whining and complaining. |
| 9. Child's "poor me" behavior appears only with one parent and not with the other; only with some teachers and not with others. With some teachers or with the other parent, the child functions fairly well independently. | Although the child's "poor me" behaviors may only appear with one parent or with solicitous teachers, performance is not adequate even when behavior is acceptable. |
| 10. Child learns only when given one-to-one instruction but will not learn in groups even when instructional mode is varied. | Although child may learn more quickly in a one-to-one setting, he/she will also learn efficiently in a group setting provided the child's disability is taken into consideration when instructions are given. |

Some children who are truly disabled have also become dependent. The key to distinguishing between disability and dependence is the children's responses to adult support. If the children perform only with adult support when new material is presented, they are too dependent, whether or not there is also a disability.

SOURCE: *Why Bright Kids Get Poor Grades and What You Can do About It* by S. B. Rimm (New York: Crown Publishing. Group, 1995).

ers also encourages dependence. However, if they can listen to test questions and answer them on audiotapes, children can feel much more independent while coping with their disability.

In the same way, reading while listening to a recording of the book is helpful and can even facilitate reading skills. Reading to themselves in a whisper or just reading aloud often helps children understand instructions or concepts better. Adults reading required lessons to children maintains dependent patterns and is not a good idea.

**Test Anxiety.** When children's test scores are consistently worse than they expect, they tend to become anxious at the thought of testing. Then they may find themselves forgetting material they've learned and understood. They may find it difficult to think during a test. Standardized tests can be even more frightening than classroom tests, and continued poor test performance perpetuates the cycle of anxiety.

Poor test performance is usually the result of poor study efforts and skills, but it can also be caused by too creative an approach to test taking. Creative thinkers often read more into questions than is intended, then provide answers that are unique and original but not at all what the teacher is looking for. The teacher may be looking for facts that seem too obvious to the student. Creative students often assume that teachers want unusual responses because these students think in unusual ways.

The study skills discussed thus far aim to make your children better students and also to help them view tests from a teacher's perspective so their creative interpretations don't interfere with good test performance. Figures 3.13 and 3.14 include some better approaches to taking objective tests and suggestions for handling text anxiety.

**Attention Deficit Disorders.** Dependent children are daydreamers and are sometimes diagnosed with attention deficit disorders (inattentive type). Their apparent inability to focus attention and concentrate causes them to absorb information poorly in the classroom and to have poor study skills. Their staring out the window, looking off into space, and restlessly moving hands and feet are annoyances to both parents and teachers. If they are engrossed in an activity, they do show complete concentration, and although this may happen infrequently, it does provide indisputable evidence that they're capable of paying attention.

PARENT
POINTER

As these children's motivation and goal direction improve, their attention span is likely to increase. **Involvement in intrinsically**

Figure 3.13

# Tips for Taking Objective Tests

There are many different kinds of objective tests—multiple-choice questions, true-false, fill-in-the-blank, matching tests, etc. True-false and fill-in-the-blank are the trickiest.

## TRUE-FALSE

- If *any* part of a statement is false, then *all* of the statement is false.
- Watch for absolute words like *all*, *none*, *only*, *always*, and *never*. They can be clues that an answer is false. Few things are "always" or "never" so.
- Watch for weasel words like *usually*, *generally*, *often*, *seldom*, *some*, and *may*. They can be clues that an answer is true.

## MULTIPLE-CHOICE

- Read each possible answer *with* the stem. This will help you focus on the right answer to the question you are given.

    *Example:*

| | |
|---|---|
| (Stem) | Many teenagers like: |
| (Possible answers) | A. to listen to loud music |
| | B. to wear clothes that are "in" |
| | C. to be on their own |
| | D. to go to parties |
| | E. all of the above |

You would read this question five ways:

A. (Many teenagers like) to listen to loud music.
B. (Many teenagers like) to wear clothes that are "in."
C. (Many teenagers like) to be on their own.
D. (Many teenagers like) to go to parties.
E. (Many teenagers like) all of the above.

- Read *all* choices before picking an answer. In the example above, A seems okay, but it's not the *best* answer. E is.
- Use the process of elimination. If you know that B, D, and E are wrong, then the answer must be A or C.

continued on next page

Figure 3.13 (continued)

## Tips for Taking Objective Tests

- When in doubt, guess. Your guess may be right; leaving a blank won't be. *Exception:* Some standardized tests have a penalty for guessing. Check with your teacher.
- If one choice is much longer than the rest, and it seems likely to be right, go with it. Longer answers tend to be right more often than shorter answers.
- If two of the choices are exact opposites, pick one of them.

*Example*

What happens when you add salt to water before boiling?

A. It makes the hydrogen in the water change to helium.
B. It makes the water boil faster.
C. It makes the water boil slower.
D. It turns to salt crystals.
E. Nothing happens.

B and C are opposites. Pick B.

- When you don't have a clue what the right answer is, pick C first. If you think C may be wrong, pick B or D. Teachers like to sandwich the right answer between other choices, so avoid A and E.

SOURCE: *School Power* by J. S. Schumm, Ph.D., and Marguerite Radencich, Ph.D. (Minneapolis, Minn.: Free Spirit Publishing, Inc., 1992).

**rewarding activities also enhances their concentration.** However, parents and teachers may want to devise some special signals for assisting children in paying attention.

Explaining the importance of eye contact for communicating is one effective means of improving children's attention to a teacher's oral instructions. Teachers can also arrange a secret signal to assist children in looking directly at them while the teacher is speaking. For example, if the teacher touches her eye or eyeglasses or taps the desk with a ruler, that signal may help the willing child who is attempting to improve concentration. **It's only effective if the signal is considered a secret between the teacher and child.** It will cause children to feel as if the teacher is constantly noticing them.

PARENT
POINTER

Figure 3.14

# Suggestions for Relieving Test Anxiety

### BEFORE THE TEST

- Study regularly, using tips in this book.
- Don't cram the night before, but do review.
- Go to bed early; wake up in plenty of time.
- Dress for success; make sure you look confident.

### DURING THE TEST

**SELF-PRAISE:** Tell yourself you've studied well and can therefore do your best.
**OVERVIEW:** Look over the test; answer questions you know first to gain confidence.
**BECOME INVOLVED:** Concentrate on the actual questions and not on your grade.
**IMAGINE:** If you feel too tense, close your eyes for a few seconds and imagine a pleasant, restful scene like a beach, sunset, or park.
**BREATHE:** Take a few deep breaths and concentrate on breathing.
**RELAX:** Tighten up those muscles that feel tense, then relax them one at a time.
**DON'T RUSH:** Don't get tense if others finish before you. Use all your time. Fast does not mean smart.

Attention deficit–hyperactivity disorder (ADHD) can be caused biologically, environmentally, or both. There is no biological test for diagnosing this disorder, although scientists are trying to develop one. Rating scales, such as the *Conners' Rating Scales* or the Achenbach *Child Behavior Checklist for Ages 4–18,*[1] are based on the descriptions given in the *Diagnostic and Statistical Manual of Mental Disorders* (4th ed.) and are used for diagnoses. Figure 3.15 includes some of the main characteristics of ADHD. **Six of these characteristics, which must have originated before the age of seven,** are required to qualify children for each diagnosis. These characteristics **should be present in at least two settings;** for example, home and school. Of course, actual diagnosis of attention deficit disorders should be done by professionals who are qualified and experienced.

PARENT POINTER

Although parenting inconsistencies almost always accompany ADHD, **this does not mean that ADHD is caused by poor parenting.** However, high-energy children are especially difficult to rear, so good parents may require some special assistance.

PARENT POINTER

Figure 3.15

# Characteristics of Attention Deficit–Hyperactivity Disorder

314.00 ATTENTION DEFICIT–HYPERACTIVITY DISORDER, PREDOMINANTLY INATTENTIVE TYPE*

A. Often fails to give close attention to details or makes careless mistakes in schoolwork, work, or other activities.
B. Often has difficulty sustaining attention in tasks or play activities.
C. Often does not seem to listen when spoken to directly.
D. Often does not follow through on instructions and fails to finish schoolwork, chores, or duties in the workplace (not due to oppositional behavior or failure to understand instructions).
E. Often has difficulty organizing tasks and activities.
F. Often avoids, dislikes, or is reluctant to engage in tasks that require sustained mental effort (such as schoolwork or homework).
G. Often loses things necessary for tasks or activities (e.g., toys, school assignments, pencils, books, or tools).
H. Is often easily distracted by extraneous stimuli.
I. Is often forgetful in daily activities.

314.01 ATTENTION DEFICIT–HYPERACTIVITY DISORDER, PREDOMINANTLY HYPERACTIVE-IMPULSE TYPE*

**Hyperactivity**
A. Often fidgets with hands or feet or squirms in seat.
B. Often leaves seat in classroom or in other situations in which remaining seated is expected.
C. Often runs about or climbs excessively in situations in which it is inappropriate (in adolescents or adults, may be limited to subjective feelings of restlessness).
E. Is often "on the go" or often acts as if "driven by a motor."
F. Often talks excessively.

**Impulsivity**
G. Often blurts out answers before questions have been completed.
H. Often has difficulty awaiting turn.
I. Often interrupts or intrudes on others (e.g., butts into conversations or games).

*Must show at least six characteristics that have begun before age seven.
Source: *Diagnostic and Statistical Manual of Mental Disorders*, 4th ed.

Stimulant medications, such as methylphenidate (trade name Ritalin), are often prescribed for children with attention disorders. At this time ADHD is often overdiagnosed, and Ritalin may be overprescribed. Don't hurry to your physician to ask for medication, even if your children's characteristics match those on the list. **Try behavioral changes first. Ritalin can have serious effects and should only be used under the careful supervision of a physician.** Although side effects occur in fewer than 50 percent of the children using it, Ritalin, or any other stimulant, should not be taken freely. For some children, these medications are dramatically helpful in both calming them and heightening their ability to concentrate. On the other hand, many other children are helped without medication.

PARENT
POINTER

Only a small percentage of children with symptoms of ADHD require medication. Telling children that drugs will make them feel better may convince them even when they don't need them. Here's a case example:

Taylor, a second-grader, was restless and inattentive in class. His teacher recommended he be assessed for attention deficit–hyperactivity disorder, and Ritalin was recommended by a psychiatrist. The teacher observed improved concentration, and Taylor told me that the Ritalin had improved his handwriting.

After counseling with Taylor's parents, he began the new school year without medication. The new teacher noticed no attention problems for Taylor, who no longer seemed to require Ritalin. A sample of Taylor's handwriting without medication showed his work to be as legible and neat as it had been with the medication.

**Blind-controlled tests are best for determining if children require medication.** However, research reminds us that a positive response to Ritalin doesn't confirm ADHD. Normal children's responses to Ritalin can be similar to those of children with ADHD.[2] Most important, ADHD children who are taking Ritalin and their parents should also receive behavioral help. Figures 3.16 and 3.17 include some tips I provide to parents who have young children with ADHD symptoms to use for themselves and to give to their children's teachers.

PARENT
POINTER

Figure 3.16

# Important Suggestions for Home Encouragement for Children with Behavior Problems or ADHD

- Positive support between both parents is critical. Children should not be hearing arguments or disagreements on how to handle them. There is no one right way to parent, so doing it the other parent's way, even if you don't like it, is better than children's hearing either of you criticize the other parent. Overt disagreements will both overempower children and make them feel insecure.
- Suggested indoor activities include reading to your children, talking with them, answering questions, doing puzzles, and playing games together. Playing for some time alone imaginatively, listening to children's music, and dancing are also excellent for improving children's concentration. Dot-to-dot books, coloring, and writing are excellent for small-muscle coordination.
- Time-outs should be used for aggressive behavior like hitting or kicking. See page 41 for a description of time-out.
- Praise your children's kindness, good manners, sensitivity, helpfulness, and perseverance. Praise sets expectations for children. Use praise words that reflect your realistic values for your children.
- Children thrive on one-to-one work projects with a parent.
- Minimize roughhousing and rough talk. When you play with or teach children something, consider how it will sound or look in their school environment. What can seem like fun wrestling may look like aggressive behavior in school. Sports activities generalize well to school.
- Eliminate TV violence as much as possible. Actually television watching should be confined to a few hours of children's shows and no more than two videos a week. Research tells us that television viewing one and a half hours before bedtime interferes with sleep.
- Try to stay firm but as positive as possible. Follow through on threats, but stop and think before you threaten, so you don't get a negative punishing environment.
- Never refer to your children as your "ADHD kids" either directly or referentially. It will cause them to feel they have no control over their inappropriate behaviors.

Figure 3.17

# Teacher Suggestions for Children with Behavior Problems or ADHD

1. Use *moderate* praise words to encourage your children when you find them behaving well. The praise should be geared to the characteristics you're trying to encourage, e.g., gentle, kind, caring, sharing, good thinking, loving, good helper, persevering, good concentration, creative thinking, etc. Extreme praise is not helpful.
2. Inappropriate behavior should be handled privately. Overt negative comments will only trigger more negative behavior. I realize that it isn't always possible to ignore or signal children privately without drawing negative attention, but it will be helpful.
3. Check my book *Why Bright Kids Get Poor Grades* for instructions when to use time-out in the classroom (p. 364). It's helpful to explain to children when they're in a good frame of mind about how you plan to use time-out. You can also permit them to use time-out voluntarily if they feel as if they need a little time to themselves. Quietly escorting them to time-out will be appropriate if they're out of control. Be sure that they understand that it is your way of helping them to get themselves under control and that it won't be for very long. If the child has hurt another, have them apologize to the child privately after time-out.
4. It's also possible to use a sticker or star system for children for good days. The stickers can be awarded at home where they can be placed on a calendar or in a sticker book so children can see their improvement. Again, this sticker system should be private with absolutely no class attention. Don't ask the class to help the child with his problems. It seems to make children's problems worse.
5. Using positive signals is another helpful way to encourage children's concentration. Explain to the child that you're watching how well he's concentrating and paying attention. When you notice him working hard, you might wink your eye at him or scratch your head (pick one). Although no one else will know, he'll know that you've noticed his good behavior. He will feel as if you're watching for his good behavior and it should increase.

Here's a case example of how these tips can help a child:

Brian had been asked to leave a Catholic school kindergarten unless he
was put on Ritalin because the teacher was frustrated with his behavior
and was certain he had ADHD. He would fight with other children on the
playground, hit others in the class, and moved from task to task without
completing anything well. Brian's parents brought him to see me for an
all-day appointment.

It was immediately apparent that Brian was tall for his age, highly en-
ergetic, and quite aggressive. He was attentive during our conversation
and very verbal. He explained that his favorite thing to do with his dad
was wrestling, and sometimes he could almost pin his dad. He also loved
jumping up and down on his bed as if it were a trampoline. He said he
was older than his cousins and could protect them if anyone wanted to
hurt them, and he acknowledged that he enjoyed fighting on the playground because he could beat up most of the kids unless the big kids
picked on him. He told me that he was a lot like his dad, and that his dad
got in trouble in school, too, when he was little. He said his mom was a lot
easier than his dad. He said when his dad told him to stop, he'd better do
it, but if his mom told him to, sometimes his dad told his mom she was
too strict with him. In my brief conversation with Brian, this bright, verbal
child conveyed the many mixed messages he was receiving.

Brian's parents told me that Brian had been the first and only grandson on both sides of the family for quite a while before his other brother
and cousins were born. Aunts, uncles, and grandparents had nicknamed
him "the little devil" and freely referred to him that way. His dad, a highly
successful businessman, acknowledged he had been much like Brian as a
child, and both parents shared with me their many disagreements about
discipline. Dad assumed that "boys will be boys," and Mom tried to set
limits firmly and found that Brian totally ignored her rules. She admitted
he was a delightful child if he and she were alone together but extremely
difficult with her if his brother or his dad was around.

While I was talking to Brian's parents, I noticed him sneaking upstairs
to listen to our conversation, and I immediately demonstrated some referential speaking. I changed the conversation quite suddenly and mentioned
that I had noticed Brian had excellent manners. Brian arose from the stair-
well and in his most polite tone asked if he could please have a glass of
water. When his parents and I agreed that he could, he thanked us politely

and quietly walked downstairs. His parents were astonished at the effectiveness of my referential speaking.

I reviewed with his parents the suggestions for parents and teachers one step at a time. They realized how Brian's problem was perpetuating itself. Certainly there may have been some genetic propensities to high energy, but Brian is a much better behaved child now, and he does not require medication. His parents are getting better at the teamwork necessary for guiding their high-energy son, who had been a king (and a little devil) before he was dethroned by siblings and cousins.

Before you decide that medication is the answer to your child's behaviors and concentration problems at home and school, ask yourself these questions.[3]

1. Do you and your child's other parent(s) disagree on how to discipline your child?
2. Do you frequently find yourself being negative and angry with your child?
3. Do you lose your temper often and then apologize and hug your child afterward?
4. Do you find yourself in continuous power struggles with your child after which you feel quite helpless?
5. Do you find yourself sitting with your child to help with schoolwork because it wasn't finished in school and your child can't concentrate at home?
6. Do you find yourself disorganized and out of control much of the time?
7. Does your child spend two hours or more a day in front of the television or computer?
8. Is your workload so overwhelming that you have little time for quality parent-child time?
9. Does your child concentrate well in areas of special interest or high motivation?
10. Is your child's schoolwork too easy or too difficult?
11. Is your child involved in appropriate out-of-school activities for energy release?
12. Does your child function well in competition?

If your answer is yes to most of the first ten questions and no to the last two, your child's symptoms of attention disorders can likely be improved by home and school adjustments. More effective parenting and school changes will help you and your child and, unlike medication, will cause no negative side effects.

As always, helping parents and schools work with this challenging generation of children can make a great difference and help us to avoid medicating high-energy, intense children automatically. Some children require medication to improve their concentration, but the National Association of School Psychologists recommends that medication be considered only after appropriate home and school interventions are attempted for a reasonable time. The NASP's position statement regarding students with attention deficits can be found in the appendix of this book.

Although food allergies and additives have not been found to cause attention deficit disorders, some children definitely exhibit ADHD-like symptoms rooted in allergies. If there is a history of allergies in the family, it's certainly worth checking with an allergist to determine if an allergy is the cause. Here's another case example:

> Sally, a bright first-grader, seemed to be having difficulty sitting in her seat during work time at school. She tended to wander around talking to friends, and her work was incomplete. During a parent assessment, I asked if the family had a history of allergies. The parents acknowledged there were, but Sally had not shown symptoms of allergies. An evaluation by an allergist revealed that Sally was allergic to milk, her breakfast drink of choice. Eliminating milk from Sally's diet quickly restored Sally to a quiet, capable student who concentrated on her school tasks.

Finally, it is important to emphasize that some children improve their concentration and behavior dramatically with the use of Ritalin. The improvement facilitates parenting and teaching, and for those children, achievement and self-esteem increase. Some children only require medication temporarily, while others seem to benefit throughout adolescence and into adulthood.

PARENT
POINTER

**Behavioral approaches that will help these children include all the suggestions given in this book.** Time-outs, united parenting, and firm consistency are important. Redirecting children's energy toward constructive activities is a high priority. However, overscheduling can cause problems for these children. They require structure and consistent expectations. Too hurried a pace will cause stress for them and for you and will lead to overreaction and impulsiveness.

Parents with ADHD children need support. Parent support groups and regular counseling are helpful. Some adolescents and adults continue to have ADHD symptoms. Others seem to outgrow the problems. The right home and school environments make an important difference for children with ADHD.

## MORNING, NOON, AND NIGHT

You may wonder why routines that describe waking up in the morning, eating meals, and putting children to bed at night are included under habits and routines for parenting for achievement. Imagine children who are awakened by parents in the morning half a dozen times, scolded to get up, nagged to get dressed, scolded to eat breakfast, reminded to get their school books ready, and nagged again to get out to the bus. As these children enter school, they have already fallen into a nag-dependent pattern. They feel negative about themselves and have learned that other people will take responsibility for them. That pattern will be generalized into the classroom, and these children will expect teachers to take responsibility for them throughout their day. Therefore, home nagging leads to school nagging, and that's why I've included the discussion of morning, mealtime, and nighttime routines in this book. Of course, if you have other more effective routines for your children, you needn't change what you're doing. These routines are only intended for families where the parents are often nagging now.

**Morning Routine.** Routines are more effective if they are arranged so that a natural positive consequence occurs at the end of a sequence of required activities; for example, morning responsibilities are followed by breakfast, which means children don't eat breakfast until their obligations are accomplished. **Be as positive as possible when you explain these routines.** For example, "I'm looking forward to breakfast together" is a better statement than "If you don't do your chores, there's no breakfast." Parents and children may

PARENT POINTER

NAG-FREE MORNING

make a list of morning responsibilities together and hang them on the bathroom mirror as a reminder. Some children may even prefer checklists, and preschoolers who don't read may use pictorial reminders. When you establish these routines, you move the responsibility from (nagging) parent to child. Figure 3.18 gives an example of bad and good morning routines.

**Mealtimes.** Difficulties during meals are often inspired by negative attention. If mealtime behavior is inappropriate, timing your children out until after the meal can be effective. They may then eat the *cold* meal *alone*. Don't feel sorry for them—you needn't feel at all guilty because their meal awaits them. Even if they skip a meal, they won't starve (contrary to the belief of some parents). When you establish clear expectations for proper behavior at mealtime, behavior will improve. Continued power struggles over eating are much more harmful than occasional time-outs. Be calm, but not picky. Dessert and evening snacks come only after a reasonable meal is consumed. These old-fashioned rewards are still effective.

Sometimes picky eaters have arrived at their pickiness because parents have given them too many choices and too much power.

Figure 3.18

# Morning Routine #1

(DEPENDENT)

**MOM:** Bobby, are you up?

**BOBBY:** *(No answer)*

**MOM:** Bobby, it's time to get up!

**BOBBY:** Um—awfully tired—a few more minutes.

**MOM:** Bobby, you better get up, you'll miss the bus! *(Repeated with increasing volume three to ten times)*

That's only the beginning. Admonitions to wash face, brush teeth, eat breakfast, hurry, wear different clothes, remember lunch money, schoolbooks, notes, and finally warnings about the soon-to-arrive school bus or car pool add to the din. Arguments between siblings on bathroom use, clothes exchange, and breakfast choices punctuate the distressing beginning of the day. If two parents are awake, interparent debate about the degree of nagging reinforces the hassled start to each new morning.

# Morning Routine #2

(INDEPENDENT)

**STEP 1:** Announce to your children one at a time the guidelines for the new beginning. From this day forth they will be responsible for getting themselves ready for school. Your job will be to await them at the breakfast table for a pleasant morning chat.

**STEP 2:** Preparations the night before will include the laying out of their clothes and getting their books ready in their book bags. An evening checklist will let them prepare without your help. They should set the alarm early enough to allow plenty of morning time. They will feel just as tired at 7 A.M. as they will at 6:30, but the earlier start will prevent their usual rush.

**STEP 3:** Children wake themselves up (absolutely no calls from others), wash, dress, and pick up their room. A morning checklist can help them to remember each task. Breakfast comes only when they are ready for school. Absolutely *no* nagging!

**STEP 4:** Parent *waits* at the breakfast table and is not anywhere around them prior to their meal together. Then, enjoy a pleasant family breakfast and conversation about the day ahead!

**STEP 5:** (Optional) If the children are ready early and enjoy TV, they can watch until it's time to leave.

continued on next page

Figure 3.18 (continued)

## Morning Routine #2
(INDEPENDENT)

QUESTION: What happens if they don't dress in time for breakfast?
ANSWER: No breakfast. (That will only happen two or three times for children who like to eat.)
QUESTION: What happens if my children don't like to eat breakfast?
ANSWER: Fifteen minutes of TV after breakfast, when they're ready for school, will probably be an effective incentive.
QUESTION: What happens if they don't get up?
ANSWER: They miss school and stay in their room all day (that will happen no more than once), or you drive them to school and they pay you for taxi fare out of their allowance or they ride their bikes or walk. They deal with the school consequence of being late. Don't write them notes to excuse them.
QUESTION: What happens if they don't have enough time in the morning?
ANSWER: They go to bed thirty minutes earlier and set the alarm thirty minutes earlier until they find the right amount of time necessary for independent mornings.
QUESTION: Does this routine work?
ANSWER: Absolutely, with elementary-aged children; they hate to miss school. Sometimes, with high school students.

SOURCE: *Why Bright Kids Get Poor Grades and What You Can Do About It* by S. B. Rimm (New York: Crown Publishing Group, 1995).

After all, many of us associate food with love, so parents often worry about depriving their children of food and love. Here are a few illustrative cases:

## Case 1

Miriam was six months old. As her grandmother (me) fed cereal to her, she moved her head to the side. Grandmom's spoon followed. Miriam led. Grandmom followed. "Why?" thought Grandmom to herself. "I'm not hungry, she is." New design. Grandmom stopped following and just held the spoon. Miriam was hungry and Miriam ate. Miriam stopped turning her head; that game wasn't working. Notice Miriam's age was six months—yes, that early.

## Case 2

Mother gave the children choices for lunch. Stephen liked peanut butter sandwiches. He ate peanut butter sandwiches daily. However, dinner had a more prescribed and well-balanced menu. One day Stephen tried peanut butter power: "Mom, I don't like ravioli. How about if I make a peanut butter sandwich?" Mom thought that was better than arguing, and it was Stephen's choice. Soon, Stephen chose peanut butter sandwiches two days a week, then three days.

Mom caught on to Stephen, and one day she announced, "I'm afraid you'll turn into a peanut butter sandwich, so I'm changing the choices. At lunch, you choose. At dinner, I choose. At lunch, it can be peanut butter. At dinner, it's whatever everyone eats or nothing." That precipitated a bit of anger and a few time-outs, but Stephen got the idea and, after a few weeks of battle, discovered that there was more to dinner than peanut butter.

Although sometimes it seems that children are born as fussy eaters, in reality they usually become fussy eaters because they've been given too many choices. They've learned to wield power through their fussiness. It's natural for children to want to eat, although many children prefer simple foods repetitively.

Of course, I have no exact prescription for every family's mealtime. Some parents insist on children eating everything; others are just as happy if their children eat a reasonable amount and variety of food. Most important is that the adults at the table, including grandparents if they're present, don't constantly disagree or argue about children's food consumption and which manners are appropriate. Power struggles between parent and child, with the other parent providing an easy way out for the child, are an invitation to the problems I've already described and even to eating disorders. It's only when we teach our children to play power games with food that mealtimes become problematic.

**Try to keep mealtime pleasant. Give children reasonable choices. Remember that children should have small portions.** They can always ask for more, and you shouldn't become a short-

PARENT
POINTER

THIS IS NOT A RESTAURANT

order cook or cater to your children's whims. They can have more options when you take them to a restaurant.

**Bedtime.** Many children are extraordinarily talented in avoiding bedtime. Somehow that talent disappears by parenthood, and you're thus left finding yourselves more tired than your children each evening. If your children's talent at avoiding bedtime exceeds your ability to stay awake, you'll find yourselves without any private adult time. This delayed bedtime produces tired children during the day and discontented partners in a marriage. **Reasonable and consistent bedtimes produce happier adults and more alert, intelligent children.**

PARENT
POINTER

Although there's no exact time for children to be in bed, and their sleep needs may vary with their energy levels, the following suggestions will guide you in deciding bedtimes on school nights. Be flexible enough to consider your children's energy levels but firm enough to provide yourself with some adult time:

Preschool: 7:00–8:00, but may vary because of nap schedule
Grades K–2: 7:00–8:00

Grades 3–6: 7:30–9:00
Grades 7–12: 9:00–10:00

For the last group, particularly in senior high school, the ten-o'clock guideline means that children must be in their rooms, although not necessarily asleep. Of course, this schedule doesn't include weekends. If you follow the routine described in figure 3.19, you'll find that getting children to sleep is a pleasant ritual instead of a battle. Don't forget to turn the TV off early, or you'll find the bedtime struggle far more difficult, and I don't recommend ever placing a TV in a child's bedroom.

Bedtime fears become an issue only if you let them. Don't permit them to become an avoidance technique. If children are afraid or worried about ghosts, permit them to leave a hall light or night-light on. Finding a way for them to handle their fears without becoming dependent on a parent is important. That means that you don't go to sleep with them at night or tuck them into your bed or permit them to sleep on the living room sofa. Of course, an occasional exception is always acceptable. It also means that you don't spend a lot of time discussing their fears, although brief explanations can be reassuring. A light will serve to dispel all ghosts, and when they feel ready to be brave, they can turn it off.

Sometimes very young children manipulate parents into rocking them or carrying them around until they fall asleep. That *used* to be called "spoiling" a child, and it still *is* spoiling the child. Of course, there's nothing wrong with comforting or holding a child when he or she isn't well. All children should have plenty of hugs and cuddling. However, they should learn to fall asleep on a regular basis independently. This means that you will probably have to permit your children to cry themselves to sleep once or twice, which is usually all it takes. It's harder on you than it is on your children. Blankets, stuffed animals, or anything else that comforts them is fine, but when the responsibility for your child's falling asleep becomes yours or your spouse's, then bedtime becomes an ordeal.

A baby that cries once in a while at bedtime probably needs comforting. If he or she cries regularly, you probably need the comforting. Give yourself permission to let your baby cry him or herself to sleep. If you're hesitant about letting your children cry too long, go to their room every fifteen minutes at first and pat them without tak-

Figure 3.19

# Bedtime Routine

- Bedtime becomes less stressful for everyone if a night routine is set up for children. Our children used to call it their "ceremonies." That framework permits children to expect bedtime and prevents their making it into a nightly exercise in avoidance. If there's a regular structure, children actually respond more flexibly to exceptions.
- To establish a bedtime routine, make a list with your children of prebedtime tasks; for example, the list might include bath, dress in pajamas, get books ready for school next day, take clothes out for next day, etc. Ask them to tape the list to their mirror or wall. The final activities on the list might be snack, a story, chatting time, and quiet reading to themselves in bed. The last three can vary with family preferences and age. Some parents don't like to provide a bedtime snack. Some parents may prefer to stop reading to children eventually, although it's appropriate as long as it remains an enjoyable activity. Some children will stay up all night reading to themselves if no time limit is given.
- Now ask your children to follow their list and be sure that you don't nag them through it. The last parts, snacks, story time, etc., are dependent on whether the first are accomplished on time. When you explain this to your children, please be positive. Don't threaten. Just say, for example, "Hurry and do all the things on the list so we can have more time for reading tonight."
- Once children have completed their ceremonies, explain that they *must* stay in their own rooms. If they insist on calling to you every few minutes or coming out to interrupt you, warn them once that if that continues, you'll have to close and latch their door until they fall asleep. Assure them that you'll open it once they're asleep. Usually the warning is enough for them to know that you're serious, but for some children you may want to use that latch once or twice. If they're frightened, they may leave a light on. Your intention is not to punish, but to set a definite limit (and to give yourself some evening peace).
- Be sure to make exceptions for special occasions, weekends, or summer. Children respect fair rules better than rigid ones. However, *enforce* the bedtime rules regularly for their sake and your own.

SOURCE: *Learning Leads Q-Cards, Parent Pointers* by S. B. Rimm (Watertown, Wis.: Apple Publishing Company, 1990).

ing them out of the crib. Then extend that time by five minutes each time until they finally fall asleep on their own. You may find your-self more comfortable with this approach. Both approaches work, but parents are often hesitant about using the cold-turkey approach.

## CHORES AND WORK

One of the most frequent complaints I hear from parents is "they never make their bed." Making beds must be a symbol of children's rebellion against chores. I recall as a child wondering why my mother put so much value on getting my bed made. As I listen to the unmade-bed syndrome described by so many parents, I find myself wondering about the state of my own bed that day. Whether or not I managed to hastily arrange the covers and spread depends on the time of my first commitments of the day and my last ap-pointments the night before. I never feel great concern for chil-dren's unmade beds; I know that children and parents will survive that degree of disorganization. However, if your children don't as-sist with home responsibilities willingly and aren't required to maintain their own rooms to at least minimal standards, then I be-lieve that there is a problem. For example:

> Bobby said, "I believe I have a right to have my own room exactly as I like it, and I prefer the mess." Bobby's parents initially concluded that he should be allowed this freedom. However, they soon felt concerned. He slept without sheets rather than make his bed. Crumbs all over the floor attracted ants. He picked up his laundry only when he was out of clothes, and he stopped inviting friends to their home because he was ashamed of his room.
>
> Bobby's room had progressed beyond reasonableness; so had his schoolwork. His parents kept a very neat household. His father was a per-fectionist; his mother was passive aggressive. In response to his dad's power, and in symbolic rebellion with his mother, Bobby was determined to hold his room as a bastion of power (and mess).

How do you encourage your children to cooperate? It isn't easy! Some tasks are not all fun, but really must be done. Again, personal attention is your most powerful reinforcer. **You can best teach**

PARENT POINTER

**your children good work habits in one-to-one partnerships.** If they share a job with you or your spouse, you will be modeling the skills, showing your appreciation for their cooperation, and giving them a sense of importance and self-confidence that comes from completing a difficult task. If you can establish this pattern as early as the preschool years, your children will be willing coworkers and will eventually move toward independence. Early parental patience results in good work habits, perseverance, and a good attitude about work. While you're working as an adult-child team, don't let the child quit until the job's complete.

Our own children, who are now young adults, report that they remember their work experiences as being a joyful, positive part of their growing up. Although I also remember my husband's and my occasional scolding, impatience, and frustration, I know that working together was really a good experience for all of us. Pitchers of lemonade on hot days, listening to a ball game on the radio, tea parties after clearing the dinner dishes, and lots of family laughter were all part of the atmosphere that guided our children toward becoming hard workers. Although there were certainly frustrating times I'd be embarrassed to describe to you, our children and we have conveniently forgotten those and so will you.

PARENT
POINTER

**Giving two siblings a task to share is their invitation to compete.** Either they will compete to make one the "worker" and the other the "shirker," or they will vie for who can get away with the least work. Don't expect motivation or cooperation. Siblings sharing chores have a hidden agenda. Getting away with as little as possible is the typical goal. Even when you work in a partnership with your children, you'll find that they are all more effective if you work with one at a time, at least until they know how to be effective workers. Of course, as children become more effective and efficient workers, they will be able to work together as a team, either with you or alone. Here's a case example:

> David and Scott were three years apart. David, the older boy, was an underachiever, while Scott, the younger of the two, was achieving well in school and appeared to be positive and well-adjusted. When I asked David how he felt about work, his response was, "I hate work." I asked him if he meant all kinds of work, and he adamantly declared that he meant all kinds of work—schoolwork or work around the house. I asked him if he ever did

WORKER, SHIRKER

work with his dad and he said yes, and he hated that as well. I asked him further if he recalled if he had ever done work with his dad without his brother around. He thought about that for a few seconds and said, "Yes, I did work with my dad once all by myself and I really enjoyed that."

What quantity and quality of work should you insist on? Please don't expect your own standards of excellence; something below what you'd expect for yourself is reasonable and fair.

Should you pay for chores accomplished? **Paying children to work is debatable and optional.** Certainly children should do some tasks without salary as part of family responsibility. If you do pay them, use children's standards for salary. (Too much money is more than they can manage.) Savings accounts are a good diversion for their funds. Invent some special jobs as a means for children to earn some money. If they require some extra funds for Christmas or birthdays, you might have them wash the kitchen floor or clean the basement.

Avoid getting into a nagging mode. Two reminders are enough. Beyond that, children aren't listening. **Use written checklists and clear, consistent consequences;** for example, you can hold Friday

PARENT POINTER

PARENT POINTER

room inspections before you permit any weekend activities. If the children's rooms are clean, they can go out; if not, they stay home until their room meets predetermined standards. As children develop good, regular habits, such consequences and inspections won't be necessary, but you may want to use them to get them started. Most important, stick to the promised consequences if tasks aren't completed. They can be removed immediately upon completion, and no further punishments are necessary. Children may resist at first, but your persistence will pay off in reasonable, responsible behavior. Teaching your children to be effective workers is an important component of teaching them to be persevering learners.

## PRACTICE IN THE ARTS

The purpose of providing music, dance, drama, or visual-arts lessons for most children is to give them exposure to learning in the arts. We assume that if they learn to love and appreciate music or dance by their involvement, they will appreciate those arts, either as part of their recreational activities or as members of an appreciative audience when they become adults. Actual experiences with the arts not only increase children's appreciation of the arts but improve other learning and concentration skills.

Some of you may believe that your children are sufficiently talented in the arts to develop it as a career. Whether you see the arts as an opportunity for enrichment or as a career will make a difference in the kinds of opportunities to which you will want your children exposed and in the expectations you'll have for them. Only time and experience with good teachers can help you and your children determine if a career is a realistic goal for them.

Although most parents want their children to love music, a visitor from another planet who observes music practice in most homes would surely assume that the real purpose of music is to let Mother develop her nagging expertise and to teach children to improve their arguing. There are few families in which the "practice battle" doesn't take place on a regular basis. Although the parents' original assumption about music was that children would enjoy it and would want to take music lessons, only rarely do lessons continue based on that assumption.

I'm a firm believer in encouraging musical opportunities for children. However, I'm equally firm that parents must remember the purpose of music lessons. Although the music teachers of the world seem to have joined together to proclaim that children must practice a minimum of one-half hour a day, parents should unite and tell music teachers that one-half hour doesn't seem to be on the agenda of many children.

Do you remember when you were a child and had to practice piano, trumpet, ballet, or whatever art form for one-half hour? Do you remember how you practiced the first ten minutes, stared out the window, made silly noises, looked at the clock, wasted a few minutes here or there, got a snack, and then went back to practicing a few more minutes? Do you recall how you manufactured ways to fill up that half hour with such statements as "I have to go to the bathroom" or "My nose is running" or "I forgot my book in the other room"? Children haven't changed much in their ability to fill up the required half hour by procrastinating and avoiding practice. Perhaps this story about music lessons and kids will cause you to rethink insisting on lessons:

> Roger began his first piano lessons enthusiastically, but unlike some other children, Roger's enthusiasm was extremely short-lived. His parents insisted, and lessons continued despite his protests. Roger discovered a foolproof retreat. He would dip his hands into the cold snow until they were swollen from the cold just before he went for his weekly lessons. His fingers wouldn't move at all, and that's enough to cause any music teacher to recommend discontinuing lessons. It worked!

Hopefully, your children will not need to get that desperate. When your children request music lessons, I suggest you negotiate the minimum number of times they'll play a piece and ask that they make a commitment to that. For example, if they're playing piano, they should promise to play a particular piece four or five times each day they practice. If they select the number of repetitions, they're more likely to rehearse their music as agreed. After you've negotiated with them the number of times they'll play their pieces, the next important recommendation I would make is that you leave practice to them. Don't let it become your responsibility.

If children continue to take responsibility for some regular practice, even though it may be less practice than their teachers suggest, you'll discover they'll be willing to increase their practice time as they achieve great proficiency in their music. They'll be motivated by their intrinsic interest, preparations for concerts and contests, involvement in a musical peer group, or by their relationship with an inspiring teacher. Accomplishment in the arts is not motivated by punishment or parental nagging.

As they begin their lessons, negotiate a three- to six-month agreement that if they practice responsibly for that time, they may continue with their lessons. Tell them that if they prefer not to practice, you'll be happy to discontinue their lessons after the experimental period. Say that you'll be willing to give them another opportunity at a later time when they may feel more ready to practice on their own.

PARENT
POINTER

If you would like to do something to encourage your children's arts practice, **you may want to set aside time for family concerts or performances by your children.** For example, establishing Friday night as children's performance night and inviting aunts, uncles, or grandparents to listen might be fun. Weekly concerts or a concert every two or three weeks may motivate children to prepare their favorite pieces. The brief concerts can be made a bit more formal by having the children announce their pieces and earn some applause; after the recital, you can serve cookies and tea.

Parenting so children will learn includes teaching them about the arts. As in other routines and habits, encouraging children to take responsibility, focusing your attention on their accomplishments, and giving them support for carrying through their practice independently will encourage them to enjoy their performance and will increase their appreciation of the arts.

## WHY DO *WE* DO IT? WHY DO WE NAG?

Why do we do for children what they could do for themselves? Why do we take on their responsibilities and then remind them dozens of times that the responsibilities are theirs? Why do we worry so at their slightest discomfort or the possibility that they might not eat enough or sleep enough? Why are we concerned that they will not feel loved when we love them so? Why do we nag them to wake, to eat, to study, to do chores, and finally to go to sleep?

Sigmund Freud described the infant as being ruled by the pleasure principle that demands immediate gratification,[4] and Erikson described the infant's need to accomplish the developmental task of trust during the first year of life.[5] As parents, we define our role as meeting our infants' needs so they will trust us and intuitively feel they are loved. We may think of love as immediate gratification of our children's needs.

Out of love we may rock them, nag them, overfeed them, do their homework for them, study for them, learn for them, and work for them. All these we do immediately to satisfy their needs. In so doing, we steal from them their initiative, their confidence, and their ability to delay gratification. Children's learning to postpone gratification is an important predictor of intellectual and social success later in life.[6]

Can it be that loving our children so much is what gets us into trouble? No, not exactly. It isn't the loving, but it is our concern with demonstrating our love immediately. We do what makes our children (and us) feel good at the moment instead of thinking about the big picture. Thus, we teach them to demand from us immediate gratification, and they become accustomed to it. If we can learn to wait patiently while they learn and struggle just a little, we can teach them patience, perseverance, independence, and self-confidence, and we won't have to nag them, at least not quite so frequently.

## THE COMMUNICATION HABIT

Of all the habits that encourage learning, communication is probably among the most important priorities. Despite parents' recognition of the importance of communication, our frenzied lifestyles seem to leave little time for listening and conversation. **Plan talk time each day with your children.** Although you may not always fit it in, at least your children can learn that communication is valu-

PARENT
POINTER

able. One-to-one conversations are especially positive. Taxiing a child to lessons can sometimes provide an ideal environment for special talk. Conversations centered around food (such as tea parties) seem to enhance them. If conversations are scheduled before bedtime, children seem to be especially willing to talk (remember, they seldom want to go to bed). Turn the TV off for best results. It absolutely interferes with communication.

PARENT
POINTER

**Listening to one another is an especially key part of communication,** and if parents model listening, children are also more likely to listen. Successful communication with your teenagers comes only after years of investing time into building a relationship. If you aren't having regular conversations by preadolescence, a wall between you and your teenager will expand a generation gap to a generation gulf. Learning falters. Underachievement may be the secondary effect of poor communication.

## FUN AND GAMES

You may wonder why I include fun and games under habits and routines that encourage learning. As I think back to when our own children were growing up, I recall with the most nostalgia the times of family game playing, the smell of popcorn, the humor, the joking, the competition, that sense of kidding, winning and losing, and acceptance of challenge that took place during game playing. Game playing is relevant to learning and relevant to life. In addition to the intrinsic motivation that comes from the experience of accomplishment when children do homework or chores, there should be a motivation that's based on the realization that after the work is over, there's time for fun.

For young children, play is the main vehicle for learning. Figure 3.20 gives some examples of the skills children learn from play. Be aware that cultural stereotypes may predispose girls and boys to choose different toys. You should encourage young children to play with toys they might not ordinarily select in order to introduce specific learning skills that they might otherwise miss.

Family game playing provides a good exercise in learning to handle competition. Humor helps children to cope with losing. Don't give a lot of attention to poor losers. Label it "poor sports-

Figure 3.20

# Play as Learning

Children learn through play—creative and educational toys are their tools. Here is a list of types of toys and some of the main skills learned through their use.

| Toys | Skills |
| --- | --- |
| Art materials (paints, markers, crayons, scissors, tape, etc.) | Creativity, small-muscle coordination, spatial skills |
| Puppets, dolls, dress-up costumes, masks, etc. | Imagination, role-playing, emotional expressiveness |
| Blocks, puzzles, tangrams, building materials, and dominoes | Imagination, spatial skills, organization, planning, number concepts |
| Music, tapes, nursery rhymes | Spatial, prereading, rhythm, listening skills, large-muscle coordination |
| Letter and number cards, games, and lotto | Prereading, math, cooperative and competitive skills |
| Books | Imagination, verbal and attention skills |

manship," ignore the loser, and go on with the fun of the game. If dependent children feel as though they're missing fun by withdrawing, they'll soon rejoin you. Permit them to do so without a lot of attention or explanation, and they'll soon get over their disappointment. Absolutely don't try to persuade them to return to the game; that will make it difficult for them to rejoin you without losing face.

Game playing should be designed as fair competition, which may mean you should give children a handicap, but don't just let them win. That takes away their sense of control and teaches them to depend on winning for fun. Learning the balance between winning and losing is the goal. Anytime winning is fixed before the game is played, children lose the chance to learn how to compete. Games encourage children toward risk-taking by providing a safe and fun environment in which they can compete with family members. Games will help children build confidence. Below are some tips for game playing:

- Don't just let them win.
- Don't feel sorry for them or overreact when they lose.
- Don't pay a lot of attention to their fear of trying.
- Don't let their avoidance of competition keep the rest of the family from having fun.
- Humor and laughter help!

Make time for family fun and games! Outdoor play, camping experiences, bicycling, sports, indoor board games, or throwing a Nerf basketball into a basket hung on the side of the door all qualify as possibilities.

The family that surrounds itself with family play, fun, and laughter is more likely to motivate its children to learn, work, and accomplish. Play should be as much a habit as homework and chores. Finding time for fun is probably harder for parents with hectic schedules than it is for children. So I ask you, as parents, to try to develop this most difficult habit of all. Have fun with your family!

## QUESTIONS AND ANSWERS

**Dear Dr. Sylvia,**
*Is it always necessary to have a quiet place to do homework? Some psychological research indicates some extroverts like to study with noise and do better.*

*Noise-Loving Parents*

Dear Noise-Loving Parents,
It is true that there are confusing contradictions in research on the impact of noise on effective studying. I can't say for sure that some

children wouldn't learn better with noise; however, research clearly indicates that students learn more from study without the distraction of television. The reality of the world of learning is that examinations have never been offered with the option of noise. Although some business offices are noisy and some provide music, most insist on reasonable quiet.

If you're preparing your children for academic success, you must help them to develop habits that will open educational doors for them. After they've learned to concentrate in quiet, they may certainly introduce higher noise levels gradually and experimentally, provided the noise doesn't interfere with their concentration.

The problem when students request socialization and music during study is that the students mainly enjoy the distraction more than the study. For the most part, they are avoiding the concentration and discipline they should be learning at this time in their lives. However, you can be flexible and allow for children's preferences once they've proven their own flexibility and commitment to study.

## Dear Dr. Sylvia,

*I have a thirteen-year-old daughter, a fifteen-year-old stepson, and a sixteen-year-old son. Some of their bad habits are already established, such as studying on beds while listening to music, TVs in rooms, etc. My husband and I are both teachers and should know better, but we walk into the house at the end of the day really tired. Is it too late to change those habits? Will I take the chance of the kids rebelling?*

*Tired Parents*

Dear Tired Parents,
You may wish to target one teenager for improvement at first. The oldest one is likely to be your best choice. If you can convince him to change his bad habits, the others may be inspired to follow, and that may make the entire reversal more doable.

Your sixteen-year-old is the closest to graduating into the real world. At about his age, teachers and counselors begin guiding students toward college and career selection. His peers may be starting to think about the future, and even as your son reminds you that the future is centuries away, he occasionally thinks about his life after high school. Because he is your biological son and your husband's stepson, there is a slightly improved chance of your communication being effective if you, his mother, talk to him in private about your concerns.

You could make this a get-ready-for-college tête-à-tête. Explain how college felt to you, including the study skills you had to learn and how high school best prepared you. Take him on a trip to some university campuses and, particularly, explore the libraries, where he will see hundreds of students busily studying in quiet environments.

On your drive home from your college tour, ask him how you can help him study for his last two high school years. You might offer to purchase a desk or table or a brighter lamp to use while studying. Remind him of how much you would appreciate his being a good example for his younger siblings, although you should assure him that you won't make comparisons. You may convince him to make a commitment immediately, or he may only wish to think about your study recommendations. Stay in a persuasive and positive alliance, and be sure not to make this a battle.

I can't promise this will work, but it is likely to be more effective than taking on three entrenched teenagers at once. As to the TVs in their rooms, I hope the televisions are old enough to break soon, and you may even wish to help that happen! Please don't replace them.

I am hoping that your teenagers are, at least, doing some homework and studying. If they manage to be accepted into college, you can hope that maturity and a challenging college environment will help them to understand the importance of real study before they've closed the doors to that important higher level of education.

### Dear Dr. Sylvia,

*You have said that "capable high school students should be studying and doing homework for two to three hours a night." I feel that two to three hours of homework every night is an unfair burden to put on a high school student. This kind of guideline applied to every high school student makes school and homework a tiresome chore. What about the other areas of our children's lives?*

*Confused Counselor*

Dear Confused Counselor,

Two to three hours of homework nightly is far less than the average high school student spends watching TV, and much less than they will be expected to do in college. It's hardly an unfair burden for young people who are approaching adulthood. If you consider that many students can complete some of their assignments in study hall, there is still considerable time for relaxation, social life, and even part-time jobs.

It's especially unfortunate when adults set expectations for high school students that are too low and place social life before learning. Of course, high school students are willing to accept that priority and will then complain about the boredom of homework. If kids spend a little more time studying, they'll do better in school and enjoy it more. Their parents and teachers won't feel so frustrated by their underachievement, and kids would be better prepared with the work ethic that college and the workplace will expect.

More than half the students who enter college do not graduate. They are simply not prepared for the required study or the competition. Many college students on academic probation have asked me why they weren't better prepared by their high schools.

Although I do agree that high school kids should have some fun, they should also take their education seriously. When a school counselor doesn't believe high school students should invest much time in study, it really worries me, but perhaps that is one component of our epidemic of underachievement. You are probably not alone, but our country needs educators and parents to prioritize school learning first. It's fair to our kids and to the taxpayers, who underwrite a large educational investment.

## Dear Dr. Sylvia,

*My ten-year-old son forgets to give me phone messages, information from school, homework assignments, etc. Do you suppose there is something wrong with his memory?*

*Wondering Mom*

Dear Wondering Mom,
If he remembers "important" things like baseball scores, football records, etc., you'll know he doesn't have a memory problem. Some issues are not on his agenda, and either he's in a little power struggle with you or he just has some bad habits.

It's usually a good idea to get children actively involved in inventing strategies for remembering. If your son makes a commitment to his own techniques, he's more likely to follow through. A pad and pen left near the telephone may help him remember phone messages, and designing a special folder or special pocket in his school bag may help him remember communications from school.

Be reassured. It's unlikely your son has a real memory problem. On the other hand, you can request a school evaluation if you continue to have doubts.

### Dear Dr. Sylvia,

*How do you overcome the writing problem that so many underachieving boys have? My son hates writing and so did I.*

*Frustrated Father*

Dear Frustrated Father,
When I ask elementary-school-age children who the smartest students in the class are, they usually give me specific names. Then I ask them why they think those children are smartest. Almost every child answers, "Because they're the first ones done." There appears to be unanimous agreement among kids that "fast means smart." Sometimes this causes problems for children.

In many elementary-school-age children, the small-muscle coordination needed for writing seems to develop more slowly than other thinking and learning abilities. This seems to be a more frequent problem for boys than for girls. Whether or not assignments are timed, these children are anxious about written work because they may lag behind their classmates in completing it. They equate fast with smart, and they search for a way to avoid feeling dumb. They may not finish their work, or they may do fast and careless work and make excuses about written work being boring. These easily become bad habits that may cause children to learn to dislike writing and to develop anxieties about written assignments.

Here are some general suggestions that may help your son and other children who have "pencil anxiety":

- Encourage your son's use of a word processor for all drafts when doing story or report writing.
- Permit him to use fine-line markers instead of pencils for assignments.
- Have him practice my "speeding" exercise, which can be found on page 187.
- Change his expectations by making specific comments that intelligence and speed are not the same.
  Some examples of things you can say follow:
    - Although some intelligent children finish work quickly, other very intelligent children are slow workers.
    - Quality is more important than quantity.
    - Authors always write many drafts before they feel satisfied.
    - Scientific discoveries and major inventions take great amounts of time and meticulous research.
- When your son has creative writing assignments, explain to him that authors usually write several drafts of their stories. Handwriting and spelling are unimportant for the first draft, which is only intended to get creative thoughts down on paper. However, he needs to plan two or three more drafts for reorganizing ideas and correcting his work, and then a final draft in an attractive format to be hung on the bulletin board or the refrigerator.

There is a place and a value for intelligent slow thinking as well as intelligent fast thinking. Because almost all young children seem to miss this important point, you and your son's teachers should emphasize that smart is not always fast, or he will lose confidence in his intelligence.

### Dear Dr. Sylvia,

*I read an article on dyscalculus and found that I have had many of the same problems when doing math, retaining numbers or letters when somebody would spell, or attempting to play the piano. I am an older adult and always felt like something was wrong with me. When I was in grade school, my parents had a tutor for me, but it never really helped. Can you tell me where I could receive some help?*

*Frustrated and Embarrassed*

Dear Frustrated and Embarrassed,
*Dyscalculus* means to have inordinate difficulty learning mathematics. Although I can't diagnose your problem exactly by your letter, your symptoms sound typical of persons with spatial disabilities. Teachers often describe their feelings about tutoring such a person in these words: "When I explain the mathematics concept to the student, they seem to catch on to the explanation. However, two hours later they no longer seem to understand it, almost as if I had never taught it."

Children who have spatial problems tend also to have problems counting money, telling time, understanding maps, geography, and directions, solving math story problems, doing geometry, and working with computers.

For adults and children alike, it is important to identify strong learning areas so they can be used to help with weak areas. For example, one boy with strong verbal abstract-reasoning ability talks aloud to himself to solve the steps of a math problem. Some children draw pictures or use tokens to help them understand spatial concepts. Written and oral repetition also seem to help. Turning a map sideways or upside down to follow directions works well for finding one's way in a strange city, and having both written and visual directions seems to help when lost.

There are vast differences in people's spatial abilities. Because the problem seems to be at least partially genetic, you can't expect to change it completely but only to compensate with practice or by making creative adjustments whenever you require them. For children, and even for adults, this disability may cause you to lose some self-confidence. Emphasizing and using your personal strengths can help you. After all, none of us are equally capable in all areas.

## *Dear Dr. Sylvia,*

*My son is repeating kindergarten and was tested last year for LD (results were normal). He is doing poorly, and the school is recommending that testing be repeated. In considering private testing, can you suggest where and what I should look for?*

*Confused Mother*

Dear Confused Mother,

When children do poorly in kindergarten, there is good reason for them to be tested for learning disabilities (LDs). Furthermore, it is reasonable to test them a second time a year later because testing can be unreliable when children are under the age of seven. Actually, it isn't really the tests that are unreliable, but the children. Shyness, lack of confidence, and difficulties with concentration can all interfere with a child's correct responses. Nonetheless, test results can provide some important hints as to the source of your son's problems. Although the school did not find a learning disability from the first testing, a year of growth could help to reveal a disability in the second testing.

Other problems, unrelated to your son's ability to learn, could cause him to have difficulties in his second year of kindergarten. Behavioral and attentional problems cause many other difficulties for children in the early grades. Either a school or private psychologist can help you identify the underlying causes of your son's problems and make suggestions as to how you and the school can help him. It is, of course, not possible for me to recommend a specific psychological clinic; however, below are some questions you can ask before taking your son for a psycho-educational assessment:

- Does the clinic specialize in working with children who are having school-related problems?
- Will the clinic work with you in guiding you to help your child at home?
- Will the clinic serve as an advocate for your son and interpret his needs to his school?
- Will the clinic work with your son's teacher to make recommendations of effective approaches to use for your son in the classroom?

• Will the clinic evaluate psychological as well as learning issues involved in your son's problems?

When you have asked these questions of the clinic's reception-
ist, and if you feel satisfied with the initial responses, you can make
a first appointment to meet and get to know the counselor or psychologist who would be working with your son. Although there is
much that psychologists can do to help your son in school, they
need family cooperation in the therapy. Even with professional
help, you must be patient and recognize that not all problems are
easily solvable.

Many children who begin with early problems become excellent
students. The best-known learning-disabled child was Albert Ein-
stein. Although your child may have learning disabilities in kindergarten, there is hope for his future.

### *Dear Dr. Sylvia,*

*Our son does very well with completing his assignments and homework,
but this quarter he was having problems with test scores in four of his
classes. His self-esteem was way down, and he commented that he was
"stupid." Warning lights came on, and we want to know how to help him
prepare for tests. He told us he never expects to get 100. He does just
enough to get by.*

*Parents of Test-Anxious Son*

Dear Parents of Test-Anxious Son,
Summertime may be the ideal time to help your son deal with his
test anxiety and/or his lack of study skills. Either or both of these
may be causing his problems and could eventually discourage him
from doing his homework. His statement that he does just enough
to get by may be accurate, or he may be using it to protect his fragile self-concept because he feels so bad about his grades.

Explain to him that understanding how to study for and take
tests is a special skill that he is capable of learning. The better he
gets at the skill, the less anxious he'll become. Furthermore, the
ideal way to learn about test taking without anxiety is in the summer when grades don't count for his report card. During the summer, he can concentrate on the test-taking skill without pressure.

Three alternative ways for him to focus on test taking are through (1) a specific summer-school class, (2) a study-skills tutor, or (3) a book or computer program specifically designed for that purpose. The first two will probably be easier to attend to during summer and may be sufficiently effective to reduce his anxiety and build his confidence for many years to come.

His goal need not be perfect scores on tests, but only improvement compared to last year. His test scores should approximately match the scores on his daily work if he is studying appropriately and his anxiety is diminished. Summer is a good time for pressure-free catch-up, which can make an important difference for your son.

### Dear Dr. Sylvia,

*In my country, children in the ten-to-twelve age group take an examination to determine the type of high school they will attend. Those with scores in the top 15 percent have their names published in the newspapers and attend the best schools. Those who "fail" attend other schools and become disheartened and sad. This is a stressful situation for children and parents.*

*How can I help the children cope with the pre-exam and the postexam anxiety?*

*Test-Anxious Mother in Jamaica*

Dear Test-Anxious Mother,

It is clear that Jamaican schools leave little opportunity for children's later reversal of underachievement, which may indeed cause pressure for families. Of course, your own feelings of anxiety will be conveyed to your children, and they will feel even more anxious. Perhaps you should begin by asking yourself if passing a test is truly so serious when 85 percent of these children fail. Are the alternative forms of education really so terrible, or will your children also be able to achieve happiness with a somewhat lesser education? Hopefully, your personal responses to these questions will assure you that intelligent children can survive and thrive without successful scores being published in the newspaper. However, they do not survive well if they fail in pleasing their parents. Your children need reassurances that you will love them regardless of their test scores, although you will be very disappointed if they don't study hard. Please explain clearly to them that there are many good ways to be happy in life, and that you will celebrate with your children both their efforts and their accomplishments, whatever their scores are. They will need convincing reassurances to compensate for the pressure they and you must feel.

Of course, no one likes to fail, but everyone fails many times. Children who fail need comfort and support first, then they require guidance for regrouping and changing their goals. It is most important for them to realize that failing does not make them "failures" because both success and failure are normal temporary experiences.

Whether or not your children fail the exam, it would be good for them to learn to be sensitive to their friends who may not pass. Indeed, it seems to me that such fierce competition is unfair to many children. Perhaps you should join with other parents in trying to change the educational system to allow for more flexibility and educational opportunity.

### Dear Dr. Sylvia,

*My nine-year-old son has been diagnosed as having an attention deficit–hyperactivity disorder (ADHD). He is also an underachiever. We're not sure whether or not to try Ritalin. The doctor has indicated he thinks it could help him.*

*Faithful Reader with ADHD Son*

Dear Faithful Reader,

Children with attention deficits and hyperactivity are difficult to parent and difficult to handle in the classroom. Most of them also underachieve in school. As you probably know, ADHD is characterized by high energy, difficulty with concentration, distractibility, impulsivity, disorganization, and a large number of the characteristics that are typical of many children with underachievement syndrome.* However, all tests for ADHD are observational and behavioral. There are absolutely no biological tests for ADHD, al-

---

* Underachievement syndrome and the Trifocal Model are explained in Dr. Rimm's book *Why Bright Kids Get Poor Grades and What You Can Do About It* (New York: Crown Publishing Group, 1995).

though many parents believe that a score based only on a parent or teacher observation scale is the same as a biological test for diagnosing ADHD. They therefore assume that ADHD is a biological disorder.

The symptoms of ADHD can be caused biologically, environmentally, or most likely, a combination of both. I don't consider it appropriate to treat these symptoms with medication unless parents and teachers have also worked with these children behaviorally. High-energy children have always been harder to parent and teach, but high energy is also (although not always) a characteristic of intellectual giftedness. Also, children of normal intelligence are born with a broad range of personalities varying in concentration, impulsivity, and energy levels.

In the past few years, there has been a growing interest in attention deficit–hyperactivity disorder, one sad result of which is the overdiagnosis of the disorder by parents, teachers, and physicians. Ritalin is the medication most frequently used for ADHD children. I believe that it is often overused and misused. One teacher recently told me that more than a quarter of her students were taking Ritalin, and a teacher of the gifted in Florida told me that fully half of her students were being medicated for ADHD. These examples are even more dramatic because estimates of the prevalence of the disorder are only 2 percent. It is almost as if Ritalin has been hailed as a magical cure, but we can't fault doctors entirely. Parents and teachers put heavy pressure on physicians to medicate children who are difficult at home or school. Although Ritalin may calm and benefit a great many children, it would be better for these children to learn to focus attention and discipline themselves with motivation. Ritalin has side effects for some children, including loss of appetite, insomnia, depression, loss of energy, stomachaches, headaches, and tics.

Attention deficit–hyperactivity disorder and underachievement are complex problems and can't be cured by a "wonder drug." They can best be reversed when parents and teachers work together. Many of the symptoms of ADHD can be controlled behaviorally; medication can therefore be avoided for most of these children. A few of them will need both medication and behavioral help to work to their abilities in school. Teaching these children to achieve in school is certainly part of the cure.

When we work with ADHD children in my clinic, we find great success if parents and teachers are guided in setting clear limits. Teaching adults to take charge and not to overreact is helpful. Consistency between parents is extremely important. Attention to the positive is also critical. Guiding appropriate styles of affection and play can be taught. Specific classroom approaches to foster in-seat behavior and withdrawal of negative attention are important. There are also techniques for teaching children to help themselves concentrate and avoid impulsiveness and behavior problems. Modeling problem solving by thinking aloud often helps children to organize their own thinking. At home, lists that guide organization and chore completion are helpful. You can see that there are many alternative strategies.

Nonetheless, despite my concerns about overmedication, I would like to make it clear that some children do benefit significantly by the use of Ritalin and, therefore, should be using it.

### Dear Dr. Sylvia,

*I have a son in college. He has excellent study skills but fails his tests. When he was in fourth grade, I wanted to have him tested for learning disabilities, but his father wouldn't allow it. I'm afraid he may have ADD (attention deficit disorder). He studies all weekend but still fails his tests. What should I do?*

*Mother of Persistent Son*

Dear Mother of Persistent Son,
Your son has a most important quality for success in life, persistence, but all of us must come to terms with limitations. Your son needs help in determining whether his failures are due to learning disabilities or inefficient study habits. It is possible that he is at a school that is too demanding or is taking courses that are too difficult. Counselors abound on college campuses, and your son requires professional help in learning how to cope with the challenges of college.

Fortunately, because of his attitude, many alternative opportunities may be available; for example, he could take fewer courses each semester and graduate in five or six years instead of the customary four. He may be able to find a tutor to assist him in learning to study more efficiently. He could choose a different major or a different college. However, as long as he perseveres, he will eventually find a path that will lead him to a satisfying career.

As a caring parent, try to be encouraging and try not to blame his father for your son's undeserved learning-disability problems. If you do that, it will give your son an easy way out of responsibility and will rob him of a potential male role model that could build his confidence. You, too, by your encouragement, can also be an important inspiration to your son.

## *Dear Dr. Sylvia,*

*My seven-year-old twins have been taking piano lessons for two years. They started at their request. Now the twins don't want to practice anymore. How should I respond to their desperate pleas to quit?*

*Musical Mother*

Dear Musical Mother,

Five-year-olds may well express a wish to play music but, unless they follow the Suzuki teaching method, are typically not ready to read notes and cope with regular disciplined practice. Neither can five-year-olds be expected to make long-term decisions. Two continuous years of commitment shows pretty impressive follow-through at that age.

Give your children the choice of discontinuing lessons for a little while with the intention of returning if they wish or undertaking their lessons with only brief daily practice. If you are convinced that music should be an important part of their lives at this time, you may wish to reward them with a sticker or star for each practice day, but it would be preferable to save the rewards for more important issues.

Although many prodigies began their musical careers early, for normally talented children, music teachers typically recommend third grade as the time to begin piano lessons. Contrary to this recommendation, recent research has found that teaching preschool children on a musical keyboard dramatically improves their spatial ability. Although it is too soon to conclude that these gains are permanent, there's no harm done. However, a continuing mother-children battle could exacerbate the problem and take away from an enriching musical experience.

### Dear Dr. Sylvia,

*We have a daughter in a four-year-olds' kindergarten. In the morning, we have to remind her over and over to get going. She dawdles. It's hard to get her attention. We talked to her teacher, who didn't think it was a problem except that she tends not to finish projects that she starts.*

*Patient Mother*

Dear Patient Mother,

Your daughter's kindergarten pace doesn't seem to be disturbing her teacher; therefore, you probably need not be worried by the school problem except to ask the teacher about her progress as the year continues.

Facilitating her home problem may actually improve her school speed as well, even though you do nothing at school. I've developed a morning routine that is very effective. You will find it in chapter 3.

A few special adaptations should be made for your preschool daughter. When you list her morning responsibilities, illustrate each one with a small picture, which she may help you design. Also, show your daughter how to use a mechanical timer so she can visualize on a dial the time she has left to complete her morning tasks. Finally, she may leave hard-to-reach or hard-to-tie fasteners until breakfast, at which time you may help her with the final touches.

### Dear Dr. Sylvia,

*My daughter, age eleven, eats nothing but peanut butter sandwiches for lunch and dinner. Five years ago, I took her to a pediatrician who deals with food disorders, and he told me to "leave her alone. Peanut butter is nutritious. She'll grow out of it." She hasn't. My forty-three-year-old husband eats only the same eight or nine things over and over again. I make a separate dinner for my son and me. Sharon eats her sandwich*

*and my husband has his separate meal. My husband has insisted that
Sharon eat what the rest of us are having, and my daughter argues back
that he gets his own special meal. She has gone with nothing to eat for
the rest of the night. She is also thin, and I have gained nothing in this
battle.*

*Mom Who's Caught in the Middle*

Dear Mom in the Middle,
Normally I recommend that children eat what is served at dinner
and not be allowed to select off a personal menu. In your case, I believe the battle has gotten out of hand, and everyone is losing. I
suggest that you continue to cook a regular meal for you and your
son and offer your husband his preferences, sometimes cooking the
same meal for all three of you.

For Sharon, who has long been embroiled in a food battle
with you, follow your pediatrician's advice by giving her the
choice of eating what you're eating, eating what her dad's eating,
or making her own meal. If she asks you to prepare a meal especially for her because you prepare it for her father, remind her
that wasn't a choice you gave her. It would be helpful if your husband were more flexible in his eating, because he would then be
a better role model; however, kids should know that adults earn
special privileges by their increased responsibility. Don't insist
that your husband become more flexible; he might feel controlled, and you would find yourself in another no-win power
struggle.

As to your husband, explain to him privately that girls who
find they can manipulate their parents against each other about
food are at high risk for serious eating disorders such as bulimia
and anorexia nervosa. Both of you could someday seriously regret
the issue you've made over peanut butter sandwiches. From now
on, it would be best not to notice or talk about Sharon's eating
habits. If she chooses to make her own, ignore her, and if she se-
lects either of your meals, be very matter-of-fact about that
choice. At this point, the less attention your family gives to food,
the better. Instead, make an effort to make your meals a time of
pleasant conversation. You're embattled now, and if it continues,
eating disorders could become a major problem.

**Dear Dr. Sylvia,**
*My six-year-old grandson sleeps with his parents regularly. My daughter
sees nothing wrong with this, but my son-in-law objects. Are there problems that can arise from this? Is this unhealthy?*

*A Concerned Grandparent*

Dear Concerned Grandparent,
Almost always the answer is yes; however, there are some exceptions. It's all right if there is a thunderstorm or if your grandson has
an occasional nightmare. It's all right if he's not feeling well or if he's
having fun in bed on a weekend morning. However, it is *not* all
right if it becomes a regular sleeping pattern because your grandson says he can't sleep without his parents. An adult and child
sleeping together on a regular basis is too controlling, overprotective, and intrusive. Under some circumstances, it may also be too
sexual.

Most parents initiate the pattern of sleeping with a child in an
attempt to help the child feel more secure during a difficult period,
such as during or after an illness or divorce. They and the child are
feeling the trauma of the illness or divorce, and sleeping together
may feel safe.

Unfortunately, that need for sleep security may become a habit.
When Mom or Dad wants to leave the bed, the child awakens and
begs, whines, or cries for the parents to stay. Mom or Dad feels
needed and believes they are providing love to that helpless child
so warmly and contentedly snuggled in their arms, but their child's
dependence and insecurity increase the longer the sleep pattern
continues.

The days become weeks, the weeks become months, and the
months become years. Mom and Dad find that their seven-year-
old, or even preadolescent, is unable to sleep without them. Sometimes the parent becomes so comfortable in the sleep relationship
that even his or her relationship with a spouse does not feel as inti-
mate. More often the parent feels torn between the child's apparent
requirement for security and his or her own need for adult privacy
and intimacy. The pattern often alienates the spouse, or if a single
parent becomes involved with another adult, he or she feels torn
between the potential new partner and the child. Now we have a

dilemma that the parent never predicted the first night of sleeping with the child. Parents fear it will cause the children insecurity if they insist that they sleep alone.

In my clinical practice, it usually takes only a simple explanation from me to the child in the presence of the parent to resolve the problem. I might say to the child that because he or she is growing up, it is time to learn to sleep alone. I explain that the parent will not sleep with him or her anymore, and it will be better that way. He or she will feel more grown up. The child usually nods his or her head in agreement, although a painful tear often slips down a cheek. The child always seems to understand the appropriateness of what I've explained and usually expresses tenuous confidence in his or her ability to sleep alone.

The most difficult part is convincing the parents not to sleep with the children again. After a night or so, children always learn to sleep on their own. Sometimes they complain about difficulty falling asleep, but that hardly ever lasts. The parents are happier and freer to have a normal adult relationship, and the children are free to become more independent. It is a difficult habit to break but easier than parents would believe, and much healthier for children.

### Dear Dr. Sylvia,

*I'm going to have a baby boy any day, and I also have a four-year-old daughter and a seven-year-old son. We would like to put the baby in the same room with my seven-year-old, but he sleeps with a light and a TV on. I would like to break him of this habit before we put the baby in with him. Any suggestions?*

*Expectant Mom*

Dear Expectant Mom,

Neither the light nor the TV is likely to keep your new little guy awake, but they are not habits your seven-year-old son should have. It may be better to change these patterns before the baby comes rather than after, when he may be more likely to feel the stress of sharing attention with another sibling.

Because the TV is the more serious problem, I would suggest you remove it from his room first. TV watching is better in a family or recreation room where it can become a shared activity. Dependency on TV at bedtime encourages teenagers to become "night people," and it often prevents them from falling asleep in a timely way, which leads to late rising. Teenagers who have become night people may become tardy at school or truant. Although night TV watching is of little risk to seven-year-olds or newborn babies, the habit shouldn't be encouraged, so your son would benefit if it was eradicated early.

When you take the TV out of his room, be sure not to use his baby brother as the reason. I've already given you a better rationale, which you may wish to explain to your son. If you use his brother as the reason, it may initiate some unnecessary resentment. Because he'll find enough other reasons for resenting his brother, there's no need to add fuel to the fire.

The light is much less of a dependency. While most kids find it dispels fears of ghosts and monsters, I know of no teenagers who insist on keeping a light on in their rooms at night. Therefore, I suggest permitting your son to keep a light on as long as he wishes. A dim night-light will most likely be sufficient and may actually be helpful when you're in and out of the room for the new baby. Leave the responsibility of turning it on to your son. He'll soon forget occasionally, and the habit will gradually disappear.

Don't worry too much. Your son will undoubtedly learn to love, lead, and care for his little brother, and you and he will surely experience many more joys than resentments.

### Dear Dr. Sylvia,

*Do you think I should give my children an allowance, or should I expect them to work for it? Also, money seems to "burn holes" in my children's pockets.*

*A Thrifty Mom*

Dear Thrifty Mom,
In teaching your children how to value and handle money, you will struggle with the issues of allowances, earning money through chores, and even how to deal with monetary birthday gifts received by your children from their grandparents. Your value system will, of course, guide you in making final decisions, but keep in mind that your real goal is to teach your children about money manage-

ment. It is also important to teach your children the principle of working and waiting for the things they wish for.

Early small allowances by the time your children reach kindergarten or first grade are mostly helpful for teaching them about counting money and making change. However, even a ten- or twenty-five-cent weekly allowance can be useful for a treat or can be deposited in a piggy bank. Actually, banks encourage children to start accounts early.

Children of primary-school age can help wash a car, weed a garden, or vacuum a carpet. They can do some simple folding of laundry and will be delighted to accrue nickels, dimes, and quarters. They can count their savings and buy some small items.

Be sure not to pay children for all their chores. Making their beds, setting the table, and picking up toys or laundry in their room should continue to be regular household responsibilities they do without pay. If you pay children for everything, you'll soon hear them ask for money for everything.

Gradually increasing allowances with age will permit you to continue to emphasize savings. Dividing allowances and earnings into three or four parts often works well. For example, the first part can be spent; the second saved for special purchases or gifts for family and friends; and the third can go to a college fund. Parents can also encourage a fourth—contributions to church or charity.

By the middle-school years, preadolescents can devise a great many ways to spend "their" money. It may be time to remind them that it is only partially theirs, and as their parents, you can determine the limits to their spending. Some music, movies, and videos might be off-limits even if it is their own money.

Middle-school students have many ways to earn money, including baby-sitting or gardening for neighbors. However, even when the money comes from outside sources, your bywords can still remain "freedom within limits." When your children remind you that you didn't give them this money, you might tactfully point out that you've not charged them for their room and board either. Try to avoid money strife.

Teenage money matters become much more complex. Providing spending money and clothing allowances may continue to be appropriate. If you prefer not to give a clothing allowance, at least give your adolescents some "not to exceed" guidelines for their shopping trips. They may prefer to do some shopping on their own or with their friends, which may actually be healthy for their sense of growing up and becoming independent. Teenagers can even learn to use their parents' credit cards and charge accounts carefully. Of course, trust involving money depends on general trust in the family and should be explored carefully with your teenager.

If your teenagers work part-time or during the summers, they may earn paychecks that can disappear more quickly than they're earned. If you've taught them three- or four-part distribution of their earnings earlier, they'll handle larger amounts of money appropriately. However, instant gratification can be tempting to all of us, so teaching teenagers the "wish, work, and wait" principle of delayed gratification applies as much to their hundreds of dollars in paychecks as it did to their earlier twenty-five-cent allowances.

Grandparents' monetary gifts, whether they're given to your children at ages two or twelve or twenty, should be carefully discussed with grandparents first. They may have some specific intentions or may wish to leave it up to your guidelines. If grandparents allow it, spending some and saving some continues to make good sense for your children regardless of age. Do include grandparents' gifts in the children's education fund. Those who save toward college are more likely to expect to get a higher education.

# In Chapter 4
## YOU'LL LEARN HOW TO

- become a good role model for achievement.

- introduce your children to other achieving role models.

- help your children adjust to negative models you can't control.

- set flexible gender expectations.

- teach children about surviving in competition.

- help your children set expectations for higher education.

- model the love of learning.

CHAPTER 4

---

# SETTING POSITIVE EXPECTATIONS

PARENTS set expectations directly by what they say they expect of their children and indirectly by how they describe their own work. If you loved school and enjoy your adult work, you can be an ideal role model for your children's love of learning. However, if either work or school has not been good for you, here's your opportunity to try a little playacting.

## HOW TO MODEL ACHIEVEMENT

Children copy much of what they see. For better or worse, they watch and copy you, although they don't copy what you think or feel unless you express those thoughts or feelings.

**You Are Their Models.** Three influences cause a child to imitate an adult: (1) similarities between the child and the adult, (2) nurturance or a special warmth that's felt between the child and the adult, and (3) adult power as perceived by the child.[1,2] You can increase your children's unconscious copying of achievement-oriented behaviors by describing yourself, your spouse, and their teachers in ways that emphasize power and achievement. A secondary benefit to doing this is that your own attitude toward achievement improves by means of a "self-fulfilling prophecy."

**How Do You Like Your Work?** Children can't copy you when they don't see you. If they don't see you at work, they can't copy your activities on the job. You may be terrific in the workplace, but that will not necessarily affect your children's achievement. You may love your work, but your children will not necessarily know that. However, when you arrive home, your descriptions of your job or that of your spouse provide a model for how your children should feel about work. How do you walk into the house? What do you say? Here are some typical examples:

> "I'm exhausted—another impossible day at work!"
>
> "My boss is horrible. I really must find another job."
>
> "Twenty more years until retirement! Do you think I'll ever make it?"
>
> "The more I do, the more they expect."
>
> "Could anything be more pressured than my work?"
>
> "Did you make the bed/buy the groceries/do the laundry? You can't expect me to do everything. I'm already working fifty hours a week. So much for women's liberation."
>
> "I'd like to go on strike. No one appreciates me anyway."
>
> "I could earn more on unemployment."
>
> "Fifteen years of education and I hate my job."
>
> "Why don't I get a different job? Mine isn't worth the hassle."
>
> "Medicine sure isn't what it used to be!"

All these comments are from adults who are successful, and some who are even happy, in their careers. Imagine what children might hear if their parents were failures or if they were out of work.

**Change the Work Script.** Home is your support system. It's a safe place where you should be able to say what you feel. However, if your children are listening and copying, perhaps it's time to give a more balanced view. You're allowed 20 percent of the time for griping. **Put a smile on your face and try these for a change of script:**

PARENT
POINTER

THE IMAGE OF SUCCESS

"It's been a hard day, but a good day."

"I really helped someone today."

"My education really paid off. I'm doing a job I enjoy."

"This may not be an ideal job, but I'm learning."

"I guess you have to pay your dues. I don't mind doing a little extra."

"Let me tell you about my interesting day."

"It feels good to make a difference."

Of course, no one expects you to lie about your work to your children. If you've done a good day's work, you're likely to be tired. That's all right and expected. Try to get beyond your low energy level to describe your accomplishments and satisfactions. It will have a remarkably positive impact on your children, your spouse, and even on your own attitude about your work. It's not really an act, but a more balanced script. Children truly do unconsciously copy their parents, their teachers, their friends, and any other people whom they value and observe.

**If You Hate Your Work.** It's sad but true that many parents hate their work, either temporarily or permanently. How can you then become an achievement model? How can you emphasize the positive? Of course, that is much more difficult. Here's a case story:

> Roger was invited to be part of the gifted program in his school despite the fact that he was a poor student and had behavior problems. His parents had agreed with Roger's desire not to join the program. Roger hated school and so had his parents. Both his parents had dropped out of high school. Roger's father was a foreman in a large printing business, and his mother was a waitress. Neither was happy with their jobs, but both were responsible and successful in their work. They actually wanted their son to graduate from high school, and they wanted him to behave in school. They did not care whether or not their intellectually gifted son chose to go to college.
>
> To help them improve their modeling, I suggested that they both tell Roger of their wish for him to complete high school and let him know about their responsibilities and their positive attitudes about work. Roger's dad brought him to work for a day so he could see his dad's important leadership responsibilities as foreman. Furthermore, he brought home some of the beautiful magazines he was printing.
>
> I could not convince the family to enroll Roger in the gifted program, but they took responsible modeling more seriously, and Roger's behavior and school achievement improved quickly. Although Roger did not achieve up to his abilities, his improved grades provided him with better choices for his future and enhanced the likelihood that he would graduate from high school.

PARENT
POINTER

If you really do hate your work and feel that you're in a dead-end position, **emphasize your responsibility on the job.** Tell your children you do at least a full day's work for a full day's pay. Don't glorify trying to get away with less work. Also remind them that you regret making the bad choices that closed doors for you. If you have some plans for a more interesting future, share these with your children, emphasizing the hard work and motivation involved. There may be real sacrifices for you at this time of life that you could have avoided had you applied yourself differently earlier. **Be extremely open and honest when your descriptions can inspire your children to avoid the mistakes you've made.**

PARENT
POINTER

**How Was School Today?** You and your children arrive home after a long day at school and work. You ask, "How was school today?" They go for the food, turn on the television, grunt, and respond:

"Terrible. It was boring."
"My teacher expects too much."
"The teacher's always yelling."
"More homework. Work, work, work."
"Boring, boring, boring!"

Here's how some parents respond to these "enthusiastic" children:

"I don't know what's wrong with teachers these days."
"School was pretty boring for me, too."
"All you ever do is complain."
"I don't know why we pay all those taxes."
"Teachers put too much pressure on kids."
"I wish they'd challenge you instead of giving you all that busywork."

Dan, an eighth-grader, responded to my question about which parent he was the most similar to in this surprising way: "I guess I'm like my mom, because she doesn't really want to work but she wants more money. I don't want to work, but I'd like all A's." He was hearing a message that this hardworking mom didn't realize she was giving.

**Changing the School Script.** Children's attitudes about teachers and school will improve if you change your descriptions of their teachers and your former teachers. If you've changed your work script, your children's school script may already have begun to change. Try these positive script modifications:

"Teachers really have a hard job. They must really care about kids."
"I remember my fifth-grade teacher. He was really special. I even remember what I learned."

"Study can really be boring, but there's that good feeling that comes from really knowing your stuff."

"I bet that teacher doesn't realize you'd like a challenge. Why don't I talk to her about that?"

"I have some really good memories about school."

"Some of the things I never thought would be useful turned out to really help me."

Specific descriptions of incidents will help make your own positive school experiences real to your children. Here's my story about Ms. Peterson:

Ms. Peterson taught senior English at my high school. She was strict and picky about our writing. She gave us more homework than other teachers, and it was hard to earn an A in her class. Ms. Peterson hardly ever smiled. She was a classic no-nonsense teacher whom almost no one really liked except when we left to enter college. Then, by our first Thanksgiving and Christmas breaks, most of us found our way back to thank Ms. Peterson. She prepared us well for our first semester of English composition, and as we thanked her, I remember detecting an almost imperceptible I-told-you-so smile. Thanks, Ms. Peterson.

THANK A TEACHER

**If You Hated School.** Some parents devote all their descriptions of school to talking about what they got away with, how they avoided working, how their teachers were, or what a waste of time school was. **Instead, pick and choose the experiences that really made the most positive differences in your education.** Don't lie and tell your children that everything was wonderful, but do give a balanced view that focuses mainly on your good school experiences. You'll probably remember that there really were a lot of them. It will be good for you and even better for your children to recall those positive stories together.

PARENT POINTER

Suppose you were an underachiever. It would be better if you'd save that confession for someone other than your children. If you brag about what you didn't do, you can also expect at least one of your children to do the same. As a matter of fact, they may be doing even less work than you did, and their grades are also probably lower.

If you've already, in your outspoken way, managed to give your secret away, tell your kids that you wish you had worked harder and about the disadvantages it left you with. If you didn't feel any major disadvantages, think of some. There definitely have to have been a few. If you can't find any, your children will continue to underachieve based on your rationale.

If your spouse, in trying to prove what a good student he or she was, emphasizes *your* underachievement, expect your child to identify with your postschool underachievement as well. A model for finding the easy way out is tempting to children regardless of who describes it.

**Designing an Achiever Image.** Modeling achievement is so important to your children's learning that you'll want to specifically act as appropriate role models. Not only should you be achieving persons, but you should **share with your children a realistic and positive view of achievement.** They should learn from you the ways in which efforts and outcomes are related. They must understand that you sometimes fail, but that you survive that failure, persevere, and succeed again. They should see both your creativity and your conformity. They should understand the intrinsic and extrinsic rewards that come with effort. There should be a balance between the posi-

PARENT POINTER

tive and negative in their view of you as achieving models. If you're an achiever, that balance probably exists, but sometimes parents unintentionally show only a biased, negative perspective to their children.

Modeling achievement and describing it in your spouse make a critical difference in your children's achievement motivation. If it sounds idealistic or impossible, listen to what your children are saying about school. You'll know that they're watching you and listening to you. They've received your messages about your work and your spouse's work. If you expect them to change their efforts and attitudes, you should change both your personal modeling and the description of your spouse's work.

Parents, what I'm asking you to do on your home stage is to show your children you value your work and take pride in it. Let me share with you my humble attempts:

In the old days, when my first children were little, it was expected that good mothers stayed home full-time to take care of their children. I tried to be a good mother and did just that. So when Ilonna was born (she's in her thirties—I gave birth to her when I was in kindergarten), I stayed home with her and then started graduate school. Soon after I began, I became pregnant with David. I left graduate school and stayed at home with Ilonna and David until they were both in school, then returned for the second time to graduate school and became pregnant with Eric. (I was beginning to think that pregnancy was somehow caused by attendance at graduate school.) I left graduate school until Eric was in kindergarten and returned for the third time. I was determined that my third return to graduate school would continue until I earned my degree, but sure enough, Sara was born. I didn't dare drop out again. I took two weeks off from classes to give birth and returned to school.

You can understand that our older children were brought up in a very different parenting environment from our younger children's. While parenting Sara, I was always either attending school or working part- or full-time. She learned early how to make her mother feel guilty. I recall her lying on the bed at age three looking up at the ceiling as I worked on one of my interminable papers saying, "When I grow up, I think I'll just be a mom." Do you suppose she was giving me a message? When I drove Sara to gymnastics, swimming, or Scouts, she would ask, "How come you gave the other kids more time than you give me?" Then from the backseat of our station wagon Eric or David would chime in, "We remember when you used to cook, Mom."

For years I apologized, and for years I felt guilty. Their complaints only increased. Accidentally, I changed my response. When Sara reminded me of my mothering inadequacy, I assured her that she was a lucky child to have such a good role model. I told her that I loved my work and was making my small contribution. I even convinced her that she was probably better off growing up as an independent latchkey kid. To our sons in the backseat, I reminded them that at least at McDonald's they could make choices. Their complaints diminished. My guilt decreased. My modeling act had improved. I felt better. They saw me in a positive light.

When I returned home from my clinic after speaking to adolescents or their parents most of the day, I faced a special challenge. My adolescent daughter awaited me impatiently. As I drove up our driveway, I would remind myself of the importance of my example to our daughter. At least some of the time I would walk into the house, place a smile on my face, and say, "Did you have a good day today, Sara?" And sure enough, Sara was there to greet me with her good day. Sharing our experiences, including stories of my clinical work and of her adolescent relationships, was part of our evening conversation. She heard about my good days, as well as about a few of my discouraging ones. Soon, Sara was thinking about majoring in psychology. She concluded, "I guess I was born into it." In graduate school, she admitted she experienced déjà vu. Indeed, much of her early childhood took place during my graduate education. My education and career were important parts of her life and provided a positive sharing for both of us. Sara is presently in graduate school studying child development. She's chosen an academic career and loves research.

**Describing Your Spouse as an Achiever.** You should also create an achiever image of your spouse. Here are some common pitfalls: Mothers or fathers may complain continually about their spouse's frequent work. They may say, "I wish Dad (or Mom) wouldn't have to work so hard. He (or she) has no time to be with the family." Sometimes they describe Dad's (or Mom's) career as terrible or blame their frustrations on their spouse's job. They may attribute family problems to the spouse's boss or blame the work for their marital or financial problems.

To avoid these pitfalls, convey to your children the financial and other satisfactions of your spouse's hard work. Although you can be

PARENT POINTER

honest about the parts of a career that you don't value, you should also emphasize the positive components of that career and explain why your spouse has chosen it. Remember, be positive at least 80 percent of the time.

In some circumstances it may seem either extremely difficult or trivial to build up a spouse's career. However, once you see the parallel between your spouse's achievement at work and your children's attitude about achievement at school, you'll be convinced. If you continually denounce your spouse's awful career, you will hear similar attitudes about school from your children. By adolescence, you're likely to find the comments quite intolerable. They will sound like this:

> "I don't see why I have to do all this schoolwork; I need time for fun."
>
> "I'm not anything like my dad (or mom), and I'd never choose a career like his (or hers)."
>
> "I don't know what I want to be or do—something in which I don't have to work all the time."
>
> "The bad grades aren't my fault; that teacher is terrible; he expects too much."

Whatever attitude you show toward your spouse's work, your children will mirror that attitude about school, because school is your children's workplace. At times during your life it may be impossible to avoid negativism and pessimism. However, if parents provide a more positive and balanced view of their spouse's career, they can certainly expect more positive attitudes about school achievement in their children

If you or your spouse is a full-time homemaker, the responsibility of adults to describe that work positively still applies; however, the pitfalls are somewhat different. The common problem is that homemaking is not valued. Comments like "Didn't you do anything today?" or "All you ever do is run around and shop" (as the family sits down to a delicious home-cooked dinner in their parent-cleaned home in their parent-laundered clothes), imply the unsalaried homemaker is lazy. Parents may describe volunteer activities, which take effort, creativity, and responsibility and make important contributions to the community or to the children, as a "waste of time." If a parent decides to return to school, the other parent may describe that education as "busywork" or point out that the schooling is interfering with the family meals and activities. This puts the parent's education (as well as education in general) in a negative light. If a mother begins a career later in life because she has waited for the children to grow up, she may have a salary disadvantage due to her late start, her lesser training and experience, her inability to travel, or to the generally lower salaries paid to women. Her husband may disparage the financial contribution she makes as well as the lesser prestige of her job.

The main danger of the parent's commentary is that it weakens the other parent's authority and status. Frequently the wife has the primary responsibility for disciplining the children, communicating with schools, and providing educational guidance. Although Dad hasn't directly told his children not to obey their mother, he has, in fact, modeled disrespect without being aware of the seriousness of his communication. Not only has he devalued his wife, but he's also underrated all that she represents: caring for the children empathically and lovingly, concern with education and learning, and the tremendous initiative it takes to combine an education or a career with homemaking. His children will judge their mother, at least partially, through his description. Boys may ignore or put down their mother and may underachieve. Girls may compete and argue with her and may also underachieve. Children don't copy powerless models. **Dad should explicitly describe his respect for his wife's efforts, contributions, satisfactions, and commitments to the community and to education if he expects his children to achieve in school and to respect their mother.** Mothers who see me in my clinic love this part of my recommendations.

PARENT POINTER

In most families, it is the wife who postpones her career to be at home part- or full-time to care for the children. However, I have also worked with families in which the mother has been the primary wage earner, and the father, the primary child-care giver. In this reversal of traditional roles, it is even more important that the working spouse show open respect and admiration for the homemaking father. The mothers with whom I've worked have often expressed such mixed emotions about releasing the main parenting role to Dad that they've tended to be harder on their husbands than most working husbands are on their homemaking wives. I've particularly noticed that career mothers may be openly critical of their husband's parenting and correct them within their children's hearing. This, of course, disempowers their husbands, who have the responsibility for guiding the children, and reduces the likelihood of the children's choosing Dad as a role model.

## WHEN PARENTS ARE IMMIGRANTS

This country has always been a nation of immigrants, so the special issues related to children looking to immigrant parents as role models while adapting to a new culture are not new. If the parents are employed in low-status jobs, they can use their work experiences to encourage their children to move up in status by emphasizing that they get a better education, which is, after all, the American dream. However, even when immigrant parents have excellent careers, their children may doubt their parents' competence at interpreting American culture.

Immigrant parents who don't speak English often ask their children to interpret for them. This sometimes implies that the children know more than their parents. The children may feel ashamed of their parents' accents or culture. Immigrant parents need to emphasize to their children that despite their accents and their cultural differences, they are good role models. Nevertheless, it is more difficult to be an effective role model in a different culture. Teachers and American friends who know you and can tell your children of your wisdom and effectiveness can help give your example more credibility.

With each passing year, it is increasingly difficult for immigrant parents to inspire their children by their own lives. Nevertheless, children of immigrants are often motivated to move out of poverty through educational opportunity. So if you are an immigrant parent, don't despair. Make it clear to your children in your own language, whatever it may be, that you are smart enough to know that their education should be their first priority. If possible, find a concerned educator in the schools who will reinforce your message.

Here's a personal experience:

My parents immigrated to our country as young adults, and they strongly emphasized to me the importance of education. However, they also believed that education was most important for men, and they hoped that I would marry an educated man. My sister often expressed her regrets to me about not going to college and even offered to help my education financially. However, it was my guidance counselors, Ed and Henrietta Herbert, who called me to their office and advised me that I should go to college. They lent me a large directory of scholarships, and based on their encouragement, I applied for every possible scholarship. Their vote of confidence, together with my family's valuing of the American dream, made all the difference in my life.

Immigrant families may need additional support from educators; however, educators are usually happy to provide that assistance if you reach out to them.

## WHEN PARENTS CAN'T CONTROL THE MODELS—OR CAN THEY?

Children can copy many possible models while growing up. They may identify with relatives, including grandparents, uncles, aunts, cousins, or siblings. They may copy stepparents or a birth parent with whom they don't live because of a divorce. They may select teachers, religious leaders, Scout leaders, music or drama teachers, or athletic coaches as models. Television and literature also provide models for children. Some are appropriate for encouraging their learning and some are grossly inappropriate. Finally, and not least of all, children, and particularly adolescents, select peers as models. You can't control most or many of these models; at least it seems that way. Here are some suggestions to help you encourage your children's selections of appropriate role models and to influence the models they've already selected.

**Special Talent Teacher or Coach.** When your children select role models who combine excellent qualities with negative characteristics, you'll want to communicate with those people carefully to reinforce the beneficial relationship while preventing potential harm. The case of Kurt provides an example:

> Kurt was a talented violinist. His music teacher encouraged him and was an inspiration to him. As she shared her musical career and experience with Kurt, she provided him with messages of his competence that inspired him to many hours of disciplined violin practice. She served as an appropriate role model for his musical dedication. However, in a conference with Kurt, after he described his poor grades in science and math, subjects in which he was also extremely talented, his teacher assured him that he needn't worry about his grades. She explained that if he concentrated on his music, colleges would excuse his poor grades in light of his musical talent. Kurt's grades became worse. He used his teacher's comment as an excuse for not completing homework assignments.

PARENT
POINTER

**Here's what you could do if your children are in a similar situation,** whether it involves a music teacher, sports coach, or drama director:

- Contact the teacher or coach and ask for a private conference without your child.
- Tell the teacher or coach how much you appreciate the inspirational model that he or she has provided for your child.
- Explain that your child is misinterpreting part of what he or she is being told and has used that to avoid school responsibility. Be assured that the teacher will understand and probably had no intention of giving an inappropriate message to your child.
- Point out to the teacher that he or she is very important to your child's life and that you want to encourage this positive relationship.
- Ask the teacher to rephrase the message so that your child may better prepare for alternative careers. Explain to the teacher your concern about leaving other avenues open should your child not be successful in highly competitive fields, such as music, sports, or drama.

**Family Members.** Sometimes role models are grandparents, aunts, uncles, or relatives who care about your child but unintentionally set an inappropriate example. This can be difficult for you because these important others may be sabotaging your messages about the importance of school learning. Here's an example of grandparent sabotage:

> Terrance was an only child and the first and only grandchild. Terrance's parents came into my clinic because they found his behavior impossible to control at home. His mother, who worked full-time, found herself avoiding coming home because her son was so difficult. Father's attitude wasn't much better. I gave the parents some simple control techniques that effectively set Terrance's limits (see chapter 1). However, I wasn't surprised to find out that a major component of Terrance's overpowering behavior was caused by grandparent sabotage; for example, if Mother was disappointed at Terrance's poor behavior at school, Grandmother's response would be, "Well, he can't be perfect. He's just a little boy. You weren't so perfect at school either."

**If you have a relative who is providing an inappropriate role model or negating your good modeling, try the following:**

PARENT POINTER

- Tell your relative in a firm, loving way that you value them as role models for your children.
- Explain that your children are also hearing negative messages and ask your relative to change these.
- If the messages are very negative and if the important adults ignore your request, you'll want to take a firmer stand. Tell them that if they continue, you'll prevent your children from seeing them. Inform them that you don't want to do that, but their actions must stop. Be firm, but loving and caring to those people who love your children so much. It would be sad to discontinue these relationships and much better if you can improve the example these important relatives set for your children.

**After Divorce.** If your child's role model is the child's other birth parent, whom you wish the child would not even have to know, **point out the good qualities of that person and de-emphasize the negative qualities. Don't discuss your frustration with the other person's power over your life.** For example, constant reminders

PARENT POINTER

to the children of your dependence on your former spouse's financial support maintain that spouse's power and make you appear powerless, and children are more likely to select powerful people as role models. **Never remind your children of how they exhibit your former spouse's negative qualities. Instead, point out your children's similarities to other important relatives whom you see as positive role models.** Tell your son he reminds you of your own dad or your daughter of your mother. Tell either that they remind you of yourself—or at least describe the positive characteristics that you share.

**If your former spouse chooses not to visit with your children, don't encourage or persuade him or her.** Don't remind your children of your spouse's neglect, because that will only make the children feel rejected and make the former spouse seem more powerful. A loving parent is important for your children. A rejecting parent who seems all-powerful and is the cause for anger is a negative role model for your children. It is better for your children to have one good parent than to be part of a conflict that's caused by your trying to harness a parent who prefers not to be in a relationship with his or her children.

**When a Spouse Dies.** When parents die, they may continue to be role models for their children and may even be more powerful than when they were alive. Of course, if children are very young at the time of the death, they will have only a few or no actual memories of the parent. If the child is older, his or her memories may be limited to times of greatest emotion. For example, if the parent-child relationship during adolescence was an embattled one, the stress engendered by that time may be remembered with guilt and pain. Grieving then becomes a confusion of anger, sadness, and guilt and causes much conflict for an adolescent in search of an identity and role models.

**The remaining parent can choose to keep a spouse's memory alive and powerful by his or her descriptions of the other parent, thus providing an effective role model.** However, some risk occurs if the deceased parent is idolized too much after death, because the parent then becomes an impossibly perfect role model. It may feel to the child as though he or she is expected to fulfill impossibly high expectations. A balanced view of the parent is important, although that balance is not always easy for the remaining grieving parent. **Real-life stories of the departed mom or dad can go a long way in easing grief for the family, as well as providing a reasonable basis for emulation and inspiration** without placing unreasonable pressure on children to follow in a deceased parent's idealized footsteps.

## Television and Literature Heroes.

**If your children have chosen good role models from television or books, point out the similarities between your children and those role models.** Provide a more in-depth picture of those heroes. For example, children often assume that television role models such as rock stars or professional football players have had effortless success. **You may want to point out the tremendous amounts of practice and effort they had to invest for their success.** In that way, the child can learn to work and make real effort in a chosen direction. You might also point to others in these particular career fields who, despite tremendous efforts, have not been successful and have had to select other options. In this way, you'll be preparing your children not only for effort and hard work but for selecting alternatives should they change their first career choice or not have sufficient talent. Don't emphasize these heroes' lucky breaks, or you may find your children sitting around doing nothing, waiting for their "lucky breaks."

When children's TV or sports role models fall, children need assistance in understanding and adjusting to their disappointments, or they may try to deny that their heroes have gone astray. It's important to help them to understand that heroes are human and sometimes have frailties that are related to receiving power and adulation. Because they are in the limelight, their failings are often highlighted by the media. **Be sure not to excuse their faults because of their heroism,** but at the same time you must also help your children cope with their disappointments.

When a sports or rock star gets publicity about drug abuse, it's important to explain to your children that drugs have destroyed, *not* enhanced, their careers. Although you should discuss the implications of heroes' crimes with your children, **you can permit them to value the characteristics of those heroes that continue**

PARENT POINTER

PARENT POINTER

PARENT POINTER

PARENT POINTER

PARENT POINTER

THE LUCKY BREAK

**to be admirable.** Of course, whether children can comprehend the complexity of their heroes' multiple roles depends on their developmental stages.

Literature, particularly biographies, can provide especially good role models because books are usually written in ways that emphasize hard work, learning, resilience, and other important values. In the back of this book you will find a bibliography that includes books that may provide role models for women who select unusual careers and for African-American, Hispanic, and Native American families that may wish to provide a more balanced view of role models within their communities. If your children are Caucasian males, don't feel left out. There are many biographies for them already. Any public library can guide you to a shelf of biographies that are at appropriate reading levels for your children.

**Peer Role Models.** During adolescence it's normal to view peers as at least partial role models. If parents have resigned from providing a model by not building alliances or appropriate identification with their children, if adolescents have become completely oppositional, or if they're not exposed to other appropriate role models, peers may become their only role models. That may or may not be positive, depending on the peer group that surrounds your adolescents. If you have emphasized popularity or adjustment to peers to your children, it's even more likely that their peer group will take priority as role models. In today's society, "popular" students are not necessarily safe friends or competent role models.[3] **Communicate the importance of self-reliance when your children are young**. By adolescence your children will have internalized much of your early advice. If you teach the priority of "social adjustment" to friends, it may backfire by your children's preteen years—they may become more social than you wish.

PARENT POINTER

Here are some messages that parents and teachers often give children when they're in elementary school that can cause them problems later:

## Case 1

Bobby is working alone on an independent science project or reading a book. It's recess and his teacher reminds him to go out to play because all the other children are on the playground. Bobby asks permission to stay in, saying, "I'd like to finish my project if I may." The teacher thinks Bobby is a loner and insists, "No, it's time for play. You should be with the other kids." He interrupts his intrinsically rewarding, independent learning to go out and join the other kids at play. The teacher believes she is teaching socially appropriate behavior and good social adjustment and preventing him from becoming a nerd or geek.

## Case 2

On the weekend, Damien chooses to play at home with the family. You're concerned about his friendship adjustment and say to him, "Damien, you haven't had a friend over since last week. Don't you think it would be good to have a friend over?" Your son responds, "I had a friend over last week, so I thought this week I'd be with the family; but if you want me to, I'll call my friend." Based on Mom's or Dad's suggestion, he invites a friend over. He's been given a message about how important it is for good social adjustment to have a friend over on the weekend.

# Case 3

Denise comes home from school and says to you, "Mom (or Dad), Marlene didn't invite me to her birthday party. She invited eight girls and didn't invite four, and I was in the group that wasn't invited. Marlene was my best friend, and I feel really sad."

You, in an attempt to help Denise with her social adjustment, say, "Well, I'm sorry you weren't invited to Marlene's party. Do you suppose there's something that you did wrong that caused Marlene not to like you anymore? I know you like her."

Denise responds, "Well, the last time Marlene wanted me to play kick-ball, I told her I'd rather play on the swing set with the other kids. Do you suppose that might be the reason that she didn't invite me?"

And you say, "Well, Denise, that's probably the reason. You should be more willing to do what a friend wants you to if you want to be invited to a party." Denise hears your message and internalizes that as good social adjustment.

When these children reach middle school, where there seems to be the greatest amount of peer pressure, they act on those internalized values and repeat them to parents and teachers. However, neither parents nor teachers recognize the origin of the behavior, nor are they happy about the effects.

Teachers ask me, "Why is it that our middle school youngsters are not willing to work independently or learn for the sake of learning?" When Bobby doesn't work by himself, they say to him, "Bobby, why aren't you able to follow through on an independent project?" Bobby responds, "But I'd rather be outside playing with my friends. This project is boring."

When Damien is busy all weekend with his friends and can't find time to do anything with the family, Mom or Dad asks, "Damien, why don't you make time to be with the family?" Damien says, "I'd rather be with my friends. Family stuff is boring."

When Denise comes home from Marlene's party and her mother can smell the alcohol on her breath, she questions Denise in distress, "How could you do something that you know is illegal and unhealthy?" Denise looks up at Mother with a tear rolling down her cheek and says, "But, Mom, Marlene wouldn't invite me to the party if I didn't drink like the rest of the kids."

Your children often internalize the advice that you give during childhood for good social adjustment and adopt it as the standard by which adolescents abide, although they may not realize that you've taught them these standards. In the name of friendship, they have been taught to identify with, feel close to, and value their peers as their most important mentors and models. **The message that you should give your children most frequently and most diligently is to be independent, to do their own work, to develop interests, to enjoy their family, and to be able to say no despite peer pressure.** Otherwise, the emphasis on popularity and an antinerd, antigeek, and antilearning standard will begin influencing your children by grade five and usually continue through grade eleven. Among African-Americans, children who are good students may be called "acting white," and Native Americans sometimes tease good students about being "apples," red on the outside but white on the inside.

PARENT POINTER

Peer pressure to underachieve interferes with your children's love of learning and their adoption of positive adult role models. We can only fight that empty value system by teaching our children that **popularity is temporary and disappears as an important value right after their senior year in high school.** In college and in careers, although people continue to value leadership, sociability, and friendship, the concept of popularity disappears. Popularity is only a competitive form of friendship. Having the most friends with the most parties is not required for most careers, for successful marriages, or in creative and happy lives.

PARENT POINTER

As parents you'll find that the popularity message is difficult to combat. We often identify with our children's desire for popularity; we see it as a symbol of their success (and our success as parents). I ask you to **overtly devalue popularity to your children. Instead, value the qualities of good friendship, including shared interests, support, kindness, and wholesome fun.** Reasonably similar values should be the number one priority for friendship, or you'll find your children being controlled by peer groups you would definitely not choose for them. You obviously shouldn't select all your children's friends, but do give them some values upon which to base their friendships. Friends will influence your children's progress toward self-confidence and accomplishment.

PARENT POINTER

# PLACING YOURSELF AND/OR YOUR SPOUSE BACK ON A PEDESTAL

Be aggressive in presenting yourself or your spouse as appropriate role models. Parents are often hesitant about using their power as role models for their children. They prefer to tell their children that they don't want to choose for them. They want their children to find their own way and their own career, and children often accept that as a message not to choose a parent's career. Children may even feel it is a sign of dependence should they select a career similar to that of either of their parents.

What's wrong with children following in their parents' footsteps? Has that become "un-American"? In efforts not to limit their children's options and independence, parents often resign as role models for their children. This leaves a role-model vacuum. Adolescents spontaneously search out role models in an effort to establish their identities. If parents refuse to inspire their children as role models, the children must seek others and may choose them by chance or proximity. **Parents should make a deliberate effort either to establish themselves as potential role models or to guide their children toward a circle of appropriate role models from which to choose.** Mentors, teachers, religious leaders, business acquaintances, or your friends may provide excellent role models. A lawyer or educator friend may be happy to take a little time to share information with your children about their careers, as you could also do for your friends' children. Don't disqualify yourselves, particularly if you have interesting careers.

PARENT
POINTER

# SETTING EXPECTATIONS

My mother expects me to get all A's.
My parents put too much pressure on me.
I'll never be able to satisfy my father.
My parents expect me to be as smart as my sister.
They expect me to be perfect.
All my parents want me to do is work, work, work.

MOM AND DAD HAVE THEIR ACT TOGETHER...

PARENTS MAKE GOOD ROLE MODELS

These descriptions of parents' expectations are typical of those voiced by children who visit my clinic. Most are difficult to trace, although the last one, about work, came from a sixteen-year-old who was required to do the family dishes nightly (and a very small family at that). Parents can rarely understand how their children have such mistaken understandings of their expectations. It takes some detective work to uncover the relationship between what parents are saying and what children are perceiving. The discrepancy between the two emphasizes the importance of clarification of expectations by parents.

**Your expectations about moral values, social behaviors, home responsibilities, and schoolwork should be clear.** Frequently, parents assume that children know what's expected and that explicit information is not needed. On the other hand, some parents talk so much about expectations that there is continual family argument and debate. Sometimes so little is expected that even a small request feels monumental compared to what children usually accomplish. Expecting either too much or too little may cause misunderstandings for parents and children.

PARENT
POINTER

If you don't set explicit expectations for your children, **they will assume that those behaviors that you praise represent your expectations and those that you condemn or punish them for are those that disappoint you.** Your praise and condemnation of others' behaviors are also incorporated into their perspectives of your expectations. Here's an example:

Alison often refused to go to school. Even when she attended, she skipped classes and sat in the library reading. When she discussed her feelings about school with me, she said that she was disappointed in herself and felt sure that her mom and dad were disappointed in her as well. She stated that she thought her mom expected her to get all A's.

When I talked with her mother about realistic expectations, she responded that she would be delighted if Alison got B's and C's. She wanted mainly for Alison to attend class and get her schoolwork done.

In our next session, I again discussed with Alison her perception of her mother's expectations. Alison asked, "Why else would my mother say, 'If you would only do your work, you would surely get A's'?" Her mother's attempts to build Alison's confidence were interpreted by Alison as her mother's expectations.

Alison's older brother was mainly an A student, and she had observed the praise that he was given for his excellent grade point average. She assumed there were similar expectations for her. Despite my clarification of her mother's expectations, Alison was not convinced. Alison had already internalized a set of personal expectations for A's and was blaming those on her mom.

Children also become confused and may believe that expectations they have of themselves are the expectations their parents have of them. Thus, when they're disappointed in their performance, they may say that they haven't lived up to what their parents expected of them. Sometimes they blame one parent and bring their complaints to the other; for example, "I can never satisfy Dad" may become a request for Mother to provide an easy way out. Mom, here's your counterstatement: "I know Dad expects a lot of you. You wouldn't want him not to. If he didn't, it would mean he thinks you're not that smart. Just the other day he was mentioning to me how pleased he is with your hard work." That will send your daughter or son back to the workplace with new confidence and no easy way out.

And for you, Dad, when you hear, "Mom expects all A's," you can say, "Mom does set high standards for you. She knows you're really smart. She was just telling me how pleased she was that you were able to bring your C in honors math to a B. It puts a little pressure on all of us to do hard things well. Keep up the good work!"

Notice that these statements (1) diffuse the conflict, (2) build an alliance for children with you *and* your spouse, (3) give a message of confidence to your children, and (4) clarify expectations. If you really are concerned about too-high expectations your spouse may have set, after you've made these diffusion, alliance, confidence, and clarification statements, talk to your spouse about your concerns (review chapter 2 if this is an area in which you need more practice).

You can see that expectations can become quite complex if they aren't specifically stated. It's critical that your expectations be realistic in terms of your children's abilities and that you establish expectations in ways that enable children to follow through effectively.

**Basic expectations should be stated clearly, briefly, and simply to children.** They should understand exactly what their parents' value system is, which values they are expected to follow through on, and where they can make their own choices. You don't want to give children a hundred rules. The more rules you give, the less they assume you trust them. Stay positive and simple.

PARENT
POINTER

Once you've stated your expectations clearly, follow through to be sure children complete their home and school responsibilities. When they don't meet your expectations, avoid arguing with them. Simply state that you're disappointed about their lying or dishonesty or poor effort in school. Indicate what you expect in the future and what negative consequences will follow if they don't meet your reasonable standards. **Stay in a positive alliance with your children but follow through with promised punishments if necessary.** A note of caution, however: **Don't state your expectations in front of their adolescent peers; that's an invitation to opposition if their peers are oppositional. Don't state your expectations in front of their siblings;** that exacerbates sibling rivalry and embarrasses your children.

PARENT
POINTER
PARENT
POINTER

INVITATION TO OPPOSITION

Be aware that your expectations about siblings and friends will be generalized and assumed by your children to be expectations you have for them. They will compare themselves to their siblings and friends even when you don't compare them. Definitely *do not* compare your children to each other.

Also, don't be surprised if your children and adolescents check out your expectations by telling you a story about a friend. That friend may be themselves, but they want to know your expectations and response before they admit to their behavior.

**Expectations for Adolescents.** The teenage years, which form the bridge between childhood and adulthood, often lead to a set of new expectations that direct young people from their achievement course. Even intelligent parents assume that they can expect at least three or four years of horrible rebellion, and many seem to be willing to accept almost any behavior from their teens, putting their behavior down to adolescence.

Although parents should expect teenagers to test limits, to explore new relationships, and to try on new roles, teenagers continue to need parental guidance and limits. **If you expect and accept irresponsible rebellion, you will find that your teenagers fulfill those expectations.** If you've guided them with the V of Love (chapter 1) from little power and freedom to more, the teenage years can be relatively problem-free. On the other hand, if you've given them too much power too early, you can expect some difficult negotiations. They'll try to oppose you.

**Be willing to negotiate with them in an alliance up front, but stay firm and positive in all your agreements.** Staying positive will be difficult if you overempowered them early. However, if you overpunish your teenagers, these years will become difficult. Remember your feelings when you were a teenager, and let your memories assist you in guiding your adolescents during this time.

**Gender Expectations.** For many generations, boys were expected to develop careers and girls to become mothers (although they could also teach or be nurses after their children were grown). Expectations for your children of both genders have changed, but parents need to be sensitive to the subtle ways that boys are deprived of learning about the world of emotions, and girls prevented from selecting an achieving route.

Gender expectations begin with dress and toys, and although children may in fact have preferences, it's important that children be provided with toys other than those that are gender stereotyped. Playing with dolls and dishes teaches different skills from those they learn from playing with building blocks or in team sports. It's important for boys to learn nurturing and kitchen arts and girls to learn spatial relations and how to compete. **Children learn from their play, and encouraging them to have a variety of play experiences encourages the learning of many skills** (see chapter 3). Don't be too disappointed, however, if despite your efforts, your children prefer gender-stereotyped toys.

Of course, we need to go far beyond toys and games. **Your messages to your daughters and sons need to be clear about your expectations for their thinking and intelligence.** Don't turn your girls into beautiful "airheads." They can learn math and science, and they can play sports and learn to take criticism.

PARENT POINTER

PARENT POINTER

PARENT POINTER

PARENT POINTER

An American Association of University Women report tells us that the gender gap in math and science continues to increase, and even girls who are highly competent in math and science are less likely to choose careers in science and technology.[4] The decline in girls' confidence and achievement begins in middle school. Of course, both parents' and teachers' expectations for girls play an important role in this decline.

Your boys will learn to be nurturers best from dads who are nurturing and communicative. Fathers need to feel comfortable about communicating on their own terms. **Mom should not attempt to teach or mediate Dad's communication to his children unless he asks for help.**

PARENT
POINTER

Girls and boys don't need to be the same, but they can have a broad range of overlapping interests and understandings. If we can give that permission to our children, perhaps they'll understand each other better as adults and will be able to work together better in their homes and places of work. Consider how far we've come in just one generation. Your expectations can increase the progress in the relationship between the genders.

**Schoolwork Is Central.** The most important expectation relative to school achievement is that academic learning is *central* while all other school-related activities are of lesser importance or *peripheral*. Band, chorus, sports, and drama are important in that they provide a full and enriched life for children and adults alike, and developing interests and involvement in competitive activities in those areas is appropriate and should be encouraged. But schoolwork and study should have first priority. If that message is clearly stated when children are young, they will know by the time they reach high school that geometry homework is to be completed even though play rehearsals last until nine-thirty, and that a heavy basketball schedule is not an excuse for skipping a class because homework isn't finished.

Actually, many parents inadvertently send the opposite message. For example, one parent informed me that she had told her gifted, academically challenged daughter that the most important part of school was her extracurricular activities. She unintentionally gave a clear message to her child to underachieve.

Here's another case example:

Jessica, a fifteen-year-old sophomore, was underachieving slightly in school. Her grades were a little above average, although her IQ indicated she was intellectually gifted. Math and science were her least favorite subjects, although she had strong potential in these areas. Jessica was a social leader. She had many friends and was well liked by everyone. The symptoms that brought her to my clinic were anxiety and feigned illnesses, which resulted in absenteeism. Her parents were simply not sure if they were expecting too much or too little of Jessica, and they surely disagreed openly on the topic.

In my interview with Jessica, the reasons for her anxiety became clear. She explained that she identified with her mom because her mom put more emphasis on having a good social life, and her dad thought she should study more and be more serious about her studies because she was so intelligent. She said she preferred the more casual approach to school.

Jessica was fulfilling both her mother's and father's expectations. She was proving she could be both social and intelligent. She could only stay popular by prioritizing a school social life, and she could prove her intelligence and remain popular by missing school and not studying but continuing to get respectable grades. The clarification of her parents' mixed message did much to remove the anxiety. Expectations were clearer for her for the next year. Schoolwork was central.

**Parents who take children out of school for shopping trips and sports events are sending messages about the lesser importance of schoolwork.** When children are excused from school, it should be for an educational or medical reason. Field trips or family trips that provide unique learning experiences obviously qualify. If other family events make it necessary for you to take your children out of school, emphasize the importance of school by requiring your children to collect and complete all school assignments, preferably beforehand. This will provide reasonable flexibility for you while you continue to communicate the value of academic responsibility.

PARENT
POINTER

The central versus peripheral message is especially important to children because their special areas of talent, expertise, or show-manship feel so much more enticing than the mundane activities of the classroom. **If your children demonstrate unusual competence in a talent area, you could ask the school to make allowances for their special training or practice needs.** It may be that such gifted children should have a lightened number of academic requirements. However, they should be cautioned to maintain at least the minimum number to permit them to select alternative career options. High standards should be expected for all subjects. It's difficult to know which may be important for alternative careers. For example, the aspiring dramatic actress may eventually be forced to compromise and teach drama and English. Although that may seem an unlikely outcome for the star of the high school musical production, he or she will certainly have to learn math and science to acquire a college degree.

Many young people, from first grade through college, have explained to me their rationalizations for not studying in subjects they are certain are irrelevant to their future. "Why do I need science if I'm going to become a famous rock star?" I've become convinced that some parents are implying to their children that teachers don't know anything about good education. Of course, this may also represent selective listening on the part of their children. There truly is a basic core of skills that educated citizens should master by adulthood. Parents should communicate to their children that they're expected to learn to read, write, and do math even if they "hate" all of those subjects as they groom themselves for professional football or ballet.

Your enthusiasm for their activities and your attendance at their events emphasize your expectations. Parents who attend every sports event and spend little time showing interest in children's learning are prioritizing sports for children. **It's better to miss a few games if you want your children to know that sports are healthy recreation and not as important as learning.** Your enthusiasm for their good grades should be greater than for their athletic letter. When the athlete in your family gets more attention than the scholar, you are unintentionally devaluing school learning.

Sports are healthy for children. They provide physical fitness and teach how to cope with competition. However, they easily become the top of the agenda for kids. For underachieving jocks, grade twelve may be the best year of their life, but there can be a better future after high school.

I don't mean that you should not support music, art, drama, or athletics. To the contrary, all these forms of creative enrichment are extremely important. However, for most children they should be viewed as supplementary to the core of good academic learning and thinking.

**Perfectionism and Competition.** Judging by the children who come to my clinic, the related issues of perfectionism and competition are high on their lists of problems. Although many children and adolescents are affected by these pressures, only rarely do the children, their parents, or their teachers recognize these as underlying causes of their problems. Here are some case examples:

## Case 1

Glen is a bright third-grade boy who is having behavior problems in school. He's not an aggressive kid, but he talks out of turn, monopolizes class conversation, walks around the classroom, and acts out to get attention. In his gifted class, which meets an hour a week, he's quiet, subdued, and hardly ever volunteers.

## Case 2

Maria, an eighth-grader, is going to a party. She looks at herself in the mirror and says, "Gee, I look really nice." She gets to the party, looks at everyone else, and says, "I'm just not pretty enough; I'm just not thin enough; I look terrible."

## Case 3

Peter, an eighth-grader, was rebellious at home and disrespectful to both his mom and dad. He was underachieving at school and teased by other kids. We helped him reverse his underachievement pattern in one quarter of the school year. His "perfect" sister wrote a letter to her parents: "Dear Mom and Dad, I'm not going to work in school anymore because you just care about my brother and not me."

## Case 4

A student dropped out of college in the first semester of his freshman year even though he had a 3.6 average in high school. The only earlier clue that suggested he had a problem with his parents' expectations was that when he didn't make first string on his high school basketball team, he quit.

## Case 5

Ron, a college student, found himself feeling depressed whenever he didn't earn an A. He didn't understand the reason for his feelings.

What do all of these young people have in common? They are all having trouble coping with competition. All of them want to be the best, and when that doesn't happen, they either quit, are depressed, or act out in some other way.

Competition is pervasive in our society. This means there is competition in families, in classrooms, and among friends. Yet we typically only talk about competition in the sports world. Let's backtrack and focus on the competition problem for each of the young people mentioned earlier.

The third-grade boy's competitive goal was to be the smartest child in the class. In his regular classroom he tried to demonstrate this by bragging and trying to complete his work first. He would speak out of turn and talk as long as possible. In the more competitive gifted classroom, he felt like a loser and was afraid to risk contributing his ideas. He became very quiet.

The eighth-grade girl looked at herself and thought she looked nice until she compared herself to everyone else. Her wish to feel prettier or the prettiest made her feel inadequate.

I had warned the rebellious boy's parents that his change would affect his "perfect" sister. They said, "It won't. She's practically perfect. She gets all A's, she's responsible, she's just a good kid." When her brother reversed his problems and became "a good kid," she felt dethroned. She didn't understand why she was no longer number one in the family. She started acting out. In such situations, I always prepare parents for increased competition between siblings, which happens frequently.

NEVER THIN ENOUGH

For the college-student dropout, the warning signal came in basketball, where he had been a star until other students grew taller than he. He was then taken off the first-string team. As soon as he wasn't a star, he quit basketball. He was an academic star as well. When he went to college, he no longer was an academic star. The competition was too keen, so he quit there, too.

The college boy who was depressed by his B's was one of the top students in his high school class—a very bright student. He described himself as not being a competitive person. When he got a B and realized that some other students were getting A's, he didn't recognize that his depression was caused by feelings of losing in competition.

Children respond to competition directly, whether in the academic realm or in apparently unrelated areas that greatly affect achievement and intellectual growth. Children obviously compete in specific areas such as art, music, or sports. They also compete to be most socially successful (popular), most creative (different), most oppositional (rebellious), most muscular, most beautiful, and the thinnest. All of these competitive pressures shape their self-image, which may include or exclude the trait of intelligence. Some highly competitive children choose an area in which they see themselves as expert and use that excellence as an excuse for not performing in academic work where they may not see themselves as winners.

Teaching children to live in a competitive society means teaching them to handle both winning and losing, succeeding and failing. Children who have had mainly failure experiences avoid competition for fear of more failures. Schools without failure and curricula that provide only successes don't provide children with

risk-taking experiences. **Children who succeed all the time or who get all A's effortlessly are not prepared for a competitive society.** They've learned to function only in a world without challenge. Their self-confidence is dependent on being first, perfect, at the top, and always winning. When they find themselves in situations where they're somewhat less successful, second best, or surrounded by other extremely intelligent people, they may feel like failures. Their confidence falters dramatically, and they may feel defeated or depressed. If they've learned to function in competition, they reset their goals, view their failure as a temporary setback, and persevere whether in the same direction or in an appropriate alternative direction.

In teaching your children to function in competition, **first examine your own competitive style;** children may have learned maladaptive responses to failure from you. For example, you may quit too quickly if a problem gets difficult, avoid all competition, or habitually blame others for your shortcomings or lack of effort. You may be denying the effect of competition, or you may be a perfectionist.[5]

Children should learn realistic attitudes toward their losses or failures; they should recognize that normal people, even very talented ones, can't be Number One in everything (or anything permanently), but that every person has areas of talent. They shouldn't feel insecure or threatened by an occasional setback. Your **discus-**

**sion of your children's failures should wait until after their emotions subside in order to avoid their defensive behaviors.** Parents can't expect rational perception or logical thinking immediately following an upsetting defeat.

**Take a questioning approach rather than lecturing**—for example, "Are you doing okay?" or "Do you feel like you've tried your best?" It will better help your children understand that (1) they

MODELING COMPETITION

can't always win, (2) their losses don't mean they're failures, (3) the particular experience simply wasn't as successful as they'd hoped it would be, (4) everyone would like to be smarter than they are, and especially, (5) the main goal is to play the learning game at their best performance level, regardless of their competitive ranking. **Effort counts, and humor helps.**

**Comparing school to sports is a wonderful way for children to learn** about being a good team member, striving for their personal best, "being a good sport," not hogging the spotlight or hurting the team by their heroics, congratulating the winner, and coping with "Zstriking out." Parents who are involved in sports with their children can help them make the relevant comparisons between sports and schoolwork. The same rules apply.

**Teaching admiration as a strategy for handling jealousy is another means of developing sensitivity that can assist your children in the real world.** Even while your children are winning, they can learn to notice, admire, and communicate their admiration to other performers. If they're in the habit of competing, others' victories make them feel inadequate by comparison. When

PARENT
POINTER

PARENT
POINTER

PARENT
POINTER

they meet real competition, even when it's against another team, the gracious "good sport" should develop skill at admiring and respecting rather than deprecating the talent of rivals. Although it's truly a difficult skill for highly competitive children to develop, it gives them a mentally healthy way to deal with being second best.

PARENT POINTER **If you stress that winning, regardless of the game, is important, then winning at tennis, on the swim team, or in popularity contests may become too crucial to your children.**

Even as you teach a healthy attitude about competition, some television athletes, adult coaches, and other parents may demonstrate poor sportsmanship. You'll need to explain to your kids that even some adults become so intensely involved that they forget the principles of good sportsmanship. You may wish to add that you're hoping they will not copy these poor examples.

Even as you enthusiastically share your children's victories and commiserate with their defeats, remind them (and yourself) that "regardless of performance, there's always someone better than you are and there's always someone worse." This may sound like a famous quotation, but as far as I can tell, this bit of philosophy that guided our children through competitive situations was stated originally (and frequently) by their dad, Alfred Rimm.

PARENT POINTER **Explain to your children that there is no such place as Number One and that first place is only temporary.** If they're first on one level, they'll soon be competing on a higher level with others who were also first. Although it's fun to keep competing and trying, it's not reasonable to expect to stay in first place. That's true in sports, music, art, math, science, debate, or any other area. It's probably better for your children to learn to set reasonable goals, one step at a time, than to dream of stardom before they've discovered all their talents and the discipline necessary for success.

You shouldn't really pin your hopes or your parent identity on your children's becoming tennis champs, Olympic swimmers, Picassos, or Beethovens. The arts and sports field are overcrowded and extraordinarily competitive. Certainly encourage their talents, but don't permit them to bypass studies or academic requirements, or you may find yourself supporting your talented starving artists PARENT POINTER for life. **Explain to your children that they should make family life and friendships as noncompetitive as possible.** They may harbor and express jealous feelings, but they should continue to try to build support, cooperation, encouragement, and admiration into these relationships. You can teach them to feel neat about having a "whole smart family" or feel good about having a friend who is so successful. You can help them to feel caring and sensitive when a sibling or friend does less well than they and to express understanding and support. These are difficult feelings for children to work through.

**To develop a skill in which they lack confidence, children should learn to compete with their own past performance instead of with others.** For example, if they're having problems with timed math tests at school, they may take the same test daily at home, timing themselves and charting it each time. Their daily goal should be to beat the previous day's time. They may soon discover that they have exceeded teacher expectations by beating their own record. This works well with tasks of endurance as well as speed. In sports it's called establishing a personal best.

PARENT POINTER

Sometimes you may find your children shutting down in an area where they're fairly talented. You may wonder why your child who wins an art contest stops painting or your child whose writing or music you admired no longer writes or plays. Children don't understand why they shut down, so don't expect them to explain it. I see this experience commonly in children who come to my clinic: they're responding to perfectionism and competition. Here's a story from my own childhood that may help you to understand. You may have had similar experiences:

I have loved to write for almost as long as I can remember. The first books, stories, and poems that I can remember writing were in fourth grade (Ms. Shoobridge's class). Perhaps there were some even earlier. In sixth grade, I wrote a creative composition about how I had gotten lost in New York City. My teacher thought it was wonderful, and I considered it the best I had ever written. Suddenly I found myself stuck (I think that's called writer's block). Every assignment that year brought me back to the same topic. I explained to my teacher that I just couldn't think of anything more to write about. I truly couldn't. I was sure I couldn't find a topic as good as my last story.

For the remainder of that school year, I hated and avoided all writing assignments. The next school year was better, although I continued to feel inadequate until eighth grade when I wrote a story in the first person in which I imagined coming to this country as a slave. I can still remember my feelings as my class sat spellbound listening to my A+ story.

That success almost stopped me again. As a result of my slavery story, I was chosen to enter a competitive essay contest. I tried to use a creative approach comparing Washington, D.C., as the heart of our nation to the heart of a person. My teacher considered the style inappropriate for the contest. I was confused. I botched something together, which my teacher thought was poor. That stifled my creative writing throughout high school. I was asked to work on the high school yearbook and had so little confidence that I volunteered to be the class typist. It took years to renew my courage.

Some readers may feel it would have been better had I not returned to writing. That might hurt my feelings, but nothing can stop me now. I love to write, and I have received enough positive feedback from readers to know that my straightforward conversational writing style reaches many of you. I enjoy writing so much that airplanes, airports, and even vacations are improved if I have my pen in hand.

I hope that sharing my own struggle with competition and perfectionism gives you some further insight into how your children may fear that their current efforts are not as good as their past performance. You can see that reminding them of their own past excellence only increases their feeling of pressure. Teaching them about brainstorming and encouraging them to fool around with artistic ideas (see chapter 3) gives children permission to produce without always winning. **Encourage your children to create many products,** and promise them that afterward they can select their best from among those they have produced. **Remind them that even the best artists and writers do not produce masterworks every time. It takes some "fooling around" to produce creatively.**

PARENT
POINTER

PARENT
POINTER

**Boredom.** Teaching children to cope with competition may feel like a piece of cake compared to convincing them of the usefulness of boredom. Boredom appears to be the major complaint of most American children who don't like school or particular classes. Parents and teachers sometimes miss the fact that *boring* may mean different things to different kids. Interpreting what it means for your children poses a special challenge. You'll only be able to help them if you know what their *boring* means, and they may not be sure of how to interpret their own boredom. (Review "Why Do We Over-empower? How Do Children Think?" in chapter 1 as you read this section.)

Boredom may mean lack of challenge or too much challenge. It may mean sitting still too long or having too little activity. It may include too much written work or too much reading. For some children, boredom means schoolwork lacks action or humor or a creative outlet. It may mean drill work intended for overlearning (overlearning helps children remember what they've learned). Sometimes children who must sacrifice chatting with their friends consider school boring. *Boring* or *irrelevant* may be used to describe high school work that adolescents don't see as being applicable to their immediate lives or goals (and they believe that they know exactly what those are). *Boring* may also mean that the teacher's presentation lacks the action provided by typical TV programs. However, most frequently children use *boring* to describe work that inwardly they fear they will not be able to accomplish well enough to be considered smart. Thus, it serves as a defense and an excuse for avoiding effort (as described in the previous section about perfectionism and competition).

If your children's abilities and skills and the curriculum are mismatched, whether the work is too easy or too hard, don't hesitate to arrange a conference with their teachers. That work is too hard is relatively easy to communicate; it is almost always more difficult to tell teachers their classes are too easy. Bring samples of work your children have accomplished independently at home to demonstrate their skills and interests. Don't assume that the teachers aren't challenging your children. Be positive. Don't blame the teachers; share with them the concerns you've heard voiced by your children. Listen to their view of your children's skills. If the teachers don't convince you that your children are challenged, recommend permitting children to take the tests at the ends of chapters or books to determine what your children already know. Hopefully, the teacher will be willing to provide your child with individual assignments, or even better, place your children in appropriately challenging groups.

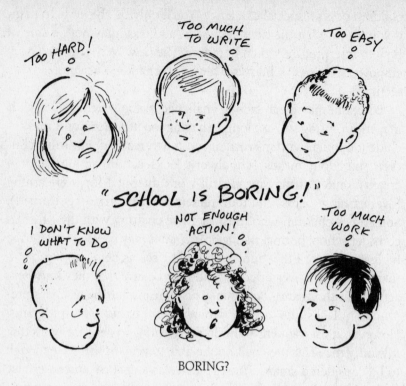

BORING?

Many teachers complain because intellectually gifted children perform poor-quality work on the pretext that they are bored. A nice technique that pleases most is shortening the next assignment based on excellence. For example, if the first math assignment is excellent, the child is only required to do three-fourths or half of the second math assignment. If that's also excellent, shortened assignments continue. If quality drops, quantity increases. Intellectually gifted children are usually delighted to be reinforced by less repetitive work and are willing to emphasize quality to get out of what they may term "busywork." This solution usually pleases their teachers as well.

**If the problem doesn't improve, you may wish to discuss your concerns with the gifted-child coordinator or principal of your school.** Be sure not to blame the problem on the teacher, but do ask for assistance.

If your children are struggling with assignments that appear too difficult, and you've tried to help them, explain to their teachers your observations about their struggles. Adjusted assignments or

PARENT
POINTER

an evaluation and recommendations by the school psychologist may be appropriate.

As you try to determine your children's appropriate academic placement, **caution your children to continue to do their best work despite their boredom.** Don't permit them to use boredom as an excuse for avoiding work. It is difficult to convince a teacher that your child needs challenge if that child doesn't do quality work.

If your children complain that their boring work is too easy, remind them that they are expected to challenge themselves. Going beyond assignments and searching for extra work is an appropriate responsibility for gifted children. They can share their results with their parents or with their class.

**Encourage your children to become involved in independent projects that reflect and extend their interests.** This is an area in which parents can also become involved. You can either explore an interest with them, facilitate opportunities for them, or provide feedback and encouragement for their work. If they can tie their individual work into a school subject or presentation, so much the better. If not, you, your spouse, and their siblings or grandparents may be the only audience for their efforts. Children do like feedback; don't expect them to keep themselves busy on individual projects if you and their teachers are uninterested.

**Foster your children's pursuit of knowledge by praise that reinforces curiosity, follow-through, perseverance, interest, and quality. Model the intrinsic interest of independent work by being interesting and interested in your own leisure pursuits.**

When children are assigned ambiguous tasks that require original thinking, like writing a story or report or doing a science project, they may describe these as boring if they're having problems getting started. Don't get into the habit of providing them with suggestions. That's easy to do, but it doesn't provide the children with idea-development techniques for the future. You produce an idea and they say that isn't any good. Of course, then they use the same pattern when they try to produce their own ideas. Instead, teach children how to brainstorm for their own ideas.[6] When they become accustomed to divergent-thinking techniques, they'll be less likely to label open-ended assignments as boring or too hard.

Children may also label long-term projects as boring if they feel overwhelmed by the size of the assigned project. Teachers often

PARENT
POINTER

PARENT
POINTER

PARENT
POINTER

break these down into subparts, which can help. If the teacher hasn't done this at school, it's a skill you can teach to your children at home. You may show them what you do when you feel over-whelmed with your own work; for example, making lists and timetables. Encourage them to check with you as they complete each task, which will provide them with feedback and attention.

**Involving children in adult-child partnerships for boring tasks is perhaps the best way to model perseverance.** Humor is a critical ingredient in moving through tasks that are boring but necessary. One of our sons' favorite memories is of tarring the inside of a silo so it would hold water for irrigating our orchard. I believe they attempted that task several times—always unsuccess-fully. The boys learned a great deal of perseverance in a boring task, which turned into a ridiculous task. (It was a ridiculous task that never worked for the orchard but did for them.)

Here are some case examples of children's experiences with boredom. All improved after appropriate interpretation of their boredom:

## Case 1

Steve, a sixteen-year-old sophomore with slightly above average ability, had done no homework since fifth grade. When I asked him how he liked school, he said he enjoyed it. Furthermore, he explained that he enjoyed learning and loved discussions. He actually considered himself an "intellec-tual." I told him that there seemed to be a mismatch between his love of learning and his refusal to do homework. He said that homework was boring, and he absolutely could not do boring work. The increasing num-ber of F's on his report card made it appear likely that Steve would not graduate from high school. Without a high school diploma, Steve might well be doomed by doing boring work as a lifetime career. I pointed out that factory assembly-line work, although surely honorable, might feel like prison for an intelligent young man. For just a moment this "tough" young man's eyes seemed to glaze over, betraying sadness and anxiety. I knew that not doing his homework had become part of a power struggle he wasn't willing to lose, and the struggle partly reflected his concern about not being as intelligent as he wanted to appear. Not doing his schoolwork was also a rather strong family tradition. His father, an acknowledged intelligent underachiever, was still providing a battery of excuses for both himself and his son.

## Case 2

Robert, an intellectually gifted seventh-grader, had been underachieving since he entered school. Furthermore, he argued with both his parents and physically abused his mother. He literally pushed her around when he could not convince her to permit him to do as he wished. After coming to my clinic, his parents worked together with his teachers, and Robert made rapid strides in his achievement. His parents learned quickly how to handle his manipulations, and things seemed to be going much better at home and at school.

Robert's mother asked about one major power struggle that didn't seem to make sense to her. Robert had been given a poetry assignment by his teacher in his enrichment class. He briefly regressed to his procrastination problem and didn't do his poetry assignment until the last minute. As he put off doing his work, he protested continually to his mom that it was "boring." His mother, not hearing the real message, tried rationally to argue the merits of writing poetry. She found herself becoming more impatient.

When Robert finally completed his poem, he received very positive feedback from his teacher. The poetry flowed thereafter and lost its reputation for boredom. *Boring* was the word Robert used for being "afraid I will not be able to do well in this new form of expression." His earlier fear of risk taking reappeared when he was faced with this assignment, and Mother, attending to his words instead of his immense fears, found herself back in the argument trap.

## Case 3

Jake was a seven-year-old first-grader. I asked him how he liked school. He said school was a "humdrum world." He said he preferred Mousey Town, the pretend world of his nine imaginary playmates. Jake scored 147+ on his WISC-R IQ test. His reading tested at seventh grade, eighth month, and his math at fourth-grade level. His first-grade teacher said he was immature, and that he would certainly adjust by third grade. He didn't read with a reading group but was permitted to read independently at a slightly more advanced level. He did math with the class. The kids thought he was "weird."

Jake's humdrum world combined a lack of intellectual challenge and peer relationship problems. He knew he was bright and was even anxious to make an effort and persevere. However, there was no place for him to fit in, either academically or socially. *Boring* meant lack of challenge and loneliness for Jake. After one grade skip and some therapeutic sessions in social skills, Jake learned to enjoy some of his schoolwork and many more peer relationships.

**Grade Expectations.** Most parents are unsure if they are being reasonable in their grade expectations for their children. They've been told so frequently that parents expect too much of their children that they tend to be somewhat defensive and fearful about expecting too much. A rule-of-thumb guideline is that intellectually gifted children can be expected to get an A–B average. More A's than B's is appropriate, but it's unreasonable to expect a perfect grade point average of your children. Obviously, if they get all A's in one quarter, kids can feel proud of their accomplishments. If that's their consistent pattern, it certainly gives children a sense of pride. However, setting consistently perfect grades as an expectation puts a great deal of pressure on them. As one boy stated it, "When you have all A's, there's only one way to go."

Schools that use a 4.0 or perfect grade point as the basis for their high honor roll are, in fact, not only causing a few children to feel great pressure, but are causing other excellent students to feel as if they can't ever work to the level of high honor roll. A high honor roll that requires a 3.5 or a 3.8 average certainly documents excellent student performance without putting excessive pressures on very bright children.

Children who have above-average ability should be expected to earn a B average. There may be some A's or an occasional C, but a B to B+ average for such children is a reasonable goal. Children with average ability can be expected to get a B- or C+ average. B's or C's could be their typical grades. An occasional A in an area of strength or an occasional D in a difficult subject in high school are also reasonable grades. Children who have somewhat below-average abilities can expect to obtain a C average with an occasional D or an occasional B. For the most part, teachers rarely give D's to children who are responsible, get all their homework in, show a positive attitude about learning, and attend class regularly. These grade ranges are based on typical schools. There may be some variation from elementary to high school, with slightly higher grade point averages expected at elementary school and slightly lower grade point averages in highly academic high schools.

Course selection may also affect grade expectation. Highly academic and honors courses may demand more of children. If the school weights these honors courses—for example, gives 5.0 for an A, 4.0 for a B, etc.—then you should adjust your expectations accordingly. The school may be able to provide you with further information to help you set reasonable goals for your children under special circumstances. Don't hesitate to talk to your children's teachers when you are not sure what to expect. Consider variations for private schools, because independent schools sometimes use a more difficult grading system than public schools. Usually their scales are approximately one grade lower than in most public schools.

Any generalization you make about grading will have its exceptions, and you should get some sense of what school expectations and grading systems represent. IQ scores should never be considered limitations to children's abilities, because IQ scores can change with children's efforts and achievements. Furthermore, IQ scores measure only some kinds of abilities; for example, IQ tells you absolutely nothing about creative writing ability. **The best and fairest way to set expectations for your children is by observing their efforts.** If they're conscientious—if they get all their homework in, prepare well for tests, and invest time in concentrated study—their grades are likely to be a good fit with their abilities. Observe their efforts and give your children a sense of expectations based on those efforts. You can be reasonably sure that your expectations fit with their abilities if they are hard workers. Study guidelines for your children should be based on the effort required and their responsibilities (see chapter 2). You should, of course, get regular feedback from teachers if your children's direct feedback is not dependable. For children who are already achievers, however, regular teacher-conference feedback is usually sufficient.

PARENT
POINTER

**Post–High School Expectations.** From early on children should have a sense of what parents expect in terms of long-term academic goals. Obviously, parents should be sufficiently flexible to allow young adults to make their own final decisions. Setting reasonably high academic expectations will make it much more likely that your children will accept the challenge of higher education. Again, those expectations can be based on early indications of your children's abilities.

Intellectually gifted children may be expected to achieve beyond a college bachelor's degree if their interests lead them in that direction. A master's, doctorate, or professional degree is a reasonable expectation, depending on the student's career choice and the degree requirements of that career. For children in the above-average range of ability, expectations for a four-year college or a technical program are certainly appropriate. For children within average ranges or somewhat below-average abilities, parents should expect them to complete high school as well as some kind of technical or post–high school training, whether it be junior or technical college or a career training program.

In our society, today and tomorrow, youth who educate themselves for careers that will provide them work satisfaction and a reasonable wage are going to be happier. There's nothing wrong with parents expecting their children to pursue higher education, but if parents don't state their expectations, children won't automatically guess them and therefore won't internalize them. They'll only be influenced by their peer group or other adults. Thus, although parents shouldn't be rigid in setting expectations, they should certainly set a range and assume that children will educate themselves within that range. That should not cause feelings of undue pressure for capable children but should, instead, encourage them to learn. Figure 4.1 will provide you with the rationale for encouraging children toward higher education.

Grading and post–high school education guidelines should only be considered *guidelines*. Don't make the mistake of not expecting your child to do well because of low IQ test scores, which you may perceive as a permanent limitation for your children. IQ scores are not engraved in stone, and there is no way to accurately measure intelligence. An IQ score may, by chance, be lower than what the

## Figure 4.1

# School, Earning . . .

| HEAD OF HOUSEHOLD | MEDIAN HOUSEHOLD INCOME, 1987 |
|---|---|
| 1–3 years years high school | $21,165 |
| 4 years high school | 29,937 |
| 1–3 years college | 36,392 |
| 4 years college | 46,533 |
| 5 years or more college | 54,492 |

# . . . and Unemployment

| EDUCATIONAL LEVEL COMPLETED | UNEMPLOYMENT RATES | |
|---|---|---|
| | MALE | FEMALE |
| 1–3 years high school | 11.2% | 10.9% |
| 4 years high school | 6.7 | 5.8 |
| 1–3 years college | 5.0 | 4.0 |
| 4 years college | 2.5 | 2.1 |

SOURCES: *Education Week*, March 29, 1989, and the "Forgotten Half Final Report," 1988, *High School to Employment Transition: Contemporary Issues*, 1994.

child is capable of producing in school. IQ scores may also have decreased over time because the child has been underachieving. Indeed, I have seen many children whose IQ scores were in the average range who were able to achieve A's and B's throughout high school, though they were rarely able to attain those high grades in advanced mathematics or advanced science courses. Again, IQ tests don't measure all abilities, only some. For example, creative thinking, artistic abilities, and insight into interpersonal relationships are not measured by IQ tests.

Before you make yourself feel guilty about expecting your children to perform better than teachers are saying you should expect, observe the process. **Remember, if your children are working,**

PARENT POINTER

**doing their homework, and being responsible, don't expect them to get higher grades than what they're already getting,** although they may benefit from learning test-taking or study skills. On the other hand, if they're not doing their work or studying, you should encourage your children to do more, regardless of what teachers are reporting to you in the form of grades. You should expect children to put forth the kind of effort that will permit you to recognize whether they're performing to their best ability.

PARENT
POINTER

**Intelligent children should be brought up with the assumption that they'll go on to post–high school education.** Saving money for college and instilling the assumption that college follows high school are appropriate. Decisions about post–high school education are among the most important that you and your children will make. It's good that children talk about career goals early. Your part of the discussion should involve positive messages about effort and perseverance as they relate to college. You should also provide an atmosphere of flexibility and exploration regarding potential careers and educational choices.

Here is an example of the importance of college expectation:

Rob and Joe, both seventh-graders, left science class together, talking as they walked. Both had received an F on their tests. Rob said to Joe, "I failed the test, again. I guess I'll drop out of high school and become a garbage collector."* Joe didn't respond, but as an adult he remembered the conversation. At the time, he couldn't figure out why Rob wouldn't go on to college, nor why he thought that a failed test could make him a garbage collector. Joe had a similar failing grade, and it had never occurred to him that he wouldn't go to college. All his friends and his family went to college. It followed automatically after high school graduation.

Although I don't know the respective abilities of Rob and Joe, I do know that Rob dropped out of high school and Joe earned a Ph.D. No doubt there was more to the case than expectation, but their views of their futures, even from seventh grade, had an effect on their accomplishments.

*I apologize to the hardworking persons who collect our trash. I believe that all work is honorable; however, this was a true story.

When your child is young, you should refer to college as a natural part of your children's education. By middle school and senior high school, you can discuss more specific college expectations. For example, financial issues and specific career directions should begin to influence your children's thinking. If a state university is your preferred direction, then the alternative levels of state universities should be alluded to. For example, higher levels should be encouraged for those planning to do graduate work and a somewhat lesser challenge for those planning to complete only an undergraduate degree. By that time, you'll have a better sense of children's capabilities. Among very intelligent children, your most important criterion will be their motivation and interest. By high school, kids should undertake serious consideration of specific colleges.

Obviously, college choices are difficult to make. How much of the decision belongs to adults and how much to adolescents is debatable, and families take very different positions on college. **Don't assume that your children should be allowed to make a college decision entirely on their own.** They deserve and need your guidance and advice, although they may not acknowledge that.

PARENT POINTER

If cost is an issue, parents shouldn't hesitate to state their financial limitations and guidelines. Although scholarships and loans are available, the extent of indebtedness to which young people may commit should be carefully discussed. Even though education is a most important investment for your children, you shouldn't be expected to make major economic sacrifices in your own lives when less expensive good-quality alternatives are available. Many good universities are more attractive to students from far away, who will pay high tuition to attend, but may not be appreciated by students within their home states. The proximity of a college, however, doesn't diminish the quality but often greatly reduces the cost, and living on campus usually permits sufficient independence.

The size of the university is frequently an issue in decision making; however, that is a matter of personal preference rather than one of quality. If your child plans to pursue graduate education, a large university is more likely to provide undergraduate research experiences that will be helpful for entering graduate school. If your child is easily intimidated by large numbers, then the closeness of a small college may provide more support. Women's colleges have been shown to provide more leadership experiences for female students than coeducational schools. On the other hand, social interaction between the sexes is more spontaneous at the latter. Figure 4.2 provides a suggested plan for evaluating and choosing a college.

Adjusting to college is frequently difficult, even for well-prepared, intelligent students. They may have a history of high school success that may be more difficult to maintain at college. Preparing for that adjustment is important for you and your children. If their grades aren't as high as you and they had hoped, don't assume that it's because of lack of effort. It is important that young adults be aware of the support people at college should they require some help. They should be assured that getting help isn't an indication of failure but a typical part of college adjustment. It may be especially difficult for you to sympathize with the pressure your adult children feel at college if you've never gone to college yourself—don't be too quick to assume that they're goofing off if their grades are poor and they claim they're studying hard. On the other hand, if they're skipping many classes, you have good reason to suspect that they need either help or a stronger commitment to college work before you invest more money in their higher education. Figure 4.3 has some tips for parents regarding college expectations.

## INTRINSIC LEARNING

If your children are to become learners, they must experience the excitement of learning. School learning can be related to winning and grades without distracting from the joy of intrinsic learning. If your children don't develop interests and enjoy noncompetitive learning, the likelihood of their being lifelong learners will diminish. Furthermore, the peer distractions and the psychological stresses that mount when children have not developed interests can diminish their self-confidence and their mental health.

How do you inspire your children to lifelong, joyful learning? **The most effective inspiration is your taking time to become learners yourselves.** Developing interests, pursuing areas of competence, sharing learning experiences with your children, and valuing your spouse's learning experiences provide examples of

PARENT
POINTER

Figure 4.2

# Choosing a College

Now that your children have been accepted to colleges, they'll have to make a choice. Hopefully, they have several colleges to choose from. Here's a step-by-step program for making this exciting choice that will affect the direction of their adult life.

1. Together you and your teenager should brainstorm for all the possible criteria to use in evaluating colleges. Here are some possible criteria: cost, size of college, major, distance from home, proximity to large city, etc. You'll find many more.
2. List criteria in order of importance. You may have some that are equally important, and you may drop some from your original list because you decide they're not important enough to you.
3. Assign numerical weights to each criterion depending on their importance. Use numbers between 1 and 3 to avoid making your evaluation too complex. Higher numbers represent greatest importance to you.
4. Make a matrix listing colleges to which your student has been accepted at the left and the criteria and their weight numbers across the top.
5. Rate each college using numbers from 1 to 3 for each criterion, 3 being most desirable.
6. Working down, multiply each college rating by the weight for each criterion. Working across for each college will cause bias.
7. Add up the scores across to determine what colleges score highest.
8. Use the matrix and the total scores for guidance as you discuss your child's college choice together.
9. Don't feel bound by numbers. The matrix is meant to help you focus your thinking for discussion, not to provide an absolute choice. Your matrix will probably be larger than the example below.

## Sample Matrix for Choosing a College

| College | Wt Cost 3* | Wt Size 1 | Wt Major 2 | Wt Distance 1 | Total Scores** |
|---|---|---|---|---|---|
| University of Michigan | (3) 9 | (1) 1 | (3) 6 | (3) 3 | 19 |
| Carleton College | (2) 6 | (3) 3 | (1) 2 | (2) 2 | 13 |
| Kenyon College | (2) 6 | (3) 3 | (2) 4 | (2) 2 | 15 |
| Brown University | (3) 9 | (2) 2 | (3) 6 | (2) 2 | 19 |

*Cost factor should include actual costs, scholarships available, etc. High numbers indicate most reasonable costs; low numbers, most expensive.
**Although this score indicates rank by your criteria, further discussion with your child may encourage you to weight criteria differently or add other criteria, which could change total scores.
( ) indicates college rating for criterion; number outside ( ) equals college rating times criterion weight.

## Figure 4.3

# Setting Expectations for College

- If your child appears to have college-level ability, make the assumption early that college will be a part of their education. This won't become a pressure for them if they're good students. If they become accustomed to the idea that education is a long-term process, they won't be as likely to be tempted by short-term gratifications, such as cars and expensive clothes.
- Be sure that your message about college and careers is no less challenging for females than it is for males. The concept that girls should "marry their education" is outdated and inappropriate.
- Don't assume that adolescents are able to make all college decisions. Certainly they should be an important part of the choice. The cost of college is the one area in which parents should take a most important advisory role. Young people don't have a great deal of financial experience by age eighteen and may burden themselves with long-term debt for the sake of short-term peer status. Don't hesitate to provide financial advice and limits.
- Recognize that acceptance to colleges and college choices become status symbols at many high schools. Sensitize your children to the peer pressure they may be feeling, and help them make decisions that are reasonable, not just geared to earning peer status. Remind them that their current boy- or girlfriend should not become the sole reason for choosing a college.
- Discuss with your adolescent the adjustments that are typical for college students. If you've attended college yourself, that's quite easy. If you haven't, you and your children may want to talk with a college counselor. College students should be prepared for (a) competition, (b) the large time required for study, and (c) the availability of and the not unusual need for counseling or tutoring during college.

intrinsic learning that will strengthen your own and your children's lives.

Some parents pursue particular hobbies their entire lives and become heavily involved in interest groups and associations. Other parents may flit from hobby to hobby or pursue one interest for a number of years and then channel their energies in a different direction. Still other parents may pursue half a dozen interests simultaneously and seem to thrive on quantity and variety. There is no right way to pursue interests and learning. **If you don't exhibit any**

PARENT
POINTER

**interest, however, your children will lack a model of the value of learning.** Encourage your children to participate with peers in shared interests. These may be summer activities and camps or special enrichment opportunities during the year. However, your messages to encourage them will be diminished if you don't show interest in other-than-work activities. If your career is also your avocation, and certainly many careers provide the depth and breadth to be both vocation and avocation, then you will want to express and describe how your career provides not only for your livelihood but for your interest in learning as well.

Whether your children are infants in your arms or teenagers looming over your head, you can expect them to enjoy learning and show them that you do, too.

## QUESTIONS AND ANSWERS

### Dear Dr. Sylvia,

*If I'm overworked and come home exhausted, should I not be honest and share that with my kids when they ask me how my day was?*

*Tired Dad*

Dear Tired Dad,

It certainly is appropriate for you to be honest with your children, but it's also important to give them a balanced view of your career. Children who hear their parents complain constantly about their work often adopt an antiwork attitude and generalize those negative feelings toward school, which is, after all, their workplace. Their words and their expressions often echo those of their parents.

Although it's fine to explain that you're tired and even feel overworked, it would be good to talk about other aspects of your work as well. For example, you could mention the contributions you make, your accomplishments, or how you've grown in responsibility or knowledge.

If you really don't like your work but can't do much to change the situation, you might at least explain to your children that you are responsible in your work. You may even wish to reframe your feelings of overwork to feelings of pride in accomplishing more than what would normally be expected of you. It's also a good idea to indicate if your education has been helpful. If you feel you would have benefited from more education, that would also be an important concern to share.

Yes, honesty is appropriate, but so is a reasonable degree of optimism. It will not only help your children but will improve your sense of accomplishment. If you are extremely dissatisfied with your work, rather than pass on a negative attitude about the world of work, you may wish to redirect your career through counseling for more personal satisfaction.

### Dear Dr. Sylvia,

*My office is in my home, and I worry about how that may affect my children's school achievement. I often feel overworked and find I must often chase my children from my office because I am too busy for them.*

*Stressed Dad*

Dear Stressed Dad,

Dads or moms who work at home are models for their kids' attitudes toward work. Because the workplace for kids is school, your children may reflect your overwhelmed attitude in their feelings toward school. If your feelings about your work are positive most of the time, you might actually be providing a wonderful role model for your children. However, if you mainly complain about the overload, don't be surprised if your children echo your sentiment and attitude when they describe school.

Your children should not interrupt you during your workday even if your office is at home. You will probably have to lock your door to protect your privacy, giving a clear message to your children that they can't interfere. Thus, you won't find yourself getting angry about their interruptions and you will actually be more efficient. You may even want to post a Do Not Enter sign on your door to indicate when they should stay away in contrast to when you're doing more casual work and they can come in for a visit.

When you invite your children into your office at home occasionally, they will realize what you are accomplishing and why you wish to keep them out while you are working. Try to be balanced in your description of your work, so they can learn balance in their reflections of their own workplace, their school.

Having an office at home is a more common problem for women. However, I think it can be effective for either men or women as long as parents realize that children are learning an attitude toward work by observing them. Children don't read minds, but they are keen observers of parent actions and attitudes. Give them opportunities to learn optimism. Try to be as positive as possible, but insist on your own private and separate time for concentration.

## Dear Dr. Sylvia,

*I am a recent immigrant to the U.S. from India, and I have a six-year-old daughter. When we lived in India, she was fluent in English as well as her other tongue, but now she absolutely refuses to speak her Indian dialect, and it is the same with all of her cousins who live in the States. All of them seem to be scared to speak in their mother tongue. Is it because they feel they will be isolated from their peer group?*

*I want her to know her mother tongue. I have a good command of most major languages of India, and I am fluent in English. I'd like my daughter to be multilingual if possible. How can I encourage her? Is her reluctance going to continue and later inhibit her ability to learn other languages?*

*Baffled Mother from India in California*

Dear Baffled Mother from India,
First, welcome to our country. Other than Native Americans, we are a nation of immigrants.

Your daughter's and her cousins' opposition to learning their mother tongue is unrelated to their abilities to later learn other foreign languages. Many immigrant children feel as if they are not a part of the majority culture. Unfortunately, they may temporarily undervalue their own culture. Your daughter may feel set apart and even embarrassed by her background only because it is different from that of her classmates. That problem may grow even worse during adolescence.

We want children of all ethnic backgrounds to value their own heritage as well as those of others. Your daughter's teachers may be able to help your daughter and the children in her classes appreciate the individual and cultural differences around them. I would suggest you communicate your concerns to the teacher. California has many cultures within most schools, and multicultural education is undoubtedly emphasized already. The appreciation of individual differences should certainly be taught in every classroom.

In addition, if your family members and Indian friends can join together to give after-school classes in your own language and culture, you will all feel better supported and so will all of your children.

### Dear Dr. Sylvia,

*You speak of the importance of two-parent families; however, what do same-sex parents (gay/lesbian couples) have to do to address the gender role-model issue besides having good friends of the opposite sex as role models?*

*Lesbian Parents*

Dear Lesbian Parents,
The research on children brought up in gay or lesbian families is sparse, but it is logical that your same-gender relationship might pose a dilemma similar to that which single parents often face with their sons. It would thus be appropriate to recruit male friends, both heterosexual and gay, or encourage teachers, church leaders, Scout leaders, or Big Brothers to serve as additional models for your sons.

Lesbian parents can be excellent role models for their daughters. However, as their children approach adolescence, they should have opportunities to understand heterosexuality from family members or friends and be encouraged to understand both the homosexual and heterosexual choices available to them.

### Dear Dr. Sylvia,

*I have a question about low-income, gifted black students. In what ways can we help those students, who may not have the resources for assistance and cannot afford private schools?*

*Concerned Teacher*

Dear Concerned Teacher,

Gifted African-American students, especially boys, are dramatically underidentified by many schools. Other minority groups from disadvantaged backgrounds are also neglected in many gifted programs. Most teachers have increased their awareness of the problem, and Javits federal-grant funding has been used nationally to identify and provide programs for gifted culturally disadvantaged youth. Programs are now using more than tests for identification. Children's work projects and teacher and parent observation checklists have increased schools' ability to identify gifted disavantaged children. Programs that accelerate learning and expand cultural opportunities, academies specifically for African-American males, mentorships in industry and science, and skill tutorials are some of the measures taken to motivate and provide opportunities to young disadvantaged scholars.

Peer pressures among minority children can be debilitating to them and frustrating to their parents and teachers. Sometimes African-American adolescents are teased as "acting white" if they are good students. The problem is widespread, but there is, nevertheless, good reason for optimism. Many of our nation's leaders have emerged from disadvantaged homes, and the American dream of education continues to motivate children to move out of difficult life situations to make distinguished contributions. Concerned educators like you make an important difference for children, who may find teachers to be their most significant role models. It's important for you to know that many value and appreciate your contributions to our country's children.

### Dear Dr. Sylvia,

*How can I turn my son away from violence when he is seventeen years old and loves violent TV, music, and weapons? What does this focus fulfill for him?*

*Nonviolent Mom*

Dear Nonviolent Mom,

Many family situations contribute to children's attraction to violence. When they are combined with television models of violence, peer-group violence, and violent music, a young man emerges who only feels powerful when he has violent outlets for his anger and he may vent his aggression on family members and peers.

The initial family patterns that can cause problems sometimes include one of the following:

- A close mother-son alliance that permits the son more power than his father.
- An angry and violent father.
- A single-mother and son relationship in which the son is considered the man of the household initially but feels disempowered later when the mother remarries or has a boyfriend.

All these patterns could occur together or they could take place one at a time. All are accidental and are not intended to teach violence. The patterns give the boys too much power initially, and when life doesn't go their way, they feel helpless, frustrated, and angry. Violence becomes a natural outlet for their feelings.

Now, what can you do? Sports, especially contact sports, are an obvious positive therapeutic outlet; unfortunately, violent young adolescents may consider sports too wimpy. Creative writing, drama, the arts, or music can dissipate the anger for a few teenagers. A powerful, nonviolent, adult male role model may assist you in redirecting your son. The right gentle female friend may also be able to redirect his interests. A good job and an inspiring boss could make a positive difference. Finally, the armed services, if your son qualifies, may provide him with a sufficient sense of masculinity coupled with the self-discipline he desperately needs.

Unfortunately, other negative temptations also entice young men who are attracted to violence. Drugs, alcohol, and crime are the omnipresent fears of every loving parent.

Continue your support and encouragement and make every effort to foster one of the positive alternatives. Although we are surrounded by violence in our society, many young men who have been attracted to violence have redirected their energies to more positive outlets. Your son may be one of those.

## Dear Dr. Sylvia,

*How do we help our son in junior high, who does not have one friend out-side of family members? We have asked him to invite a friend over or to ask someone to go to the movies at least once a month. It is like taking a bad pill for him. We have an older son and a younger child who are both extroverted and very social. This middle child is a good student and helps with everything at home (cooks, etc.). He says he is happy and doesn't need anyone else. He has asthma and allergies and has tried baseball and soccer, but doesn't want to play sports.*

*We have moved about every three to five years. He always had one or two good friends in each of our other communities before this move, but absolutely none here, where we've been for two years.*

Anxious Mother of Loner Son

Dear Anxious Mother,

Your son may be a loner, and he may or may not be lonely. How-ever, your anxiety about his lack of friends may cause him to feel more anxious and may even be preventing him from admitting to you that he feels lonely, if in fact he does.

The most intense period of peer pressure for kids is during the junior-high or middle-school years, and your son may feel he must stay away from kids who may be pressing him to accept values with which he is not comfortable. Although you should certainly en-courage him to invite friends to visit occasionally, please be careful that the invitation is not mandatory. This might only increase the pressure your son feels.

Instead, insist he select some activities for participation. Al-though team sports shouldn't be required, a regular physical-fitness activity should be expected. Swimming, biking, track, or tennis is often selected by adolescents who are less comfortable with com-petitive team sports.

Your son should also be required to get involved in at least one extracurricular activity at school. Drama, forensics, or the school newspaper are good for encouraging your son's assertiveness and expression. By emphasizing the activities instead of socializing, you can help your son develop interests, confidence, and the foundation for peer relations based on shared values and interests, which will help to prevent his feelings of pressure about friends. Kids who feel pressure about friends may join undesirable peer groups, who may be the only ones who will accept them.

A helpful learning experience for your hesitant son would be a special-interest camp during the summer. A week or two on his own will encourage him to expand his interests and foster independence and more positive peer relations. Furthermore, any negative labels he may have accumulated at his school will be erased in a new environment where others don't know of his friendless reputation. Again, select summer opportunities based on special interests. There are camps for science, computers, drama, writing, art, religion, sports, music, and most everything else. Outdoor group cooperative/challenge experiences have helped many adolescents understand themselves and others better.

Most of all, be patient and relax. Although your son may be lonely, he needs the courage to continue to be as independent as he chooses. Many parents wish their teenage sons had fewer friends because their friends are influencing them so negatively. Popularity is no measure of success and can be an empty value that puts undue pressure on kids. Although popularity may be an indication of a positive, friendly, and social person, it does not guarantee happiness. Sometimes, the most popular kids are also in the most trouble. Encouraging your son to develop interests will best lead him to self-confidence and reasonable friendships.

### Dear Dr. Sylvia,

*How can I deal with my son who deliberately underachieves because he thinks it's not cool to be smart? He doesn't want to be considered a nerd by his peers.*

*Mom Concerned about the Future*

Dear Concerned Mom,
By fourth or fifth grade, we find that children become anxious to fit in with a special crowd. When the peer norm is "casual" and uncaring about schoolwork, many bright children who wish to fit in

stop studying. Some children will copy, cheat, and be defiant to fit in with friends who are doing the same. Your son's underachievement could become much more serious as he loses skills and confidence.

You're asking about a serious problem in our country. I know you don't want your son to be without friends, but these are crucial years for teaching him your value system, which I'm sure includes achievement. Don't wimp out because you are afraid of his losing friends. Let him know early and often that everyone has to go it alone at times. Tell him that it is more important to stand tall and know that he is living by a standard of excellence and honesty than to conform to a peer standard that will in the long haul cause him problems. Let your son know that it's all right to walk alone because it will equip him to be strong. Encourage him to be selective in his friends. A few good friends with similar values and interests are healthier than a crowd who may get him into trouble. Good academic habits and independence will be critical tools for the rest of his life.

Although it is often effective for you to give your son this important message, it may be even more valuable if his father has a heart-to-heart talk with him. Sometimes boys believe that women are the only ones who prize education because they see so many more female teachers at the elementary level and because mothers often take the main responsibility for communicating with schools. A son who hears directly from his father in a one-to-one talk may consider the communication important enough to counteract some of the anti-achievement peer pressure he is feeling.

When children are in elementary school, parents and teachers alike worry too much about social adjustment and fitting in with the rest of the group. If children play alone or have only a few friends, both teachers and parents tend to encourage them to join others or invite friends to their homes almost as if they fear that children who are not popular will not be successful. If we continually redirect their independent activity to social activity, and we praise the more social children in the family, our children will receive a strong message about social adjustment that leads directly to peer conformity.

What children need most is the courage to be independent. We surely don't want them to be friendless or lonely, but peer conformity with antilearning friends can be a terrible waste of educational opportunity.

## Dear Dr. Sylvia,

*I am a single mom and have two boys, ages thirteen and eleven. My thirteen-year-old wants to shave his head and wear an earring. The group of friends he hangs around with have all done this, although they are good kids. He says he feels like he doesn't fit in with his friends, and he has low self-esteem because I won't let him do this. How can I handle this? Am I being too old-fashioned?*

*Mom Who's Worried about*
*Being Old-Fashioned*

Dear Single Mom Who's Worried about Being Old-Fashioned,
Hair fashions—short, long, buzzed, or shaved—have forever been symbols of adolescent individuality, assertiveness, and sometimes rebellion. Not surprising, either, is the adolescent desire to fit in with all the other kids. Your son's threat to you about his potentially damaged self-esteem is only a new twist on the old story. Your single-parent status may make you more vulnerable to his persuasion.

Donning adolescent fashions and going along with the crowd can be harmless for teenagers. They can have adult permission to conform to group norms under some circumstances. However, from early on, kids should be thinking about the choices they're making when they join others in any activity or style.

Your son's pleas for protecting his self-esteem shouldn't convince you, although it is true that kids with low self-esteem are more likely to conform. The most convincing part of his argument is that his friends are nice kids and up to no harm. However, if I were you, I'd check out that information before I'd accept my son's story.

Think about your response before giving your son an answer. You may wish to know which rock star or political group the earrings and shaved heads represent. You are unlikely to be tuned in to teen customs, so a neighbor, a teacher, or other kids' parents can give you some insight.

If you conclude that the statement he wishes to make is harmless, certainly you can give your permission. On the other hand, if his haircut represents an anti-authority, antiteacher attitude, tell him no firmly. Give him your reasons only once. Don't get involved in continual discussion on the topic.

If you say yes, be sure you make it clear that your decision is based on the harmlessness of the conformity and not on your concern for his self-esteem, or he may push that self-esteem button in the name of conforming to most anything he chooses.

Single-parenting is always a little harder during adolescence. You'll feel stronger and build your own self-esteem if you have supportive friends to talk with about these difficult teenage issues. However, adults are not all that different from adolescents when it comes to social conformity, so select adult friends carefully based on parenting values you believe in. Otherwise, you could find yourself being pressured by your friends to give in to your son's whims, despite your good old-fashioned feelings.

### Dear Dr. Sylvia,

*I would like your thoughts about discussing and answering questions concerning marijuana with my children, ages twelve, nine, and six. While in college, I used marijuana in moderation. I would prefer not to lie to my children about whether I had used it or not. I am curious as to what the best way to handle this discussion with my children would be. What are your thoughts?*

*Honest Dad*

Dear Honest Dad,
You share a dilemma with many other parents who were part of a generation that did a good deal of experimenting. It is not a good idea for you to lie to your children, because if they learn the truth from someone else, they will no longer trust you. On the other hand, you have no obligation to tell them everything, and you should gear your answers to their maturity levels.

Don't share tales of your drug use with your children unless they ask directly. If they do ask, you might first redirect their questions to the issues involved in marijuana use. You could say that present research indicates marijuana has an adverse effect on motivation, and you hope they will never try it or use it. If your children continue to push for answers about your own use as an adolescent, admit your use but do not glorify it. Remind them that when you used marijuana, there was no research that indicated harm. Be sure to give clear messages about recently discovered risks of marijuana. The sharing of that evidence will lead your children to respect both your honesty and knowledge.

Other questions can be answered similarly—honestly but not in great detail. If you feel a little guilty about not telling all to your children, consider that it will permit them the same privilege. Although it is valuable for parents and children to have open, honest communication, it is also important for adults and children to allow each other some privacy. It is probably healthier for your children to reserve some secrets for themselves to preserve their sense of individuality and independence and to prevent enmeshment.

Parents who brag about their past rebellious behavior, whether it be underachievement, promiscuous sex, or drug use, are likely to hear their adolescents justify their own experimenting based on their parents' experiences. Parents may find themselves giving unintentional permission for actions that hold much greater risks for this generation than they did in the past.


### Dear Dr. Sylvia,
*How do you encourage capable middle-school girls to compete in chess tournaments? They don't want to beat the boys.*

*Gender-Conscious Teacher*


Dear Gender-Conscious Teacher,
Early-adolescent male-female relationships have changed in many ways. However, girls' fears that intellectual prowess will interfere with their social lives continue to affect their educational goals and, yes, even their play. Girls tend to be less competitive than boys, and this characteristic may cause achievement problems for them later in life.

Teenage girls will certainly benefit by becoming involved in intellectual competition as well as by taking the risk of coping with male-female competition. Males, too, would benefit from valuing females as intellectual equals.

Girls' sports provide a wonderful model for encouraging female participation in chess. Start an all-girl chess team with a woman coach. Help girls learn the techniques of the game, as well as experience confidence in their skills. After the girls' chess team has thrived for a while, encourage a few special mixed-gender opportunities. Combine them with a pizza party and fun atmosphere to tempt the middle-school girls to risk the complexity and competitive challenge of chess.

Chess is a wonderful way to introduce females to the challenge of competition. After all, no guy is worth playing dumb for, and many more young men are learning the value and excitement of intelligent women.

### Dear Dr. Sylvia,

*Is there such a thing as gender-appropriate toys? I have a three-and-a-half-year-old son who, when given a choice, tends to choose toys that we would associate with girls, such as Barbie dolls. This is a concern to my husband because he had a brother who was gay. He's uncomfortable about it. Should we be discouraging this?*

*Wary Mother*

Dear Wary Mother,
Preschool- and kindergarten-age children often choose toys that can be associated with both genders. Dress-up clothes, either male or female outfits, are fun for all children and encourage their imaginative play.

Barbie dolls are not truly appropriate for preschoolers, boy or girl. Baby or child dolls of both genders are more appropriate. The emphasis on nurturance and kindness that is learned from playing with baby dolls is more appropriate than an emphasis on fashion. A boy doll for your son would probably also help your husband feel more comfortable.

By first or second grade, boys tend to be more gender selective, but even then, it would not be unusual for a boy or girl to play dress-up. It would be more unusual for a boy to become overinvolved with Barbie dolls, except in the role of brother or dad.

In an era when both males and females become involved in both child care and careers, it seems psychologically healthy for children to play with the whole continuum of toys rather than only those that are gender stereotyped.

Your husband's expression to you of his anxiety is better than his pretending he isn't worried. Building a good father-son relationship is good for boys regardless of what their sexual orientation becomes in adulthood. If your husband and son spend lots of time together doing work in and around the house, enjoying sports together, or just doing errands, your son is likely to feel comfortable with his masculinity. It's important, too, that you, as the mom, don't become the mediator of that relationship. In other words, if you keep telling your husband how to act with your son, he will soon tire of being advised.

If your son is accustomed to being a "mama's boy"—and, incidentally, that is not unusual for a three-and-a-half-year-old—when he asks to stay home with you instead of going with his dad, assure him that you are busy and that his dad requires his help. If you don't play the role of shelterer, they'll soon find each other. If you withdraw a little from their special relationship, male bonding and camaraderie will just occur.

Mainly, I'm hoping that neither Mom nor Dad is truly worried. Cross-gender play at this age is not a predictor of homosexuality. However, if this little boy does grow up to be homosexual, I hope that Mom and Dad will continue to love him and respect his choices.

## Dear Dr. Sylvia,

*I have an eleven-year-old son who gets angry, pouts, and is rude to those who try to console or help him when he strikes out or if no one passes the ball to him during basketball. I don't even enjoy going to his games because it's embarrassing to watch that behavior. I was even contemplating not signing him up for baseball this year because I don't want to deal with it a whole season. There are a lot more strikes than hits. How do I deal with this?*

*Dad Who's Losing the Battle*

Dear Dad Who's Losing the Battle,
Your consoling your angry son has probably become a habitual form of attention, so he's learned to expect that you'll "fix" his sad

feelings when he loses. He's probably learned some habits of poor sportsmanship by now, although he undoubtedly understands the way he should behave.

He could probably benefit from a brief review about good sportsmanship before the season begins. Let him know you'll understand his disappointment but will not tolerate his inappropriate behaviors. Any special after-game treats can be considered only after a display of good sportsmanship. You might also wish to add a positive signal from the bleachers on days when he handles himself well. Waving your hat to him could let him know that you see his improvement. Most important, be sure no one is giving him any feel-sorry-for-him attention.

Poor sportsmanship at age eleven may also be a sign of internalized pressure. That pressure may come from your expectations that he win all the time, although that's unlikely. It's more likely to have been internalized from a history of frequent winning experiences or from extreme praise he has received based on his skill or victories in the sport. If you praise him continuously for being extraordinary or even if you praised a brother for extraordinary skill, he might assume that's what you expect. Some moderate praise for his perseverance, practice, and good sportsmanship will go a long way toward improving the balance he needs to feel about sports and competition.

Don't give up on baseball unless he absolutely wants to discontinue the sport. Children have much to learn about competition and cooperation from the baseball diamond and the basketball court. Sports contribute both to children's physical and mental fitness.

### Dear Dr. Sylvia,

*My high school son is busy planning for his college years. We were careful that he took the appropriate college-bound courses and stressed the importance of hard work and good grades. Do you have any advice that will help him with his future college studies? We, his parents, are not college graduates, so we do not feel qualified to give advice as it relates to college studies. He plans to keep his weekend job, so he will be balancing work with study time.*

*Dedicated Parents*

Dear Dedicated Parents,

Here are some general recommendations I give to all beginning college students whether or not they were achievers in high school. You may wish to share these with your son:

- Never skip a class no matter how boring or irrelevant you believe it to be. You've paid for this education, so you might as well get your money's worth. The lecture or explanation you miss may become the exam answer you don't quite remember learning.
- Plan to study at least two hours for each hour of class time. Colleges recommend this guideline; take their advice literally.
- Structure your study time on a schedule or calendar for at least one week ahead of time. Visualizing the time allocated for study will lessen the pressure you feel.
- If you're struggling with course content, find help *before* you fail. Writing labs, tutors, study groups, and counseling abound on college campuses. No one is going to take you by your hand for help; you will have to initiate the search, but plenty of willing and free help is available.
- You may be disappointed in your grades, even when you've studied hard and have always been an excellent student. Try not to compare yourself to others who have better grades. Instead, concentrate on studying more effectively and efficiently and doing your best.
- Exercise at least three times weekly. Daily exercise is even better. Exercise will help you feel alert and in control and will release tension.
- Plan for brief social time daily and a little more on the weekend. Don't overallocate your social time. There will always be more than you plan for. Remember, alcohol, drugs, and study don't mix well.
- Keep healthy eating and sleeping habits. Fatigue and poor nourishment will only increase your feelings of being overwhelmed.

Because you didn't attend college, you may indeed worry when your son expresses normal concerns about adjustment, but the first year of college is always difficult for students. He may feel as if everyone is smarter than he is. He may wonder why he can't get the high grades he received in high school. He may realize that compared to the studying he does in college, high school study was easy. He may feel as if he doesn't fit in. All these feelings are normal in adjusting to college life. You will want to be encouraging and supportive and assure him that he is not alone with these feelings. Don't threaten to punish him if his grades become unexpectedly low. He will probably feel discouraged enough. You can help him by using a problem-solving approach.

As to your son's job, many students do manage to work while attending college, but initially, fewer than ten hours of work weekly is advisable. Most college students need to study on weekends. Working on campus usually places them in a more understanding environment than working off campus.

You are indeed dedicated parents and have guided your son well. I hope these hints will help as he prepares for the challenging college years ahead.

## Dear Dr. Sylvia,

*We live in a rural area, and my children constantly complain of boredom. There are no other children nearby, so I'm frequently driving them to friends' houses or activities in town. It seems like they expect me to entertain them, which I don't mind doing once in a while, but shouldn't children be able to keep themselves busy sometimes?*

*Tired of Driving*

Dear Tired of Driving,

Children need friends and activities during the summer, and because you live in a rural area, you must invest some time behind the wheel to provide entertainment and fun. However, it's also healthy for children to learn to play alone for part of each day. Solitude stimulates imagination, creativity, initiative, and independence. You will want to establish time alone as a routine for your children, or they will continue to believe that they must have peer or adult entertainment.

Insist that they spend at least an hour a day without peers, siblings, or adults. You may want to call that hour "independent or creative time." Brainstorm with them to develop a list of activities they can do on their own during that hour, such as reading, writing, games, imaginative play, gardening, biking, arts and crafts, or just daydreaming. Don't allow television or computer games. Once the list is completed, post it in a prominent place to inspire your children. Encourage them to choose any activity from the list for their independent time, or they can make up something of their own. Eventually your children will not only learn to enjoy being alone but may even extend it beyond an hour. You will watch your children's confidence and interests increase when you put aside time for them to get to know themselves and explore their interests. Furthermore, you'll be provided with some welcome relief from your taxiing.

# APPENDIX A

## Position Statement on Students with Attention Deficits

Adopted by NASP Delegate Assembly
September 1991

The National Association of School Psychologists advocates appropriate educational and mental health services for all children and youth. NASP further advocates noncategorical models of service delivery within the least restrictive environment for students with disabilities and students at risk for school failure.

NASP recognizes that there are students in schools with academic and adjustment problems who exhibit a constellation of behaviors commonly associated with ADD/ADHD (Attention Deficit Disorder/Attention Deficit Hyperactivity Disorder). NASP believes that attention deficits are not a unitary condition, that they are not reliably diagnosed, and that it is difficult to distinguish attention deficits so severe as to require special education from the normal range of temperament and fluctuations in attention to which all students are susceptible.

Longitudinal data suggest that the problems associated with attention deficits present at an early age may change over time, and that they may persist into adulthood. Therefore, NASP believes that interventions must be designed within a developmental framework. Furthermore, recognizing that these students are at particular risk for developing social-emotional and learning difficulties, NASP believes problems should be addressed early to reduce the need for long-term special education.

NASP believes that students with attention deficits can be provided special education services as appropriate under disability categories currently existing in EHA/IDEA. While concern has been expressed that students with attention deficits served in existing categories will not receive the most appropriate instruction for their unique needs, research indicates that disability categories or area of teacher certification have no significant effect on instructional methods or on effectiveness of service.

NASP believes that excessive emphasis on assessment and diagnosis at the expense of developing and monitoring effective interventions is not in the best interest of children. Assessment of youngsters with possible attention deficits should include intervention assistance to students and their teachers as prerequisites to a formal assessment process.

NASP believes that effective interventions should be tailored to the unique learning strengths and needs of every student. For children with attention deficits, such interventions will often include the following:

1. Classroom modifications to enhance attending, work production, and social adjustment;
2. Behavior management systems to reduce problems in areas most likely to be affected by attention deficits (e.g., unstructured situations, large group instruction, transitions, etc.);
3. Direct instruction in study strategies and social skills, within the classroom setting whenever possible to increase generalization;
4. Consultation with families to assist in behavior management in the home setting and to facilitate home-school cooperation and collaboration;
5. Monitoring by a case manager to ensure effective implementation of interventions, to provide adequate support for those interventions, and to assess progress in meeting behavioral and academic goals;
6. Education of school staff in characteristics and management of attention deficits to enhance appropriate instructional modifications and behavior management;
7. Access to special education services when attention deficits significantly impact school performance;
8. Working collaboratively with community agencies providing medial and related services to students and their families.

NASP believes appropriate treatment may or may not include medical intervention. When medication is considered, NASP strongly recommends:

1. That instructional and behavioral interventions be implemented before medication trials are begun;

2. That behavior data be collected before and during medication trials to assess baseline conditions and the efficacy of medication; and

3. That communication between school, home, and medical personnel emphasize mutual problem-solving and cooperation.

NASP believes that school psychologists have a vital role to play in developing, implementing, and monitoring effective interventions for students with attention deficits. As an association, NASP is committed to publishing current research on attention deficits and to providing continuing professional development opportunities to enhance the skills of school psychologists to meet the diverse needs of students with attention deficits.

# APPENDIX B

## Resources

Family Achievement Clinic
MetroHealth Medical System
Westlake HealthCare Associates
2001 Crocker Road
Cleveland, Ohio 44145
(216) 808-1500

Family Achievement Clinic
1227 Robruck Drive
Oconomowoc, Wisconsin 53066
(414) 567-4560

Educational Assessment Service,
   Inc.
W6050 Apple Road
Watertown, Wisconsin 53098-
   3927
1-800-795-7466

CH.A.D.D.
(Children with Attention Deficit
   Disorder)
499 NW 70th Avenue, Suite 308
Plantation, Florida 33317
(305) 587-3700

Council for Exceptional
   Children
(Also provides information about
   learning disabilities)
1920 Association Drive
Reston, Virginia 22091
(703) 620-3660

National Literacy and Learning
   Disabilities
Academy for Educational
   Development
1875 Connecticut Avenue NW
Washington, DC 20009
(202) 884-8185

Gifted Child Society, Inc.
(PING)
190 Rock Road
Glen Rock, New Jersey 07452-
   1736
Parent Information for
   Gifted (PING)
Hot line: 1-900-773-PING

National Association for Gifted
   Children
(NAGC)
1707 L Street NW, Suite 550
Washington, DC 20005
(202) 785-4268

For scotopic sensitivity:
Irlen Institute
5380 Village Road
Long Beach, California 90808
(310) 496-2550

The National Research Center on
   the Gifted and Talented
The University of Connecticut
362 Fairfield Road, U-7
Storrs, CT 06269-2007

For information about PlugHugger (TV plug lock), call 1-800-795-7466.

# Appendix C

## Booklists

### Books and Materials to Encourage Females

Boter, Mary C. *Women Who Made History*. Warne, 1963.

Boynick, David. *Women Who Led the Way: Eight Pioneers for Equal Rights*. T. Y. Crowell, 1959.

Downie, Diane, Twila Slesnik, and Jean Kerr Slenmark. *Math for Girls and Other Problem Solvers*. Eureka Catalog, 1985.

Epstein, Vivian Sheldon. *The ABC's of What a Girl Can Be*. VSE Publisher, 1980.

———. *History of Women for Children*. VSE Publisher, 1984.

———. *History of Women Artists for Children*. VSE Publisher, 1987.

*Great Women* (card games). Aristoplay.

Johnston, Johanna. *They Led the Way: Fourteen American Women*. Penguin USA, 1973.

Marsh, Carole. *Math for Girls: The Book with the Number to Get Girls to Love and Excel in Math*. Gallopade Publishing Group, 1989.

Moore, E. K., M. A. Vassell, and J. Wilson. *Beyond the Stereotypes: A Guide to Resources for Black Girls and Young Girls*. National Black Child Development Institute, 1987.

Ross, Pat. *Young and Female: Turning Points in the Lives of Eight American Women*. Random House, 1972.

## Suggested Books on Role Models for African-American Children

### FICTION

Armstrong, William Howard, *Sounder,* 1969.

Hamilton, Virginia, *M. C. Higgins, the Great,* 1974.

McKissack, Patricia C., *Mirandy and Brother Wind,* 1988.

Ringgold, Faith, *Tar Beach,* 1991.

Taylor, Mildred D., *Roll of Thunder, Hear My Cry,* 1976.

Taylor, Theodore, *The Cay,* 1969.

### NONFICTION

Altman, Susan R., *Extraordinary Black Americans: From Colonial to Contemporary Times,* 1989.

Gleiter, Jan, *Matthew Henson,* 1988.

Haskins, James, *Space Challenger: The Story of Guion Bluford,* 1984.

Hudson, Wade, *Afro-bets Book of Black Heroes from A to Z,* 1988.

McKissack, Patricia, C., *Jesse Jackson: A Biography,* 1989.

————, *Sojourner Truth: Ain't I a Woman?* 1992.

————, *The Story of Booker T. Washington,* 1991.

Myers, Walther Dean, *Malcolm X: By Any Means Necessary,* 1993.

Paulsen, Gary, *Martin Luther King: The Man Who Climbed the Mountain,* 1976.

Russell, Sherman A., *Frederick Douglass,* 1988.

Time-Life Books, *African Americans: Voices of Triumph,* 1994. Vol. 1, *Perseverance;* vol. 2, *Creative Fire;* vol. 3, *Leadership.*

## Suggested Books on Role Models for Hispanic-American Children

### FICTION

Brown, Tricia, *Hello, Amigos,* 1986.

Cisneros, Sandra, *The House on Mango Street,* 1984.

Delacre, Lulu, *Bejigante Masquerader,* 1993.

Dorros, Arthur, *Abuela,* 1991.

Garcia, Carmen Lomas, *Family Pictures/Cuadros de Familia,* 1990.

Mohr, Nicholas, *Going Home,* 1986.

Myers, Walter Dean, *Scorpions,* 1988.

Sonneborn, Ruth, *Friday Night Is Papa Night,* 1970.

Timmen, Edward, ed., *North of the Rio Grande: The Mexican American Experience in Short Fiction,* 1992.

## NONFICTION

Carson, Robert, *Hernando de Soto,* 1991.

Cockcroft, James, *Diego Rivera,* 1991.

Codye, Corrin, *Vilma Martinez,* 1990.

Concord, Bruce W., *Cesar Chavez; Union Leader,* 1993.

Garza, Hedda, *Joan Baez,* 1991.

Macht, Norman L., *Roberto Clemente: Baseball Great,* 1993.

Stefoff, Rebecca, *Gloria Estefan,* 1991.

Sumption, Christine, and Kathleen Thompson, *Carlos Finlay,* 1991.

Westridge Young Writers' Group, *Kids Explore America's Hispanic Heritage,* 1992.

# Suggested Books on Role Models for Native American Children

## FICTION

Bruchac, Joseph, *First Strawberries: A Cherokee Story,* 1993.

Connon, A. E., *The Shadow Brothers,* 1990.

DePaola, Tomie, *The Legend of the Indian Paintbrush,* 1988.

Hobbs, Will, *Bearstone,* 1989.

Markle, Sandra, *The Fledglings,* 1992.

Martin, Rafe, *Rough-Face Girl,* 1992.

## NONFICTION

Avery, Susan, *Extraordinary American Indians,* 1989.

Bruchac, Joseph, *Keepers of the Animals: Native American Stories and Wildlife Activities for Children,* 1991.

Erdrich, Heidi E., *Maria Tallchief,* 1992.

Ferris, Jeri, *Native American Doctor: The Story of Susan La Flesche Picotte,* 1991.

Hirschfelder, Arlene B., and Beverly R. Singer, eds., *Rising Voices: Writings of Young Native Americans,* 1992.

Hungry Wolf, Adolf, *Children of the Sun: Stories by and about Indian Kids,* 1984.

Iverson, Peter, *Carlos Montezuma,* 1990.

Johnston, Basil H., *By Canoe and Moccasin: Some Native Place Names of the Great Lakes,* 1992.

Poatgieter, Alice Hermina, *Indian Legacy: Native American Influences on World Life and Culture,* 1991.

Richards, Gregory B., *Jim Thorpe: World's Greatest Athlete,* 1984.
Scordato, Ellen, *Sarah Winnemucca,* 1992.
Simon, Charnan, *Wilma P. Mankiller: Chief of the Cherokee,* 1991.

*Note:* These bibliographies are by no means complete, but are intended as a starting point in a search for books of this nature at your local library.

# NOTES

## Preface

1. S. B. Rimm, *Why Bright Kids Get Poor Grades and What You Can Do About It* (New York: Crown Publishing Group, 1995).
2. S. Rimm, M. Cornale, R. Manos, and J. Behrend, *Underachievement Syndrome: Causes and Cures* (Watertown, Wis.: Apple Publishing Company, 1989).
3. S. B. Rimm, *Keys to Parenting the Gifted Child* (Hauppauge, N.Y.: Barron's Educational Series, Inc., 1994).

## Chapter 1

1. S. B. Rimm, "A Theory of Relativity," *Gifted Child Today* 13, no. 3 (1990): 32–36.
2. S. B. Rimm and B. Lowe, "Family Environments of Underachieving Gifted Students," *Gifted Child Quarterly* 32, no. 4 (1988): 353–59.
3. J. Piaget, *The Moral Development of a Child* (New York: Harcourt Brace, 1932).
4. L. Kohlberg and C. Gilligan, "The Adolescent as Philosopher," *Daedalus* 100 (1971): 1051–86.

## Chapter 2

1. M. L. Usdansky, "More Kids Live in Changing Families," *USA Today,* August 30, 1994, 1A.
2. B. Spock, *A Better World for Our Children* (Bethesda, Md.: National Press Books, 1994).

3. Rimm, *Why Bright Kids Get Poor Grades.*
4. S. B. Rimm, "A Bicycle Ride: Why We Need Grouping," *How to Stop Underachievement Newsletter* 1, no. 3 (1992): 1–3.
5. Rimm, *Why Bright Kids Get Poor Grades.*

## Chapter 3

1. *Child Behavior Checklist for Ages 4–18* (Parents and Teachers) (Copyright 1991 T. M. Achenbach, University of Vermont, 1 S. Prospect St., Burlington Vt. 05401); *Conners' Rating Scales* (Parents and Teachers) (Copyright 1989, Multi-Health Systems, Inc., 908 Niagara Falls Blvd., North Tonawanda, N.Y. 14120, 800-456-3003).
2. A. J. Zametkin, "Attention Deficit Disorder—Born to Be Hyperactive?" *Journal of the American Medical Association* 273, no. 23 (1995): 1871–74.
3. S. B. Rimm, *Keys to Parenting the Gifted Child.* (Hauppauge: N.Y.: Barron's Educational Series, Inc., 1994).
4. S. Freud, *Collected Papers* (New York: Basic Books, 1959).
5. E. H. Erikson, *Childhood and Society,* 2nd ed. (New York: Norton, 1963).
6. W. Mischel, Y. Shoda, and M. L. Rodriguez, "Delay of Gratification in Children," *Science* 244 (May 1989): 933–38.

## Chapter 4

1. P. H. Mussen and E. Rutherford, "Parent-Child Relations and Parental Personality in Relation to Young Children's Sex-Role Preferences," *Child Development* 34 (1963): 589–607.
2. E. M. Hetherington and G. Frankie, "Effects of Parental Dominance, Warmth, and Conflict on Imitation in Children," *Journal of Personality and Social Psychology* 6 (1967): 119–25.
3. S. B. Rimm, "Popularity Ends at Grade 12!" *Gifted Child Today* 11, no. 56 (May/June 1988): 42–44.
4. American Association of University Women Educational Foundation, *How Schools Shortchange Girls* (Executive Summary) (Wellesley, Mass.: Wellesley College Center for Research on Women, 1992).
5. G. A. Davis and S. B. Rimm, *Education of the Gifted and Talented* (Needham Heights, Mass.: Allyn & Bacon, 1994).
6. Rimm, *Why Bright Kids Get Poor Grades.*

# INDEX